HERBERT HOOVER

A Reminiscent Biography

BY

WILL IRWIN

ILLUSTRATED

Special Edition

THE CENTURY CO.

New York   London

Copyright, 1928, by
WILL IRWIN

Copyright, 1928, by
UNITED FEATURE SYNDICATE, INC.

First printing March, 1928
Second printing April, 1928
Third printing June, 1928
Special Edition July, 1928
Second Special Edition, July, 1928

ILLUSTRATIONS

HERBERT HOOVER . . . . *Frontispiece*

	PAGE
MRS. JESSE HOOVER	28
"TAD," BERT AND MAY HOOVER AT SALEM, OREGON, ABOUT 1888	61
CORNER OF THE INNER QUADRANGLE, STANFORD UNIVERSITY	76
HERBERT HOOVER, PERTH, WEST AUSTRALIA, IN 1898	93
SONS OF GWALIA MINE AT MOUNT LEONORA, WEST AUSTRALIA	124
MRS. HERBERT HOOVER	157
HERBERT HOOVER AND A GROUP OF HIS AMERICAN AND DUTCH ASSOCIATES, ROTTERDAM, 1915	188

HERBERT HOOVER:
A REMINISCENT BIOGRAPHY

HERBERT HOOVER:
A REMINISCENT BIOGRAPHY

CHAPTER I

HERBERT HOOVER derives from the Colonial stock. His first established ancestor was a certain Andrew Hoover, one of three brothers who in 1740 or thereabout held farms in the uplands of Maryland. Very probably Andrew was an immigrant; we have before him no record of the name in America. Certain genealogists, on doubtful or fanciful authority, say that the Hoovers came originally from France; that one Huber, a Huguenot fleeing from persecution by the king, settled in Holland and altered his surname to fit the phonetics of his adopted country. An old family tradition relates that the Hoovers sprang from Holland and were there converted by English refugees to the Quaker faith. This name is common in all northwestern Europe; but while the French and Walloons spell it "Huber," the Germans "Hoofer or Hoefer," the Dutch and Flemish alone use the form "Hoover."

Andrew Hoover was second of these three pioneer brothers and Herbert Hoover's direct progenitor in the sixth generation. When the curtain rises on him he belongs to the Society of Friends. Thenceforth for five generations his descendants remained Quakers, married "in the meeting" with women of the Anglo-Saxon-Celtic blood, followed the frontier, and broke virgin soil. Andrew Hoover passed on from Maryland to North Carolina. In 1802 his son John joined one of the Quaker treks into the virgin lands of the Western Reserve and settled, with others of his faith, near Miami, Ohio. Again in 1853 the family was on the move, driven—as was typical of American rural life in those days—by the necessity of providing farms for the growing boys. With a group of neighbors and co-religionists, Jesse Hoover, then head of the family; his wife Rebecca, his son Eli, and Eli's brood packed themselves into covered wagons and emigrated to the fat, unbroken prairie lands of Iowa. There in 1853 they founded West Branch, Cedar county. Before they began clearing land they had broken ground for their meeting-house; and for at least thirty years the majority of that small but soberly prosperous town wore the broad hat or the poke bonnet and spoke the "plain speech."

To the large Hoover faction Jesse's wife Rebecca (sprung from that good old pioneer family the Younts) stood matriarch. Born at about the turn of the nineteenth century, she lived until 1895. She was a woman of glorious energy, stern but humorous character, and strong religious convictions; and she held firmly to the observances and even the prejudices of her faith. When the inhabitants began screening their windows against flies, she opposed this hygienic measure as balking somehow the purposes of the Lord. When her son Banajah bought a parlor melodeon, she did her best to prevent such manifestation of worldliness. Next thing, she said, they would be setting up an organ in meeting. And indeed, before she died, a faction of the community had done exactly that.

Eli Hoover, eldest son of Jesse and Rebecca, held a farm like his forebears. He had, however, a strong mechanical bent. Toward the end of his life he was as much carpenter and mason as farmer; old residents of West Branch still tell of his skill in building cisterns. Following his father's inclination, Jesse the second, Eli's third son, abandoned the farm and became the town blacksmith. Until the general wave of immigration which followed the Civil War, the Friends' settlement of West Branch had practised primitive agriculture—reaping with sickle and scythe, threshing with the flail. The newcomers brought improved agricultural machinery and tools, like mowers, threshing machines, sorghum mills. Jesse Hoover was scarcely established as a blacksmith before he took on an agency for agricultural machinery which in time absorbed all his attention. Also, in his early twenties he married Huldah Minthorn.

Of the Minthorns less is known with certainty than of the Hoovers. As far back as memory ran, they had been Quakers. A family tradition holds that they came from England to Connecticut in the eighteenth century. Then they migrated to Canada; and a few generations later returned to the United States and settled in Ohio. This same tradition says that during the Canadian period a marriage with a Huguenot woman brought the French strain into the blood. That appears probable; I have always felt a touch of French quality in the minds and temperaments of Herbert Hoover and his brother Theodore—for example, their tendency in crises to think like pessimists while behaving like optimists. It is certain that both Herbert Hoover's maternal grandparents, as well as his mother, were born in the United States.

His grandfather on the Minthorn side is remembered as a bookish farmer who carried favorite volumes in his saddle-bags; and he gave his family the best education within his means. Huldah had "finished" at a young ladies' seminary and, according to some of her relatives, had attended for one term the embryo University of Iowa. Her name, however, does not occur on the existing registration list of the university. On the other hand, some of the records are lost, so this may be true. At any rate, she had a mind much better equipped than that of most women in her time and clime. West Branch remembers her as an attractive and efficient woman, serious-minded even for a Quakeress. She took literally the doctrines of her faith. In meeting, according to her surviving relatives, "the spirit moved her beautifully." They thrill yet to the memory of her inspired speech. Jesse Hoover was of a different and more sanguine temperament. By native quality or by training in his business as purveyor of reapers and threshers, he was a "mixer." Above all, he loved a joke. "And once he got one on you, he'd never let up," says his younger cousin George.

It tickled his sense of humor to play on the serious mind of his wife; to puzzle her with statements palpably absurd and to observe with that chuckling laugh of his her efforts to understand.

They lived in a one-story cottage across an alley from Jesse Hoover's blacksmith shop and machine agency. There in 1871, when Jesse was twenty-four years old, appeared their first child, Theodore, called far into his maturity "Tad." Three years later, on August 10, 1874, came Herbert Clark Hoover, born under the ministrations of his Aunt Ellen, volunteer nurse to the community. Concerning which, there is direct and personal testimony in a letter from one of Herbert Hoover's Quaker aunts, as cited by Rose Wilder Lane:

". . . I had spent a day with Huldah, visiting and sewing. Thee was with me. Jesse and Huldah always made much of thee because thee represented the little girl they hoped soon to have.

"Next morning early, Jesse came and tapped on my window and said, 'Well we have another General Grant at our house. Huldah would like to see thee.' So we went, thee and I, . . . Herbert was a sweet baby that first day, round and plump, and looked about very cordial at everybody."

Vigorous he seemed, and normal. Yet, Jesse and Huldah Hoover—to use the old-fashioned phrase—"nearly lost him." He seemed especially subject to croup, that scourge of old-fashioned babyhood. In his second winter, he had an attack so serious that Aunt Ellen came in as nurse. At the end of a long choking-spasm, he stiffened; stopped breathing; so far as visible signs went, died. Aunt Ellen was laying out the little body when she noticed signs of life and applied strong restorative measures. He revived. His mother always believed that the Lord gave him back in answer to her prayers.

Then to Jesse and Huldah Hoover came May, the little girl they wanted when Herbert was born. Just after Herbert turned six years old, the Hoover children were sent for a long and pleasant visit to their Uncle Benajah and their cousins. It ended abruptly when Benajah packed them into a cutter and drove them home.... Their mother, their aunts, and uncles were sitting round the corpse of their father. At the age of thirty-three—just when his small ventures were beginning to pay, just when, discounting prosperity, he had moved into a new and better house—Jesse Hoover was dead of typhoid fever.

CHAPTER II

SOME modern psychologists maintain that men of exceptional capacity are usually precocious as children, and that their conscious memories begin early. There are on record geniuses who remember events in the first year of life. Herbert Hoover is an exception. With him the curtain rose rather late. His mind carries no definite picture of his father, who died when he was six years old. His first teacher remembers him as "a sweet little boy," plump and with rosy cheeks, who learned readily and never made any trouble, but who seemed more interested in getting out of doors to play than in books and studies. Two episodes of this period have left permanent scars on his person. Running into his father's blacksmith shop barefoot, he stepped on a piece of hot iron, badly burning his foot. Playing with a hatchet, he nearly chopped off the index finger of his left hand. There was more croup, and serious trouble with earache, the pest of his childhood. Another memory—painful but humorous—concerns his first scientific experiment. They were boiling tar beside his father's shop. Herbert, watching the black, oily bubbles on the surface of the kettle, began to speculate on the properties of hot tar. Would it burn? Or would it extinguish fire? So he drew a brand from the fire and plunged it into the caldron. Few questions which the noble curiosity of science asks of inscrutable Nature were ever answered so swiftly as this. Jesse Hoover and his customers, finally the Volunteer Fire Department, were all needed to put out the fire before it reached the house and the store. Little Herbert, questioned, confessed his fault. He received a double dose of scriptural admonition and a sound whipping. In those days, even Quakers spared not the rod lest they spoil the child.

So much for incidents. As for more general memories—sliding down Cook's Hill in snow-time, ranging the spring fields in vain pursuit of baby rabbits, gathering wild strawberries in summer, the sonorous roll of the English Bible at family prayers, the meetings on First Day where he sat beside his father watching his mother over a partition, and trying to keep from wriggling during long pauses between the motions of the spirit. However, the old meeting-house soon passed out of the picture. New rivals brought new ideas into this set community; there was a quiet but dynamic upheaval. Presently, the meeting split into conservatives and progressives. The more conservative faction withdrew; the original congregation, with which Jesse and Huldah Hoover remained, adopted an organ and gospel hymns, installed the more progressive mode of worship of the present orthodox Friends. Still, however, Herbert Hoover's parents dressed in Quaker gray, addressed each other in the "thees" and "thys" of plain speech, and shunned the forbidden pleasures of the world.

In the summer after his father's death came an experience which left, one feels, an imprint on his tastes and character. His Uncle Laban had gone to Oklahoma—then, of course, Indian Territory—as government agent at Pawhuska, capital of the Osages. Aunt Agnes, Laban's wife, came to West Branch and took Herbert home with her for a visit. By Osage policy, which the Government heartily approved, this nation within a nation put up effective barriers against invasion by our race. Except for Uncle Laban's brood of three, they found no other white children in that most picturesque of the southwestern frontier towns. But there were hordes of little Indians, running wild as pup coyotes. All that summer little Bert enjoyed fascinating friendship with Indian boys. He watched the little braves snare rabbits and ground-squirrels; he fished beside them with a bent pin; he made his own childish attempts to draw the hickory bow; he stood in a state of exalted admiration while they cooked their prey on the lid of a tin can. This halcyon of genuine boy-scouting left marks on his tastes and character. From it, as much as from anything else—I conjecture—arises his love of hills and forests and the out-of-doors. Still, when he wants to get away from the world he goes camping or fishing, if it is only for a day; and the scent of a wood-fire burning against the evening dew raises him to a pleasantly reminiscent humor. On these expeditions he insists on doing the rough camp-cooking; and westerners have noticed with amusement that he builds a fire in the neat and economical fashion of an Indian.

His father's death set a period to his early childhood. Besides a modest life insurance and the new house, Jesse Hoover left small estate. Huldah Hoover, true to the traditions of her family and her sect, desired that the boys should go to college; and the next four years were a struggle to hold the nest egg intact for that purpose, while keeping their little bodies nourished and warm. Being a fast and artistic seamstress, she began by taking in sewing. But from the day of her husband's death she was less and less a creature of this world. In meeting, the spirit moved her more often and more beautifully. Her sermons became famous among the Quaker colonies of Iowa. They invited her from afar to Quarterly or First Day meetings; to pay her for the time lost from sewing they made contributions of money and supplies. Another sect would have ordained her a full-fledged preacher. So it went for four years, while Herbert Hoover grew from the chubbiness of his babyhood to the spindling leanness of his boyhood.

Benajah Hoover had a farm near by. He was Jesse Hoover's uncle, but of about the same age. As I have told already, his wife Ellen attended Huldah Hoover when Herbert was born. Ellen was a Methodist, and after their marriage she weaned Benajah over to her own faith. This heresy did not for a moment interrupt a cordial friendship between the two families; until Jesse's death they always dined together on Sundays. At Benajah's, Tad, Bertie, and May lived while Huldah Hoover was away on her missions of religion; and Herbert Hoover's gayest memories of boyhood have their focus in that Iowa farm. He occupied still the position of the small boy tagging along; but Tad and George, Benajah's son, seem to have tolerated him for his good humor, his willingness to enter on any adventure, and his enterprise.

Speaking before the Iowa Society of Washington in 1927, Herbert Hoover himself touched on these delights of childhood. The swimming hole under the willows down by the railroad bridge—"albeit modern mothers probably compel their youngsters to take a bath to get rid of clean and healthy mud when they come home. The hole still needs to be deepened however. It is hard to keep from pounding the mud with your hands and feet when you shove off for the thirty feet of a cross-channel swim." . . . The cracker-boxes, triggered with a figure-4, set in the woods to catch rabbits. . . . Fishing for sunfish, suckers, and catfish in the creek with a willow pole, a line of butcher's string, a cork salvaged from a rubbish heap, an angleworm, and a one-cent hook . . . sliding down Cook's Hill on a home-made sled and thawing out your chilblains with ice-water. . . . The one drinking man in the village who happened to be also the one Democrat, and therefore, according to conventional boyish ethics, fair game for baiting. . . . Collecting old iron and selling it to this same Democrat for the money to celebrate fourth of July with firecrackers. . . . Of all rough boyhood experiences and experiments with life, the little Hoovers missed only one—fighting. Quakers were still in vast majority about West Branch; and to strike a playmate was the great, almost unforgivable sin. Also, the Hoover boys helped their burdened mother about the house not only in the manly chores of chopping and carrying wood, but in sweeping and washing dishes. "And Bertie was always very willing," says one of his aunts.

Whittier, in "Snow Bound," has sung the life of a Massachusetts Quaker family a hundred years ago. In Iowa fifty years ago the customs and outlook were nearly the same. Whittier catalogues the books—the Bible, Quaker sermons, and homilies, tracts, "Paradise Lost," "The Wars of the Jews," and—

> One harmless novel, mostly hid
> From younger eyes; a book forbid.

In Huldah Hoover's household was not even a single novel, if you except fictional tracts "wherein," says Hoover, "the hero overcomes the Demon Rum." Benajah Hoover had carried over from Quakerdom some strong sectarian prejudices. He too forbade books of romance save those with Total Abstinence as hero and Rum as villain. But inconsistently he permitted "The Youth's Companion," which he considered uplifting literature for the young. Huldah Hoover disagreed with him. However, the Hoover boys used to read its thrilling narratives and anecdotes during their visits to Benajah; and Tad began to carry away old copies and to hide them in a secret nook between the sheathing of the house and the attic wall. Finally, from some worldling of a boy he borrowed a copy of "Robinson Crusoe." He and George

Hoover, to whom this strong meat was equally forbidden, used to read it lying on the floor in an upper bedroom of Huldah Hoover's house. They took turns, each squabbling when he felt that the other had read too long. Bertie got his Defoe second hand. Being the youngest and the fag, he sat on the stairs as lookout, instructed to whistle a tune if any one approached. Little-boy fashion, now and then he would forget his job, creep into the room and ask in an excited whisper, "What are they doing now?" Then the member of the guilty pair who had lost the book for the moment would rise and drag him back to his post. So, continuing on their worldly course, Tad and George read Cooper's "Leatherstocking Tales." Thereafter they acted out these romances. Bertie played the super parts. When Tad commanded the Colonial army, Bertie was that army; he was also the white maiden bound to the stake, while George as the *Indian Chief* tortured her and Tad as the *Deerslayer* came to the rescue.

They collected birds' eggs, of course; concerning this activity too they must needs be somewhat discreet, because many of their elders considered this cruel and unnatural. One day George found on his place the nest of a screech-owl; and he had an idea which he imparted to his playmates. Instead of robbing the nest, they would wait until the little birds grew up, and catch one for a pet. From a neighboring tree, week after week the boys watched until the eggs hatched and the fledglings sprouted feathers. The day came when the owlets began to flutter their wings; the boys must act at once. The tree was tall but slender, devoid of branches for some thirty feet up; the nest lay in a crotch of the lowest branch. They elected Bertie, as the youngest and most agile, to make the first try. He shinnied up the tree to the nest, laid his hand on a little bird; and the mother owl, which had been sleeping the day away in the upper branches, swooped down with a squawk and fastened her talons in his hair. He descended at a speed which ruined his breeches. He still carries on his scalp the scars of those claws. The owl-hunters held a council of war. They had one weapon—George's big pocket knife. Tad volunteered to go up, holding the knife in his teeth, and fight off the mother owl with one hand while kidnapping her young with the other. The plotters did not consider the fact that a boy needs both arms as well as both legs to hold firmly to a small tree. When the mother owl attacked again, Tad reached for the knife, fumbled it, lost his grip, and came down so fast that she did not get him. The hunters waited under a bush until mother resumed her nap. Evidently her manifestations of emotion had tired her out; for when George tried, she did not appear. He grabbed the nearest fledgling by the neck and slid down unattacked.

They tethered the young owl by the leg and wooed it. As a pet it proved a complete failure. By day, when they wanted to play, it slept. Awakened, it answered soft approaches with pecks and truculent rufflings. Experiment established that it would eat only raw meat; and in that economical family rationing became a problem. Tired of the game, the boys tried an experiment in natural history. If you walk around an owl, he follows you with his gaze, revolving his neck like a contortionist. They had heard that if you walk long enough you can make him wring his own neck. They tried; but this owl would not be tricked into suicide. Always just when his head was turned until he looked almost directly backward, with a movement so quick as to defy the human eye he jerked it round to the other side. They could never seem to catch him off his guard. They lost interest even in scientific experiment on this reluctant pet. George Hoover, who among the three has the most vivid memory of the episode, cannot remember what finally became of their owl.

In the summer when Bertie came eight years old, George Hoover was permitted to go with neighbors to the circus at Iowa City, ten or fifteen miles away. Any one knows what happened next. They began to play circus. On the Benajah Hoover place was an old site of a threshing machine. The horse which propelled it had trodden a circle; it made a perfect ring. Benajah Hoover had a white mare, docile and at leisure through extreme old age. They braided her mane, and made her a circus-horse. Bertie, standing in the center of the ring, acted as "post"—he guided her by the halter about the periphery of the ring. Tad, as ringmaster, cracked a whip behind her. And George, who enjoyed great prestige because he had actually seen the circus, was the rider. He contrived, after much experimenting, to stand up barefoot on the old mare's rump; but as soon as Tad urged her into a stiff gallop, he fell off. When he had bruised himself sufficiently, he changed places with Tad, who had no better luck.

Perceiving that circus riders are born, not made, they decided to transform the show into a menagerie. The big yellow hound-dog which was their faithful attendant impersonated a Numidian lion; an especially fierce and battered tomcat, shut in an empty apple crate, the Bengal tiger; ground-squirrels and chipmunks, industriously trapped, the panthers and leopards; a bull calf the elephant. The audience—which paid of course with pins—had just begun to assemble, when the lion broke his leash, knocked over the apple crate, and joined battle with the Bengal tiger. In the struggle to separate them the boys overturned the other cages, and the panthers, the leopards and even the elephant escaped to the jungle.

Then there was the furor over archery, which infected not only the Hoover boys but all juvenile society in West Branch. Unconsciously, Uncle Laban Miles started it by returning from Oklahoma and bringing along six little Indians to board under contract with the Government. One of them knew how to make bows. Tad, scraping acquaintance, learned from him the art of quartering a seasoned hickory pole, studying the grain, and tapering the ends; and of feathering arrows. When he flaunted his new accomplishment, all the other boys went wild over it. For a year they shaped bits of scrap-steel on the grindstone to make points, combed chicken-yards and raided glue-pots for the raw material of arrows. Tad made the best bows; he gave Bertie one of his outworn specimens. "There were also at times pigeons in this great forest and prairie-chickens in the hedges," said Hoover in his speech to the Iowa Society. "Sometimes by firing volleys in battalions we were able to bring down a pigeon or a chicken. The Ritz Hotel has never yet provided game of such wondrous flavor as this bird plucked and half cooked over the small boys' camp-fire."

Rabbits, however, were the big game of their hunting. Once of a Sunday afternoon when meeting, Sunday school, and dinner were over, Uncle Benajah permitted the boys to take a Sabbath day walk. "But leave your bows at home," he commanded. "No hunting, mind!" Soberly they started out, followed by that yellow dog which played lion in the circus. Suddenly a rabbit started from an Osage-orange hedge—another—and another. It was alive with rabbits. Forgetting their religion, the boys pursued in every direction, hurling sticks and stones. The dog caught and killed a rabbit. The boys took the carcass away from him before he had mutilated it too much. Apprehensively, they carried it home and explained that they had not hunted the rabbit; it just happened; and anyhow, the dog did it. Without any cross-examination, Uncle Benajah accepted their testimony. "Keep it for one of your barbecues—but not on this day," he said. And probably the corners of his mouth were twitching.

Herbert Hoover himself, in that same speech before the Iowa Society, told the boyish tragedy of the prey which escaped. "Rabbits fresh from a figure-four trap are wiggly rabbits, and in the lore of boys of my time it is better to bring them home alive. My brother, being older, had surreptitiously behind the blacksmith shop read in 'The Youth's Companion' full directions for rendering live rabbits secure. . . . Soon after he acquired this higher learning he proceeded to instruct me to stand still in the cold snow and to hold up the rabbit by its hind feet while with his not oversharp knife he proposed to puncture two holes between the sinews and back knee-joints, through which holes he proposed to tie a string and thus arrive at complete security. . . . The resistance of the rabbit was too much for me. I was not only blamed for its escape all the way home and for weeks afterward, but continuously over the last forty years."

Mounted on a pair of second-hand skates acquired by trade and barter, he skimmed on open winter days the frozen surface of the swimming-hole. With a shaped hickory stick and a ball formed by winding purloined yarn about a piece of rubber, he played one-old-cat and learned the rudiments of baseball. From the Mississippi River ballast of the Burlington tracks he picked up fragments of coral or agate, tried to polish them on the grindstone, kept them as secret treasure. And in his little-boyhood as in his babyhood, no one observed anything remarkable about him. His Quaker relatives, refusing conscientiously to let pride or imagination color their sense of fact, all testify to that. But he was "a good little boy," pleasant and willing, interested in everything, on the outskirts of all exciting or amusing events. And looking back over forty years, his limited world remembers that every one liked him.

Bereavement put a sudden end to his little-boyhood, as it had his babyhood. In February, 1884, his mother came back from one of her excursions to the neighboring meetings with a hard "cold on the lungs." It grew worse; it turned into a swift, unconquerable case of pneumonia. She had borne many burdens; "and the Lord had mercy and gave her rest," said her friends of the meeting. But she had done most of her work as a mother. To Theodore and Herbert, now twelve and nine years old, she had given strong, healthy, well-nourished bodies. And by gift of inheritance or by the unconsciously absorbed training of infancy, she had infused them with her own unswerving integrity, her spiritual quality. The idealism of Herbert Hoover reflects her; as his love of human contacts, his shy but unfailing sense of humor, and his interest in mechanics reflects his father.

CHAPTER III

As soon as Huldah Hoover was laid beside her husband in the Friends cemetery of West Branch, the Hoovers and Minthorns held a family council. They would take care of their own. However, none among them could quite face the sacrifice of supporting three half-grown orphans. For the present at least, the children must be separated. Uncle Davis volunteered to bring up Tad like a son on his own farm. May, still little more than a baby, would stay with her Grandmother Minthorn. And his uncle Allan Hoover, who cultivated a quarter-section in Cedar county a few miles from West Branch, would take Herbert.

Carefully squeezing out every cent, the Hoovers and the Minthorns collected the remains of the widow's hoard. With all debts and expenses deducted, it amounted to little more than $1500. Laurie Tatum, a lawyer, had closed up Jesse Hoover's estate and advised the widow in her small financial affairs. He took over this sum as trustee and became legal guardian to the three orphans. The Society of Friends has almost a mania for book-learning. Minor sect though they be, they support to-day in the United States four institutions of university rating. The boys should have a good education if they wanted it—that went without saying. Laurie Tatum was to dole out the tiny interest on this insignificant sum for necessities which their host could not afford to furnish, and hold the principal, so far as possible, for the higher purpose.

These are the mere statistics of a tragedy. When Herbert Hoover left the little two-story house behind the maples he was bidding farewell to his immediate family and entering the full state of orphanhood. He took it hard—but with his mouth shut and grief showing only in his eyes. However, his Aunt Millie was an understanding woman and just. For a long time, his elderly relatives say, she favored him—to external appearances at least—over her own brood. And the emotions of childhood are as unstable as mercury. He adjusted himself to the life of a prairie farm, most fascinating for a boy; became happy after his fashion.

Cedar county lies little more than a hundred miles from the country where Abraham Lincoln kept store, rode circuit, and ran for Congress. Though thirty years had passed, though crude machinery was replacing tools, though more and more the rural population was clothing itself from the country stores instead of from its own looms, the life had not changed in its essentials from that which Lincoln's people lived and with which his biographers have made us so familiar. "Then," said Hoover in after-years, "the farm produced eighty per cent. of what the farmer consumed—and now only twenty per cent." They manufactured their own butter and cheese, slaughtered and dressed their own meat, raised their own fruit and vegetables, carried their grain to mill, and, after giving the miller his proportion for his trouble, returned it to their cellars as flour. The women made their own clothes and even the men's shirts, boiled their own soft-soap, tried out their own lard. The motive-power of the equine engine which carried the family to market or to meeting was fodder, farm-raised; not the extraneous gasoline which the modern Ford demands. In such conditions children, and especially male children, were not all a liability.

Herbert Hoover found in his cousin Walter a kindred spirit. Together the boys walked two miles to district school; or, when winter made the highways troublesome, rode double-mounted on one of the farm horses. Together they did the farm chores. They milked the cows. They "spelled" the woman at the handle of the old-fashioned churn. They fed the stock, taught the calves to drink skim-milk, brought in the wood; in planting-time followed down the furrows, dropping corn; in growing-time weeded the kitchen-garden; in harvest-time carried water to the men or husked corn. Mounted on boxes, they curried the horses. And still they found time for plenty of play —searching the coverts for quails' nests, climbing trees for birds' eggs, pursuing rabbits, making willow whistles, or just hopping and whooping aimlessly over the rolling hills.

In two episodes of this period, remembered by the family for their comic quality, the biographer traces the first impulse of his natural bent in Herbert Hoover. Uncle Allan had a new mowing-machine.

Herbert and Walter were fascinated with its clean slice into the growing timothy, its rhythmic music, and especially its ingenious mechanism for transforming the rotation of its wheels into the thrust of its blade. About the barn or on the trash-pile behind it lay that abandoned junk common to any long-inhabited farm —warped and broken wheels, pieces of dismantled machinery, rusty bolts, nuts, and screws. Somewhere in this mess Bert discovered a crosscut saw with many teeth missing. It resembled the blade of the mowing-machine. And a constructive idea struck him. They would make a mowing-machine of their own. Uncle Allan saw them tinkering with this contraption and gave them his amused encouragement. He was, it seems, a kindly man with a special appreciation of boys; perhaps that is the reason why Herbert Hoover in after-years gave the name Allan to his own second son. It seems miraculous, until you consider what boys are doing to-day with parts of deceased Ford cars; but they produced a plaything which not only traveled on wheels but did in an intermittent and uncertain fashion move the saw-blade across its bed. That spring's calving had brought into the world a heifer of which the boys made a special pet. She should provide the motive-power. They rigged her a harness out of old rope-ends and disintegrating straps, gave her a few lessons in driving, and then tried her out on the machine. It lasted less than a minute. When the clatter broke out behind her she gave a frightened bleat and bolted, dragging after her Bert at the end of the lines, the machine at the end of the traces. After cutting a swath across the vegetable garden, she smashed it against the trunk of a tree—a total wreck.

The boys were constructing a new mowing-machine, when a passé clothes-wringer caught their attention. It embodied the principle of those sorghum mills by which the farmers ground molasses out of cane. That was hint enough. They managed to set it upon a base, so to rig it with the wheels and cams salvaged from the mowing-machine that it would grind at the propulsion of a long pole. To that pole, in imitation of the horse which motived "grown up" sorghum mills, they hitched their calf. With one boy pulling her from before and another pushing or braking from behind, she worked better. Actually, they succeeded in grinding out a few spoonfuls of somewhat tinged sorghum molasses, sweeter by far than any which Aunt Millie served them at table.

CHAPTER IV

THIS farm-life lasted until Herbert Hoover was eleven years old. Then came another of those abrupt breaks from old association which have made the rhythm of his life. With him things have always changed suddenly, completely, as by a cast of the die in the hands of fate. John Minthorn, his mother's brother, was a physician. He, like Laban Miles, had felt the Indian problem tugging at his Quaker conscience, had served as a reservation physician, as agent, as head of an Indian school. Now he was venturing into business. During the two centuries of our westward advance the Quakers have always trekked in groups. A peculiar people, they wanted to keep their own customs and mode of worship; this was impossible if they scattered themselves among other sects. Now, Quakers were passing on to Oregon—the last frontier. Infected with the boom, Dr. Minthorn conceived the idea of settling, on the land about Newberg on the Willamette, a Quaker colony with its own meetinghouse and its own academy, which he hoped some day to build into a college. Now, at last, he was opening the academy. Here was a chance for Bertie to make a start in the world while carrying his share of the family burden; paying his board by doing chores round the school, he would get a better education than the district schools of rural Cedar county could possibly afford. Dr. Minthorn wrote home to that effect.

By letter, or in conferences after meeting, the Hoovers and Minthorns threshed it out and reached a unanimous conclusion. Huldah had hoped to give her boys a higher education; next to holiness, it was her dearest wish for them. While Uncle Allan and Aunt Millie desired with their emotions to keep him as their son, their minds told them that this was his chance. Herbert knew of these plans and negotiations; and when at last Uncle Allan announced, "Thee is going to Oregon," he found himself torn between grief at parting with these tender and understanding substitutes for parents and the thrill of a venture into the world. His lips closed very tight, he bade them good-by. Oliver Hammel, a friend of the family, was going to Oregon. Allan Hoover put the boy in his charge. With a large hamper for provision, they traveled west by emigrant train. At Portland they parted company. Herbert never saw Oliver Hammel again. In charge of the captain, he traveled up the Willamette on a stern-wheel river steamer to Newberg, journey's end.

The town, and the budding agricultural region which supported it, were then just a clearing among the thick, sceptral evergreen forest which in a state of nature clothed our northwestern river-banks. For the moment Herbert Hoover was catching up with his past. Andrew Hoover, a hundred and fifty years before, had cleared the pine forests of the North

MRS. JESSE HOOVER
Mother of Herbert Hoover

Carolina mountains for his seeding-ground. John his son hewed the chestnuts of the Ohio hills; Eli his great-grandson the willows of the Iowa bottom-lands. Always they had lived and worked like these pioneers of Oregon—in Quaker colonies, soberly, fearing the Lord. It was the pioneer life without the old, accustomed trimmings of whisky violence.

To this Quaker colony Dr. John Minthorn stood a kind of *Pooh-Bah*. He managed the perplexing business of its land company; he was its sole physician. In default of funds, he served as president of the academy; later even taught a class in physiology. "A severe man on the surface, but like all Quakers kindly at bottom," says his nephew. Under his quiet surface lay concealed tremendous mental and physical energies. The first modest building of the academy —it has grown since into an institution of high academic rank—was not ready when Herbert arrived. So the boy settled into his uncle's house and went for a time to a little clapboarded public school.

When at last the academy opened, he settled into two or three years of sober routine. He was chore-boy not only for the school but for his uncle. He fed and curried the doctor's horses, fed and milked the cows, helped with the furnace, and for the rest—went to school. Now, for the first time, his relatives noticed something unusual about him. One handmaid of his greater powers is a remarkable memory, "wax to receive impressions, steel to hold them." His lessons took him no time at all. But school did not seem especially to interest him. "What was your favorite study?" some inquisitor asked him years later. "None," he replied. "They were something to race through—so I could get out of doors." In spite of school and chores, he found time to read for himself. Dr. John Minthorn belonged to the liberal branch of his sect; the growing library of the academy included classical English fiction. With the thirst of an inhibited desire, Herbert plunged into Scott, read the Waverly novels from cover to cover; then Thackeray, Dickens, and Shakespeare.

The urge for romance appeased, he took to history, and especially American history. Uncle John was a rigid Sabbatarian. On Sunday mornings, when work of necessity was done, came Sabbath school; then the long meeting; then dinner; then a period of sluggish rest followed by a Band of Hope meeting, where the lecturer or teacher displayed colored prints of the drunkard's dreadful interior on each stage of his downward path, with corresponding illustrations of his demeanor and conduct. This finished, until bedtime one might read an improving book. By inquiry and experiment, Herbert found that the definition of "improving," while excluding all fiction, could be stretched to include history.

"A boy's will is the wind's will," and especially at the age of puberty. When he was fourteen, Herbert passed from the grammar grades into the equivalent of high school. He had a bit of elementary Latin, some algebra, and a knowledge rather more thorough of physiology. Then Minthorn's affairs took a lunge forward. The northwestern land boom was on. He had merged his Quaker development with the Oregon Land Company, which had offices in Salem and Portland. He himself intended to take charge of the Salem offices. Herbert Hoover was bored with the routine of school. Business—a plunge into the world—had its appeal. When Dr. Minthorn removed to Salem, Herbert Hoover went along as his office boy.

He was to become in the course of the next thirty years the human symbol of efficiency, so perhaps it goes without saying that he made a good office boy. Those who remember the Oregon Land Company say that he had the pride of an office manager or a head clerk. Without instruction he picked up typewriting; in order to help out on the books he perfected that firm, clear handwriting of his with its tendency to a Spencerian flourish. (In later years, what with the pressure of things more important than penmanship, it has grown less legible.) This job gave him some leisure. In summers, in the long open springs and autumns, he kept his eye on the clock, and the moment he turned the key in the office door raced away to play baseball or to go fishing along the river.

A casual bit of atmosphere and an accidental meeting gave his career its direction and awoke his ambition; it was as though a bud had blossomed in a moment. Certain directors and customers of the Oregon Land Company were interested not only in farms but in mines. They displayed specimens, talked drifts and leads and prospects. The office boy grew mildly interested; this searching the blind earth for treasure had its appeal. Then one day there appeared an engineer engaged to develop one of these mines. Herbert Hoover does not now remember his name nor how they happened to fall into conversation. One conjectures that something about the boy's doings gave this stranger a clue to latent but unusual powers, and awoke a sympathetic interest. At any rate, the engineer asked suddenly, "Son, why don't you go in for engineering?" Then he talked—while Herbert stood fascinated—about his own job with its out-of-doors life, its intellectual thrills, its possibilities in the West. "We've been short on technical instruction out here on the coast," he added in effect. "But Senator Stanford is opening a new university down in California next year. They're going to have one of the best men in the world for head of the mining and geology department—John Branner. Tuition will be free; and an ambitious boy can work his way through."

By the time this stranger left the office an astonishing thing had happened to Herbert Hoover—a change as sudden and revolutionary as a sincere religious conversation. The boy was a drifter no longer. In an instant he had grown up. He wanted to go to Stanford, to become a mining engineer. Modern psychologists say of such abrupt mental and spiritual changes as this that the apparent cause is not really a cause but an occasion—a spark falling into a pile of tinder which has been long accumulating. Stored in his memory and his subconsciousness there lay inert his love of the out-of-doors, his play-experiments with machinery on the Allan Hoover farm, the delight, which he had never admitted to himself, in using his beautifully balanced mind. That talk with the stranger mining engineer fused all these atoms, set them into dynamic action....

As his affairs straightened out, Dr. Minthorn had sent to Iowa for his mother and May Hoover. To this uncle and grandmother Herbert made shy confession of his ambition. They and all his other Quaker relatives approved the object but disapproved the means. Why Stanford, a worldly institution? The Society of Friends had universities of high standing. Theodore, for example, was going to Penn College. Let Herbert follow him. Herbert, however, was fresh from the memory of his hard-working, unexciting years at the academy. Further, the Quaker colleges ran to literature, abstract learning, and the humanities, while Stanford would have the scientific and technical cast. Shrewdly he hammered in this last point, and by means of it beat down their opposition. He sent for an advance catalogue of the coming Leland Stanford Junior University. The entrance requirements filled him with despair. He had small Latin, no Greek, no modern language, no science except the physiology he had learned in the academy from his Uncle John, and little skill in writing the English language. However, one obscure paragraph gave him a gleam of hope. A few imperfectly prepared students of special promise and merit would be admitted as "specials." At once, he entered a night business-college and went to work at mathematics. In this he expressed not only his natural bent but also his shrewdness and judgment. Stanford or no Stanford, he intended to be an engineer; and mathematics is the engineer's main tool.

The opening of Stanford was set for August, 1891 —the month when Herbert Hoover would reach the age of seventeen. And in the spring, Professor Joseph Swain, engaged as head of the mathematics department, visited Portland to conduct preliminary entrance examinations. Herbert Hoover presented himself among the candidates. Swain talked to him between sessions. A born educator with a talent for evoking confidence, he drew from this shy lad the essentials of his history and circumstances. Now Swain was himself a Quaker—he died president of Swarthmore College. Just man though he was, the common faith doubtless swayed his attitude. Yet when the papers came in, Herbert Hoover had failed.

A man of less sympathy and thoroughness might have marked him simply "insufficiently prepared." But Swain took the trouble to analyze the papers in mathematics. The boy had not gone far enough with either algebra or geometry; that was the sole trouble. What he knew he knew. Besides, Swain, a mathematician who lived in the fourth dimension, perceived a special talent; just as a professional writer sometimes sees in the awkward compositions of a child the promise of form and imagination. So they had another talk. Said Swain in substance:

"I understand you're poor—expect to work your way through, don't you? Then you can't waste time on three or four years at preparatory school. We have tutors at Stanford. If you'll come down to Palo Alto a few weeks before the university opens, take tuition in mathematics and English and pass examinations in them, I think I can get you admitted." Swain knew what the boy did not—that Stanford would for a year or two go lightly on applicants for matriculation. Now, in its thirty-seventh year, it imposes besides strict entrance examinations an intelligence test—and has at that a long waiting list. But then, as it prepared to raise the curtain, the chief concern was getting enough students to justify its plant and endowment. Its roving missionaries like Swain had instructions to encourage boys of special character and native abilities. And Swain, who perceived talent in Hoover's incomplete mathematics papers, must also have felt the power under his quiet surface, the steel in his blood.

CHAPTER V

To understand Hoover's life during the next four years it is necessary to know something about Leland Stanford Junior University. It sprang full-born from the brain and fortune of Senator Leland Stanford, a memorial to his only son, who died at the age of sixteen. He owned a beautiful and famous ranch at the head of the Santa Clara Valley, thirty miles south of San Francisco—a paradise of fertile fields, vineyards, semi-tropical gardens, artificially planted forests. To westward rose the Coast Range, wooded and colorful; to eastward, Mount Hamilton shadowed glimpses of San Francisco Bay. On one side of this principality grazed the famous Stanford trotting-stud, whose glory was Electioneer and his dynasty of sons; on the other lay a stable, almost equally famous, of thoroughbred running horses. There I have myself seen the month-old Rosormonde, daughter of Ormonde and Fairy Rose—priced from her birth at $25,000—hold court to half the horsemen of the Pacific coast. However, even before he conceived the university Stanford had ceased to enter these darling hobbies of his in racing meets, and concerned himself solely with improving the breed. Marking almost the northeastern corner of the estate stood a gigantic sequoia tree, strayed by some freak of growth from those mountain meadows which are the natural habitat for this species. And the town near its foot, consisting then of a flag-station on the Southern Pacific and a few flimsy cottages, was called Palo Alto or "Tall Tree." Between that and Menlo Park, the first regular station on the line, there was not when the university opened a single house.

In an open hay-field amid this setting Senator Stanford laid out the campus for a new free university, "dedicated to make men and women useful." He had risen to wealth and power without the aid of formal education; but he had the common sense to recognize his own limitations. When he needed technical advice or assistance, he asked always, "Who is the best expert in this line?" The most famous American architect of the period was Richardson, who built Trinity Church in Boston. Stanford employed him to design the buildings. Taking his cue from the churches and cloisters of the pioneer Franciscan friars, Richardson worked out the California mission style; which, in the hands of imitators, has blossomed into beauty or degenerated into atrocity over the whole State. For ideas about curriculum and policy he consulted Charles W. Eliot, president of Harvard. Eliot had just stirred up the conservatives of the academic world by installing the elective system. For Stanford he laid out a scheme even more broadly elective. A young luminary had risen in the West—David Starr Jordan, eminent ichthyologist, poet, and executive, who had recreated the University of Indiana. Him Stanford secured as president; he brought with him almost the pick of that strong young faculty which he had gathered about him, including Swain, who had already met Herbert Hoover, and Branner, who was human focus for his young imagination.

So in June, 1891, Hoover packed and started from Salem to Palo Alto. With him traveled Fred Williams, whom he had met at the preliminary examinations at Portland, and who himself needed a little coaching before he tackled his "finals." With inherent and instilled Quaker thrift, Hoover had opened a savings-bank account as soon as he began to earn wages. Also, Laurie Tatum, his guardian, had made a modest addition from the tiny estate of Jesse Hoover. That was all, Laurie Tatum wrote; when it was spent Herbert must support himself. Altogether he had about $300. From that he must buy his passage to California, pay his tuition fees, live until September. The rest would not last far into his expensive freshman year.

He found the university in the last of its birth-pains. Workmen were putting finishing touches to the inner quadrangle, that stretch of tile-roofed one-story buildings connected by rainproof arcades which is still the heart of Stanford's serious activities. They were hurrying to complete Encina and Roble Halls, respectively the men's and women's dormitories; the power plant which, with addition of recitation rooms and huddled laboratories, was to serve for the present as home of the engineering department; a row of frame houses for faculty residence. The campus was still "all torn up" and resonant with sawing and hammering.

On the unfinished campus stood Adelante Villa, an

old country residence transformed into a boardinghouse. Here dwelt the advance guard of the faculty and a few students who like himself needed tutoring for entrance examinations. Under Miss Pearson he prepared to attack two dreaded barriers—the literature and composition of his native tongue. The composition examination became later a university bugbear under the name of English 1B. Professor Melville Anderson, selected as head of the English department, had insisted that no man or woman should enter Stanford, or at least that none should be graduated, without proving the ability to write an acceptable essay—straightforward, correctly spelled, grammatically and rhetorically accurate. Many among the early student body had been reared in pioneer surroundings; and correct academic English was not a virtue or accomplishment of the frontier. Perhaps a third of the men in the early classes—and this was especially true of the engineers—entered "conditioned in English 1B" and took examination after examination until at some time in their junior or senior years they had a brilliant or lucky day and passed. Hoover set himself painfully to perfect the art of expression. It came hard. Then and for many years after he was impatient of words. This, I think, is often a minor flaw of men who think actively and in large terms. Language seems so trivial and so inaccurate in comparison with their rich thought that they despair of it as a medium. In English he was not a promising pupil.

Mathematics, under Miss Fletcher, went better of course; and for the first time perhaps he became aware of his own exceptional memory. When, just before matriculation day, he took his final entrance examinations, he passed triumphantly in algebra and geometry and comfortably in American history—he needed no tutoring in that; it had long been his favorite reading. He scratched through in English and American literature; that, after all, is only a matter of remembering what Longfellow wrote or when Shakespeare died. But English 1B floored him. He entered conditioned; semi-annual examinations during the next few years failed to clear the condition away. He passed it only on the eve of graduation; and then only because one of his engineering professors shook a technical paper of his before the noses of the English department and demanded to know if a man who could express himself as logically as that wasn't worthy of a Stanford degree. He must assume a triple burden from now on: keeping up with his studies in a university which was soon notorious in the academic world as easy to enter and hard to stay in, making up five or six entrance "credits," and earning his living.

A fortnight before the university opened its doors, the plant—so far as it went—was pronounced finished; and Hoover moved into Encina Hall, the men's dormitory. University tradition, probably accurate in this case, says that he was the first student who ever slept there. And he was waiting by the pillars of the front piazza when the station omnibuses from Menlo Park began delivering that interesting and amusing body of students which formed the early classes.

Stanford was not only a brand-new university but a

departure in higher education. From the American men and women who stood prepared to enter college that autumn it had drawn by natural attraction such original and able characters as fixed their eyes on the future rather than the past. Having flouted tradition, they set immediately to work to create traditions of their own. They wanted to play football; but few of them had ever seen a set of goal-posts. Also, in the confusion of organizing a brand-new university, there was no time to gather and train a team that autumn. But what law prevented football at any season?

In January a scratched-up football association marked out a gridiron on a lumpy hay-field and imported an Olympic Club player to teach the game. Across the bay stood the University of California, old and established as western universities went—a Godsent rival. Stanford challenged, California accepted. The game came off in San Francisco during the green and pleasant month of March. All the metropolis attended to see what the university would do to this upstart. During its cavorting on the hay-field the Stanford team developed Clemons, an inspired running half-back —a Red Grange of his time. Round him the coach had built his strategy. The California forwards punched holes through the heavy but inexpert Stanford line. But Clemons ran the traditional rings round them. Stanford won, 14 to 10. The baseball team, assembled at about this time, for four years won not only every academic series it played, but nearly every game. The artistic element wanted college shows; but they had no theater. However, there stood the big wooden gymnasium.

Some engineer or other built a temporary knock-down stage with footlights, border-lights, curtains, and scene-loft. Thereafter, on the eve of a university holiday, engineering students employed at twenty cents an hour started a night shift which, before morning, had the stage ready for the performance. Within two years Harry Connick, sole director, coach, and orchestra leader, had presented a most creditable performance of "Pinafore."

For a year the freshman class—'95—made up the bulk of the student body. When '96 entered, there began the custom of "rushing." That is a polite name for struggles which, in ferocity and intensity, resembled war. The northern Santa Clara Valley made and used much hay. They baled, in that time and clime, not with wire but with rope. Oddments of loose but strong hempen cord lay all about the fields and farm buildings. The belligerent classes would put on their oldest clothes, gather munitionment of rope, and join battle either after formal challenge or by sudden surprise. The object was to tie the opposing army hand and foot. Sense of fair play forbade hitting, biting, or in other manner committing deliberate mayhem. Otherwise, there were no rules. The smaller and weaker members of the class were told off to slip into the mêlée with open knives and cut loose their fallen comrades. By this means the struggle was prolonged to a contest in physical endurance. The losers had simply collapsed. The victors, after a space of rest and rejoicing, piled the trussed-up captives like dressed pigs into wagons, drove forth into the farming country, and lashed them to fence-posts. There they stood like martyrs awaiting the fire, until they worked their bonds loose or some kindly farmer accommodated. It was twice as rough as our old-fashioned mass-play football and therefore twice as fascinating; and every one could get into the game. Why the faculty tolerated it so long, I have never known. Perhaps they felt that if they checked it, these wild young rough-necks would blow off their energies in some form more dangerous to academic discipline. At any rate it lasted far into the age of refinement.

That same able faculty had a slightly Puritanical tinge; and it took seriously its charge of creating useful men from this powerful but unlicked material. Failure to maintain the stiff academic pace and conspicuous departure from the Victorian code of morals meant dismissal. Probably no other university of its time had so large a proportion of what my brother Wallace has called "graduates by request."

If I have digressed to describe Stanford of that early day, it is to show the effect of this environment on the slim, shy Quaker lad, just turned seventeen, who from behind the pillars of Encina Hall watched this colorful and turbulent flock assemble. He had lived, so far as he was aware, a happy childhood. But after all, that sympathetic brooding which makes childhood supremely happy had been lacking to his life since he was nine years old; for the greater part of another seven years a repressed atmosphere, wherein his extraordinary intelligence had no proper soil for growth; and hard work at menial or mechanical tasks.

The atmosphere of freedom, of high animal spirits, the intellectual stimulus of those original young professors who went adventuring to Stanford—these struck in. Here he knew first joy of the intellect, here he felt the initial stirring of his higher powers, here he found his wife. Stanford became a kind of complex with Herbert Hoover. Within fifteen years his interests and his wanderings were to embrace the globe; but those golden hills above Palo Alto were always the pole to his compass.

But now he must take thought of pressing personal affairs. What with board and tuition, laboratory fees, and purchase of equipment, he had less than a hundred dollars left. He found that the registrar needed a temporary clerk to help enter this sudden inundation of students. On representation of his experience as an office boy he got the job. Seated at a table before a temporary office, he took down statistics of their birth, guardianship, and academic intentions; the old archives of Stanford are still sprinkled with records in that firm business hand. This over, he got the contract for handling and delivering the San Francisco newspapers on the campus. For a year he was up with the lark, making his rounds before breakfast. He kept this franchise for a year or so; however, as the university grew he found it possible to hire another man, at current student wages and a partnership, to do the leg-work; while he took a modest but steady profit for managing the enterprise and keeping the books. Finally he sold his share in the route for $40. Later in his course he obtained a laundry agency. For this he himself performed the labor, calling for the bags Monday morning, delivering the parcels Saturday afternoon. Because of the public and intimate nature of the job, most of us thought that this gave Hoover his main support at the university. As a matter of fact, it was the least of his enterprises; paying so little in proportion to the time and energy which it demanded that he was always on the point of giving up the contract.

In the meantime, a minor disappointment. Professor Branner, owing to pressure of government work, could not come to Stanford until after Christmas; until then there would be no department of geology. Temporarily, Hoover registered as a mechanical engineer under A. W. Smith, himself a professor with the gift of inspiration. He "took," that first semester, advanced algebra, shop work in mechanics, linear and free-hand drawing.

Branner arrived in time to open his department at beginning of the second semester; and Hoover changed over to the mining side of engineering and registered in geology. Almost as though by fate or the direction of Providence, he fell under direction of a great natural teacher, one of the greatest I have ever known. A scholar to the marrow of his bones, Branner's code nevertheless envisaged the application of scholarship to practical purposes. He loved intellectual contacts; and in his quiet way he had the faculty of imparting his intellectual enthusiasms. And he gloried not so much in teaching facts as in getting at the minds of his students. Association with Branner was in itself a higher education. By another benevolent turn of fate, the geology department opened with only eleven students; Branner, therefore, could give each of his charges his individual attention.

Still better, circumstances threw Hoover and Branner into personal relations even closer. The new professor needed a part-time secretary; by virtue of his experience as an office boy, Hoover got the job. Henceforth he arranged Branner's desk in the morning, opened the mail, answered routine letters on the typewriter, in general kept the office running smoothly. Before long, Branner perceived the qualities of character and mind hidden beneath the placid surface of this gangling boy. Though his sense of justice inhibited him from parading the fact, Hoover became a favorite student. Just before Branner's death, Lester Hinsdale asked him, "What first attracted your special attention to Hoover?" "A bit of laboratory routine," said Branner. "I'd always employed the working students of my classes as assistants or secretaries. Constantly we received Geological Survey reports and German scientific periodicals. These, as they accumulated, had to be bound. I'd hand them over to the ordinary assistant and he'd ask, 'How and where?' 'Send them to a binder in the city,' I'd say, and he'd ask, 'How?' I'd answer, 'By express,' and he'd ask, 'How shall I pack them?'—and so on. But with Hoover I'd say, 'Get these periodicals bound,' and the next time I'd notice them they'd be back on the shelves and the bill for binding and shipping would lie on my desk."

In the midst of his triple struggle, Hoover—probably by virtue of his prodigious memory—managed to find time for the joys of college life. He attended that glorious, unique spring football game in San Francisco. He so arranged his laboratory work that he might come out as candidate for the freshman baseball team, and "made" shortstop. But a grounder tipped the ring finger of his left hand, causing an ugly sprain. That joint remained tender for years; it is still swollen. No more baseball; this ended his career as an athlete. That spring an epidemic of measles swept Encina dormitory. Hoover, being one of the youngest, was one of the first to catch the infection. For a fortnight he endured mild sufferings in the "bull-pen" over the dining hall, which Dr. Wood had turned into a temporary hospital. This setback compelled a month of hectic work at his studies and his business affairs; but he passed all his courses and ended his freshman year with a little money still in hand.

CHAPTER VI

DR. BRANNER, who retained his post as state geologist of Arkansas, was preparing a survey and a topographical map of that State. He intended to use the summer of 1892 for the work. Needing assistants, he put a proposition to his office boy. Herbert Hoover, although he had taken only a semester of geology, was far enough advanced to make himself useful in the field. It would afford a moderate salary, much practical education, best of all a few hours of university credit for "field work." So in the summer between his freshman and sophomore years, Hoover tramped the Ozarks with surveying instruments on his shoulder and a hammer in the belt of his overalls. He returned to the university as lean as a greyhound, as hard as nails, and as brown as a berry; and, by way of starting his sophomore year, with nearly two hundred dollars in his pocket.

He was getting on personally by now. However, affection for Hoover is not a sudden, dazzling discovery but a gradual dawning. Lester Hinsdale—of his class but some years older—sat opposite him at the university commons during most of their freshman year. "Very immature in appearance," he says, "probably the youngest looking of us all. He seemed shy to the point of timidity—rarely spoke unless spoken to. It wasn't until later, when we got into politics on the same side and I began to see under his surface, that I realized how much it was possible to like him." In Sam Collins, however, he had found already a kindred spirit. Collins was one of the oldest members of the pioneer class, as Hoover was perhaps the youngest. He had taken his own buffets from the outer world before he came as a working student to shelter of alma mater. The town of Palo Alto, on the strength of the university, was enjoying a building boom; new dwellings stood available for student uses. At the beginning of their sophomore year Collins proposed that as a matter of sociability and economy they establish a coöperative boarding-house at Romero Hall. There Hoover lived through his sophomore year, walking to laboratory and classes through the shades of the beautiful Stanford arboretum. And there, under tutelage of Collins, he first became interested in university politics.

For at the moment the students of Stanford were entering a turbulent era. The university had sprung into being full-grown. During its first four years it seemed a microcosm of a nation which, having gained its independence, is learning by mistakes how to govern itself. In the first semester enterprising seniors had formed "the student body," of which every one matriculated at Stanford was theoretically a member. This took control of that major activity, football. But weekly new enterprises were starting up—a daily newspaper, a monthly magazine, a glee club, a band, an orchestra, a mandolin club, track, lawn tennis, and baseball clubs.

Over these new activities the students in general had no control; often they were managed solely for financial benefit of the promoters and with a looseness which raised unjust suspicion of graft. A "farm university," a self-contained little world, Stanford has always taken its private affairs intensely. The campus was bubbling with gossip, seething with a vague desire for change.

At the birth of the university, advanced students had brought in the Greek letter fraternities. The very masculine rawness of early-day Stanford drove these societies to extremes of fashion and refinement. When in after-years I began to get acquainted with eastern colleges, I was surprised to find poor but able students, even working students, wearing fraternity pins. Such things did not happen in the Stanford of my days! And, indeed, what with age and wisdom she too has forgotten this attitude. The fraternities combined at birth of the university to control its politics; for though only a minority of the student body, they had no organized opposition. And by virtue of that attraction which a fraternity pin holds for the feminine imagination, they could always "swing the co-ed vote."

In Hoover's second year there rose a prophet of the "barbs" or non-fraternity men whose appropriate name was Zion. His constant tilting against things as they are gave him the nickname of "Sosh"—short for Socialist. And so all Stanford calls him even to-day, when he is a staid and respected city functionary of San Francisco. He set himself squarely against the fraternity element; began to organize the barbs, announced his candidacy for president of the student body. Collins swung in behind him in this campaign, and Hoover followed. It was with him a matter of boyish conviction. He had come to Stanford to find a free and democratic university where men shone by their intellectual merit. Artificial distinctions did not fit the picture. Still less did they harmonize with those principles of the founders which he had imbibed from his reading in American history. He had been brought up a Republican in a town which included only one Democrat; the principles of the Republican party were to him ingrained, axiomatic, as much a part of one's self as his religion or his nationality. This belief that a university should be democratic was his first burning and original political conviction.

Behind the engineering buildings stood "the camp," a row of wooden shacks erected for the workmen who built the university, and for some reason left standing. There students too poor to pay even the $23.50 a month charged for board in Encina Hall slept in bunks and cooked their own meals over kerosene stoves; in a climate where the thermometer touches freezing point only two or three times a year, they had no heating problem. Now, although Hoover was making enough money to live in the dormitory or a boarding-house, this element knew his worldly circumstances and regarded him as one of their own. Collins and Zion set him to "deliver the camp." He was still rather inarticulate—this repressed boy of eighteen—but his very struggles for expression gave somehow a glimpse into his sincerity. Barbs with address and finesse worked systematically among the girls. There appeared with the class of '96 a tall, gangling freshman who kept in his room as his proudest possession a tambourine on which his elder brother, a cadet at Annapolis, had made the world's record for the high kick. As Ray Lyman Wilbur, he became a quarter of a century later president of Stanford. He organized and "delivered" the majority of the freshmen. In the course of this job he became acquainted with Hoover. Their intelligences—immature but strong and realistic—threw off sparks on contact. Also, they had the bond of common enthusiasm for science. Here began a friendship which has lasted all their lives.

An unprecedented list of voters appeared at the polls before the chapel. And by a close vote Zion won. It was not, however, a decisive victory; the fraternities still held the minor offices. Nor had the student body done anything toward controlling or centralizing its activities. The minor teams, the periodicals, and the musical clubs were still running wild. The baseball team, whose merits had given it wide advertising, was planning summer tours on its own initiative, meeting all comers. Before this finished, there was a minor athletic scandal.

In the summer of 1893—between his sophomore and junior years—Hoover, thanks again to Dr. Branner, got a job with the United States Geological Survey. He found himself under a great master of geology, Waldemar Lindgren; the work involved visiting mines and studying mineral deposits. As he ranged the Sierra on horseback, he thought not only on the bones of the earth but on this problem of the Stanford student body. He returned in September with a mature plan in his mind—his first creation in organization. All student activities should lie under control of the student body; and the active manager should be a bonded and double-audited student body treasurer. The common treasury should collect all gate receipts from athletic contests and shows of the musical clubs, and should pay all expenses. That was the essence of a constitution which, with minor modifications, still governs the student activities of Stanford and which many another western university has copied. That autumn Hoover reëntered the dormitory; Palo Alto was too far from the center of things. Collins, Kimball, Zion, Wilbur, Herbert Hicks, and finally Lester Hinsdale, whose integrity and sterling young judgment had given him much quiet standing, took up the plan, threshed it out in long night-talks, compromised on this or that disputed point, put it into legal form.

Then came the question of procedure. Should they "spring it" now? Much debate through the pipe-smoke before they decided to concentrate on electing in the spring an administration pledged to the new idea. And, as they began disputing and trading over candidates, they saw that the man for treasurer—the most important job—was Hoover. His abilities had dawned upon them, not burst. Collins had first realized his practical talents when the finances of Romero Hall became tangled and complex, and Hoover, with just a touch here and there, straightened them out. Hinsdale, who two years before had noticed him across the table as a quiet, repressed, and especially immature specimen of the raw freshman, now began to admire his judgment. "It seemed to me," he said thirty years later, "that this kid always ignored unessentials and got to the heart of any situation."

However, when they suggested it they found that Hoover needed persuading. He believed that the treasurer, alone among the student body officers, should draw a modest salary. The incumbent should be a graduate student, taking a half course; otherwise he stood to neglect either the job or his university work. He himself had his living to make and a heavy burden of university work to carry.

"But there's the salary," they said; "you can drop your work for Doc Branner and your laundry agency. The job will support you."

"No, sir!" responded Hoover, emphatically. "If I accept this nomination and get elected, there's one thing sure. I take no salary. Otherwise, they'll say I'm backing the new constitution just to get a paid job!"

As the first semester of his junior year drew on to Christmas, not only his associates but the student body in general were beginning to appreciate Hoover's qualities. "Popularity" is not exactly the word for his reaction and influence on his fellows. A better word, probably, would be "standing." The bleachers never rose and cheered when he passed; but subtly he expressed and radiated leadership. "Here I was," says Hinsdale, "older, you know, and probably better at expressing myself. But whenever I came to Hoover with a suggestion or a proposal, I found myself wondering what he'd think—and wondering a little apprehensively, as though it were my major professor." When

New Year's brought the second semester, and the "barb push" began to mature its plans, they realized that Hoover would be the strength of their ticket; that without him they could not win. They renewed their persuasions.

"Well, perhaps I can swing it—but no salary!" he said at last. And no salary did he take.

So they nominated for student body president the solid and esteemed Lester Hinsdale, for football manager that popular character Herbert Hicks, and for treasurer Hoover. Presently fences and pavements blossomed with the legend in colored chalks, "Vote the 3-H Ticket," and Stanford was in the midst of a campaign without precedent for heat and intensity. Every elector was canvassed and recanvassed; on the morning of election day corps of volunteer workers scurried over all northern Santa Clara County getting out the vote. Hoover and Hicks won by an easy margin over Grosh and Kessinger; but Hinsdale and the popular Magee were tied. This brought a special election just as hot, wherein Hinsdale won by a hundred votes. The three-H's presided at a loud rally of triumph in Encina Hall and broke Stanford precedent by opening cigars for the crowd. At once they set out to fulfil their pledge concerning the new constitution.

There had been so much politics that year as rather to alarm Dr. Jordan. "I wonder if I'm presiding over a young Tammany Hall," he remarked once. But he had greater perplexities at the moment. In the summer of 1893 Senator Stanford had died, and the Government had instituted a suit concerning the ownership of certain bonds issued to build the Union Pacific Railroad. The endowment was tied up in the courts; Stanford must for the time not only cease to expand but fight and scrimp for very existence. Also, the thing might as well be settled once for all. And so the faculty did not interfere.

No longer now was this a "barb-frat" controversy, but rather a struggle between conservatives, including those who profited by the old system, and progressives. Almost at the last moment "Sosh" Zion threatened to jump the traces. He objected to the salary for the treasurer. There were hot caucuses before he fell into line. Then came a meeting of the student body which packed the chapel. Zion read the proposed constitution and announced the beginning of the debate. Big Bill Hazzard rose. Though, oddly, he did not find it out for another year, he was a heaven-born center rush. Big as a house, he seemed just a huge pudding of a man. You had to play body-to-body against him, as I have, to realize that what looked like fat was pure muscle oddly placed, and that he was as light on his feet as a stage dancer. "Mr. President," he began, "large bodies move slowly—" The speech never got any farther than that; but it served. Laughter which lasted a full two minutes broke the tension. A hot afternoon of serious debate; and the Stanford student body passed that constitution which, with slight amendment, has stood for thirty-four years. It provided that all undergraduate enterprises should be the property of the student body and under its control; that accounts must be kept, audited, and published in detail.

A spasm of hard work for Hoover now. He carried that semester a very stiff course. He must "cram" for final examination with one lobe of his brain while organizing the new system with the other; and all the while he had his living to make. Also, on the day after the spring session closed, he must take train to his summer job. His work with the United States Geological Survey had attracted some attention. Waldemar Lindgren, who was making a survey of the interesting Pyramid Peak quadrangle near Lake Tahoe, had asked for him again. Another summer of travel by horseback, eating at a camp-fire, and living under the stars—of serene study. It was all part of a training in varied fields of engineering—from triangulation to topographic and geologic mapping. Lindgren liked so well this boyish assistant and his work that the maps and reports, when finished, bore not only his own name but that of Herbert Hoover. . . . Years later, Hoover confessed to a friend that no subsequent honor ever puffed him up so much as this. . . . The necessity of finishing the survey forced him to enter the university late. But he brought back the whole salary of three hundred dollars.

Things had gone at loose ends in the meantime, and the whole system of student government was in worse shape than he supposed. That autumn he experienced his first academic failure—he "flunked" in German. Fortunately, earning a living made him less trouble than in previous years. Stanford had a course of paid Tuesday evening lectures and concerts. Upon graduation of a student who managed it the year before,

Hoover inherited this enterprise. It fitted in with his work as treasurer; and though it involved some risk—nothing venture, nothing have. He passed over the laundry agency to other hands. . . . That year, in this same lecture course, I heard a young congressman from Nebraska express himself with empty eloquence on the issues of the day. Two years later he was world-famous as William Jennings Bryan. . . .

Entering as a freshman, my first impression of Hoover, our most eminent senior, resembled that of some great impersonal force. Jack Reynolds and Jule Frankenheimer, the uncheckable half-back; Phat Downing, the mighty football captain; Charlie Field and Edward Maslin Hulme, the university poets; Bledsoe and Magee, the statesmanlike intercollegiate debaters—them one cheered or joked from the bleachers. But Hoover, while he walked humanly among us, was a kind of legend, too; a supernally able personage. We both lived in Encina dormitory; so I must have seen him constantly at meals. I was playing football; so I have beheld him conferring with Walter Camp, who coached us that year. I knew that he was a great man just by common report. Yet I have no concrete memory of him until that day when, playing center on the freshman team, I broke my ankle most painfully and completely. Dr. Wood, after giving first aid, sentenced me to live for the next three months in a plaster cast. And presently enter Hoover to assess and authorize the expenditure for surgical supplies.

Those broken bone-ends were hurting abominably, and I suppose that pain sharpens both the perceptions and the memory. At any rate, I have carried for more than thirty years the picture of him as he stood framed by the yellow door of my dormitory room. He was tall—just under six feet—broad-shouldered, very lean of figure. He wore one of those double-breasted blue suits which have since become almost a uniform with him. He had a slight stoop which, you felt, came rather from excess muscular development of the shoulders than from the midnight oil. As he contemplated the damaged member, he carried his head a trifle to one side—another trick of attitude which marks him to this day. He had mouse-colored hair, as stubbornly straight as an Indian's, and hazel eyes so contemplative that they seemed dreamy. His round but powerful face had not a straight line in it. That oddity, I have noticed since, often characterizes the physiognomies of extremely able men—O. Henry and Lord Northcliffe, for example. He stood with one foot thrust forward, jingling the keys in his trousers pocket; a little nervous trick which he has never overcome.

Hoover consulted the rubber, who was acting as nurse, concerning needs and costs of the operation. Some piece of material was lacking to the university medicine-chest. He sent out one of the crowd—Charlie Dole, my roommate, I suppose—with a telegram to San Francisco. I made some little joke or other by way of keeping up my courage, and he laughed—in his fashion. That fashion was a deep, rich chuckle which seemed to originate far down in his chest and in his psychology; and to lose most of its force in inner mirth before it came to the surface. I cannot remember that I have ever heard him laugh "out loud." But that chuckle expresses a world of appreciation for the humors of this funny and contrary world. He did not say a word of sympathy for me—in pain and forever out of football—but I felt it nevertheless. Then, at the door he turned for an instant and jerked out: "I'm sorry." Just that; but it was as though another man had burst into maudlin tears. The crown of that personality was shyness.

Then and there, I suppose, I put myself under his leadership. That kind of thing was always happening at Stanford. Even men who opposed him in the "great frat-barb war," coming afterward into association with him, began to lean on his sane unruffled judgment. The whimsies of life have permitted some of us to follow him since in affairs and struggles whose actors were kings, principalities and powers, dynasties and armies, violences of which the nineteenth century never dreamed, incredible human sacrifices, God-like benevolences. But the game was the same. . . .

The "big" football game with the University of California—played then in San Francisco and on Thanksgiving day—was of course the main present concern not only of the team but of its financial manager. Following that unexpected victory of the spring game in '92, California had for two years tied us. That autumn we presented a remarkably strong eleven. "From tackle to tackle," said Walter Camp, "it could trim any eastern university." We scarcely believed that; in the imagination of our generation the Big Three stood unconquerable. I realize now that he was prob-

"TAD," BERT AND MAY HOOVER AT SALEM, OREGON, ABOUT 1888

ably right. California, on its part, had an exceptional line and in Wolfe Ransome an inspired back. That game was a struggle of the giants. In the first half Fickert, our left guard, broke through and blocked one of Ransome's kicks with his forehead. Guy Cochrane, left tackle, following through, forgot that old-fashioned rule "fall on a loose ball." He had the instinctive originality to pick it up and carry it over the line for the only score of the game. A privileged cripple, I watched that glorious episode from the side-lines with the team, and I retain a vision of Hoover leaping up as though touched with an electric wire, and whooping like an Indian.

The exceptional quality of our team that year and the magic name of Walter Camp brought a challenge from Stagg's University of Chicago team, champions of the Middle West. This offer came like manna to the student body treasurer, struggling against that burden of outstanding debts to every incautious tradesman of the neighborhood, which the anarchy of three years had bequeathed him. In those days, when ten thousand spectators made an enormous football crowd, Chicago could not pay expenses of their long trip out of one exhibition. With the consent of Dr. Angell, chairman of the Faculty Athletic Committee, Hoover arranged for two games—one in San Francisco on Christmas day, wherein the middle westerners walked over us; and one in Pasadena on December 29, wherein we turned the tables. And on New Year's day the weary Stanford eleven beat the Los Angeles Athletic Club. It was barn-storming; henceforth the faculty prohibited this sort of thing. But it wiped out the deficit. Meantime, Hoover, displaying even in his teens his magic skill with organization, had the new plan running as smoothly and easily as though it had been a hundred years old.

He returned to Stanford early in January and buckled down to his university work. The "flunk" in German had put him into a bad hole. What with that and checking off part of his courses against admittance requirements, he needed nineteen "hours" to finish with his class; and generally no student was allowed to carry more than eighteen. But his efficiency in straightening out student finances and his brilliant record as a scholar won him special favor; the faculty made an exception in his case. During the semester I came to know him better; especially after spring rewoke politics and the "barb element" determined that Hinsdale, who expected to take a graduate course in law, was the man to carry on the Hoover policies. I helped to line up the freshman class. In the conferences over this or that problem of our bijou party in a toy state he seemed hesitant of advancing an opinion. Then, when every one else had expressed himself, he would come in with the final wise word. . . . After all, ours was the world in miniature. I lived to see him in councils whose decisions meant life or death for millions; yet it was always the same mind and the same method.

We knew something of his laboratory reputation as a brilliant scholar; for Dr. Branner, now that his favorite student was a senior, could afford to do a little vicarious boasting. However, no one considered him a "dig."

He was in everything that pertained to university life. As a sophomore he had fought in all the rushes. One amusing skirmish, which long remained a folktale at Stanford, he had won by strategy. Hearing a subdued disturbance in a new building near Romero Hall, he made a quiet investigation. On the second floor lay a dozen of his classmates, bound and gagged. The freshmen who put them there had gone back for more. Hoover cut them loose, sent couriers to gather reinforcements and munitionment of baling-rope. When the freshmen returned with another batch of captives, Hoover's guerrilla army leaped upon them in the dark, tied them up, and left them in that plight until the carpenters, arriving for the day shift, cut them loose. His adolescent sense of humor ran in those days to practical jokes. He played his quiet part in several of our best-remembered student pranks. And this minor episode sticks in my memory:

One moonless spring night a dozen of us were sitting in Hinsdale's room smoking and discussing, as students will, all topics of human interest and concern from the origin of the universe to free silver. How the talk dropped from that level I do not remember; but presently we were betting humorously who could run the fastest. "Well, I'll call your bluffs," said Hinsdale. "Out there's the cinder track, and here's a sack of Bull Durham tobacco as a prize." We all piled out into the darkness. Billy Knowles or some other man who ran for the varsity track team, and was therefore ineligible, started us. I remember that I adopted the strategy of sprinting for a lead. I kept it up too long. Three quarters of the way round I "blew up" and finished in the rear, dragging my lame leg. I found the rest of them pounding Hoover on the back and declaring between puffs that he was a born distance runner—with those legs and that chest, he ought to be. Back in the room, Hinsdale presented him the sack of tobacco with a mock oration. Hoover gave one of his rich chuckles and tossed it back. "You fellows," he said, "are good from the hips down, but from the necks up you're nothing at all. None of you noticed that I fell back of you at the start and cut across the infield and waited for you a half hour!" "Mr. Hoover," said Hinsdale, "needs a nice cold plunge to refresh him after his exhausting intellectual exertions. . . ." We overpowered him and carried him to the bathroom.

And now, Lou Henry of the freshman class enters his life.

The magic of Branner had drawn her also to Stanford; and she too was born in Iowa. Her father was a small-town banker. In the severe winters of the Middle West her mother developed a chronic cough. At that time science had not yet identified the tuberculosis bacillus, and such a symptom meant only one thing—"consumption." A mild dry climate was the standard treatment. The Henrys moved to Los Angeles. There she did not improve. Then they discovered Monterey. Some balm in its misty climate relieved the cough; for it was not tuberculosis at all but only a bronchial trouble. So, amid the gnome-like cypresses and adobe houses of that old Spanish capital, Lou Henry grew up —an athletic, out-of-doors girl who rode her bronco like a centaur. During her senior year in high school, Dr. Branner gave a series of university extension lectures in Monterey and she attended them. She is one of those women who thrill to intelligence. Before the course was finished she found herself fascinated by the mysteries in the bones of the earth. After the last lecture, she broke to her parents the news that she wanted to enter Stanford and to work under Branner. In those middle years of the mauve decade, sending a girl to college savored of unconventionality. But the Henrys were progressive people, and they had the means to indulge her whim. She was in those days as slim and supple as a reed. Her face had and has a beautiful bony structure, regular and delicate yet firm; and her wealth of brown hair she coiled about her forehead fillet-fashion. Though she brought no horse to Stanford, she used often to rent a hack from a livery stable at Palo Alto—riding, as was then required of a lady, side-saddle with much drapery of long skirts. I first noticed her for her horsemanship as much as for her beauty.

No sooner had she settled down to her laboratory work than she began hearing about Hoover. He was the brilliant student whose original work all the geology department tried to imitate. It was Hoover this and Hoover that—the great Hoover. She being a mere freshman and he an exalted senior, Miss Henry had no present hope of meeting him. Then one day Dr. Branner was discussing with her some new specimens in a cabinet. "Hoover brought them in from the field," he said. "They've been called carboniferous, but I'll eat my hat if they aren't pre-carboniferous. Isn't that your opinion, Hoover?" Miss Henry looked up. Beside Branner stood a lean, immature-looking boy. Was this the great Hoover? She had thought of him as seven feet tall with a beetling brow and a beard! As for Hoover, he stood speechless. Presently Dr. Branner, having finished his impromptu lecture, withdrew. And Hoover and Miss Henry fell into conversation about the carboniferous period. Next Friday night he put on his best suit and called at Roble Hall. Their acquaintance went steadily and serenely toward its destined end.

So at the end of May 1895, he being not yet twenty-one years old, Hoover took his diploma and departed for another summer of education among the mines, water sources, and forests of the West with the United States Geological Survey. No student who ever walked its shadowy arcades left behind him so deep an imprint on Stanford life and tradition. Perhaps in this story of his college days I have passed too lightly over the important point—his work in classroom and laboratory. During that early period Stanford kept no "marks"; one was simply passed, conditioned, or flunked. I cannot say, then, how he might have measured against conventional standards. And such data would mean little. For according to Branner and his other instructors, the remarkable thing about his university work was its originality. He attacked all problems, even of pure mathematics, in his own way and went forward to brilliantly original results.

Dr. Branner (who succeeded Jordan as president

A REMINISCENT BIOGRAPHY

of Stanford) had ideas on the training of engineers. He believed it a waste of energy to give the so-called "practical" courses in a university. He grounded his young men strongly in the sciences of mathematics, geology, chemistry, physics, and civil engineering—more strongly than is usual to-day in our engineering schools. With that equipment, he believed, they would absorb quickly a practical education from their hard knocks. Moreover, so equipped they might shift to any branch of engineering. For all which, that group of eminent engineers who passed through his hands daily give him thanks and loving memory.

Besides the training of the university, Hoover had worked during three vacations of three or four months in the government bureaus, where he came under tutelage of great experts upon public lands, water and power resources, forests. And the hard labor of those roving summers had maintained that physique, that farm-bred stamina, which he brought to the university; and which is serving him so well even to-day.

CHAPTER VII

WHEN Herbert Hoover left Stanford he had a little less than no money at all. The lecture course, while it made a small profit, did not turn out so well as he expected. Further, one or two working students of his intimate acquaintance needed money badly. His summer's earnings went for debts and loans—this last the beginning of his extensive and well-concealed personal philanthropies. Twenty years later he remarked: "I suppose it is good for some boys to make their way through college. Teaches them to buckle down. But in my case, I'm sure I'd have made myself a better all-round man if I hadn't lost so much time just making a living."

When he finished with the United States Geological Survey, he traveled on the last of his ready funds to Nevada City—once heart of the romantic Bret Harte region, center in his own day for Californian goldmining. There he hoped to get a job on the technical staff of some mine or other. He failed. One cardinal principle of the business as it was, he had not learned in college. The "practical miner," a graduate prospector, still held the reins; and this hardy son of toil scorned the "college-bred" as impractical and visionary. Good mining engineers with fine technical training were still, by way of disguise, wearing rough clothes, chewing tobacco, and debasing their grammar. Innocently, Hoover revealed his secret. There were, indeed, college-trained engineers in camp, mostly from the University of California; but these had no present opening. His college diploma closed the other doors against him.

Partly for practical experience "but mostly," he said afterward, "because I had to eat," he took a laborer's job in the drifts of the Mayflower. In collaboration with a shift of Cornish miners, he pounded a drill, shoveled ore, pushed a hand-car for eight hours a day or night. Tommy Ninnis, one of those veteran foremen who are to mining what hardened "non-coms" are to armies, served as his shift boss. And from him Hoover picked up practical tricks which came handy in his later career—on which subject Tommy Ninnis may readily be interviewed even to this day. At his boarding-house Hoover ran against E. B. Kimball, classmate in engineering at Stanford. He also was doing "practical work" in the drifts and stopes while waiting for an opening. And George Hoffman, a young mining engineer with a real job, began to take an interest in him. Of evenings or late afternoons—according to whether they were on day or night shift—Hoover and Kimball loafed about the Nevada City Hotel, picking up the lore of mining. Out of it all came with frequency and respect the name of Louis Janin. As the world dragged into 1896, Hoover had saved a little money from his $2.50 a day on the drill. And he came to a decision. Nevada City offered him no prospects besides day labor. He would go to San Francisco and ask Louis Janin for a job.

He was an outstanding personality even in that city of individuals, this Louis Janin. French by birth, he got his technical education both in Paris and in Freiburg, Germany. With his two equally well-known engineer brothers Henry and Alexis, he spent most of his working years in San Francisco; and his interests covered the whole West. In spite of his thorough technical education, the "practical" element as well as the college-breds esteemed and trusted him. His native love of dining had given him a portly figure, and the reflection of good red wine shone in his benevolent countenance. He had conscious Gallic wit and some unconscious humor. Others of his Californian contemporaries excelled him in the money-making faculty; but none had such reputation for ability, soundness, and integrity. A young man trained under the Janins would not only acquire a most valuable post-graduate education but he would have a special cachet.

Hoover visited Janin's suite of offices over the Anglo-Californian Bank, got access to the great man, and presented his application. Janin asked about his training. "Graduated from Stanford; one summer with the Arkansas Geological Survey; three with the United States Geological Survey, and some work at Nevada City," replied Hoover. Now embryo engineers were constantly trying for a foothold in that office. Why among all the applicants Janin picked this inexperienced boy as an apprentice on his staff, he never lived to tell.

Probably he caught that subtle aura of mastery and integrity which made us at Stanford Hoover's followers all; only, with his French talent for rapid intellectual contacts, he perceived it instantly instead of gradually. Janin asked for references. Hoover offered Lindgren of the United States Geological Survey—a great name. "Well," said Janin in effect, "just now there's nothing definite for you to do here. But if you want to make yourself useful about the office until your references come and I can find something that warrants a salary—all right."

Hoover wrote to Lindgren; but he was on some far search and did not answer at once. Dr. Jordan and Dr. Banner responded promptly and enthusiastically. For a few weeks he served in Janin's office as he had in Branner's—typing out the letters, keeping the correspondence straight, smoothing the machinery. And Janin, like Branner, must have perceived that this boy not only did things but got things done. So one day—and just when Hoover saw debt or starvation ahead—the boss laid down before his unpaid assistant the papers and data in a mining suit. "I want a technical report on this situation," he said. "See what you can do." Working night and day Hoover finished the report, typed it, laid it on Janin's desk. Now although Janin used afterward to brag about Hoover to his luncheon cronies at the Poodle Dog, he was usually chary of praise to a man's face. But the report swept him off his feet.

"Good—very good!" he told Hoover. "Where did you get all this practical knowledge?"

"I worked underground in that mine pushing a car," replied Hoover.

Thereupon Janin put him on salary—a nominal fifty dollars a month while working in the office, and a hundred and fifty dollars a month while out on a job as subordinate to the senior members of the staff. Within a fortnight Janin was starting him on engineering missions to mines in California and Nevada. He visited Routt county, Colorado, to inspect a "gravel proposition"; to lay out its ditch-lines and to bring in water. Before the year was out, Janin had raised his salary to $250 a month for field jobs and sent him to New Mexico and Arizona. Here Hoover found himself assistant to the superintendent of his employer's southwestern properties.

It was the frontier still; only a few years since Geronimo spread fire and torture over southern Arizona. Amid surroundings which live to-day only in the movies, he camped for many months at a time among the sage-brush or lodged in primitive frontier hotels. Hoover avoided the movie stuff. As he said later, "That kind of adventure never appealed to me much." Janin appreciated already the boy's sound informed judgment; he began now to perceive his executive ability.

On his part Hoover, like the other young engineers of that staff, had high apprenticeship under a great master of practical engineering. Part of his work consisted of looking over new properties or new developments of old mines. But there followed large operations, begun under the difficulties of transportation which beset every new mining enterprise. For two years he lived and worked with abstruse western mining, railway, and water problems—and so, on the scientific groundwork laid under instructions of Branner and Lindgren, he began to build an education in broad practical engineering and in the management of modern industrial enterprises.

Meantime his brother Theodore and his sister May had moved from Portland to Berkeley, across the bay, where May was going to school. Theodore had left Penn College midway of his course, learned the printer's trade, and, when that newfangled machine appeared, become a linotype operator. This was only a means toward an end; his suppressed youthful desire for "Robinson Crusoe" and other worldly reading had endowed him with literary and journalistic ambition. In his leasure time he wrote. Between flights to the Southwest, Herbert lived with the family at Berkeley. "Tad, you're not endangering Kipling as yet," he remarked one day. "Probably the family talent doesn't run to expression. Why don't you put yourself under Branner and learn engineering? I'll be established by the time you come out, and we can work in partnership." Tad took his advice.

Then came a big, unexpected chance which gave direction to Hoover's destinies for the next ten years.

Western Australia had discovered gold in the Coolgardie district. A boom followed—a rush. As the surface diggings worked out, as the miners began breaking into the veins, capital for large operations was invested in this field; and capital demanded the latest and most efficient technology. That was to be had in the United States. A British firm, with international interests, knew that Americans led the world in gold-mining on a large scale and that our best technicians worked in California. Also, they held Janin in great esteem. So they cabled and wrote him, asking him to send on an expert engineer who could introduce Californian methods into their western Australian properties; owing to the trying climate, a young man preferred. And here Janin performed an act of pure decency. This boy Hoover, not yet twenty-four years old, was a find. With his capacity for learning on the job, he was mastering every branch of engineering which that office practised—prospecting, mining, metallurgy, transportation, power. Janin could trust his ability and integrity with anything. Not in ten years might he find another such assistant. But here was an exceptional opportunity for a young man—a salary of $7500 a year, all expenses, assured future increases; and in a new, expanding district. We take out of life what we put into it. Hoover has always been a creature of infinite personal kindness; and generosity begets generosity. Janin did not hesitate long. He called Hoover in from the field and put the offer. Hoover—Janin said afterward—stood for a moment so dazzled that he could not speak. When he found his tongue, he accepted on the spot.

He rushed into Market Street, hurried to inform Lester Hinsdale, now a full-fledged young attorney, and Folsom, his laboratory-mate in the engineering department of Stanford. They went boyishly wild, of course. "You'll need clothes!" said Hinsdale, and they led him to that Market Street tailor who made most of the college creations for Stanford men in funds. Hoover ordered three new suits—and at one time! Hinsdale cherished for high-colored homespuns a fancy which his poverty inhibited from expression. He cajoled Hoover into adding a "morning coat" effect of aggressive Scotch tweeds. . . . Two years later Hinsdale received an express parcel from Australia. It contained the Scotch tweed suit and a note in Hoover's hand, saying: "Since you like this damn thing, take it. I haven't worn it yet."

CHAPTER VIII

SEA transportation between our Pacific coast and western Australia was in 1897 still slow and uncertain. So Hoover traveled by the shortest route eastward, stopping for a day or so in Iowa to renew boyhood memories at West Branch. Then New York, the Atlantic London; and the passage by P. & O. steamer through the furnace-heats of the Red Sea. On the steamer which landed him at Albany in West Australia, epidemic broke out; he had ten days of uncomfortable quarantine before a newly constructed narrow-gage road carried him to railhead at Coolgardie—the Dutch Flat, the Cœur d'Alene, the Leadville of the latest Australian diggings.

As though by way of compensation, nature has generally dropped the world's richest of mineral deposits into barren soil. Australia, the gigantic island-continent, lives under three belts of climate. About the eastern, southern, and western coasts lies a moist circle, fertile and cultivated; lining that, a semi-arid circle, field of the famous wool industry; and center of all, a region where the rainfall often does not exceed one or two inches a year, where man can in no way get a living by tickling the soil. On the western side this desert runs close to the coast. Coolgardie and Kalgoor-

CORNER OF THE INNER QUADRANGLE, STANFORD UNIVERSITY

lie—twenty-five miles apart and the centers of the gold discovery—are less than three hundred miles from Fremantle, a seaport; but they lie in the "bush," a monotonous growth of dwarf eucalyptus. "A sort of aggrandized sage-brush" Hoover called it in one of his letters home. That part of the interior desert runs so flat as to make our prairies seem like Alps. Its greatest eminence is Mount Leonora—which rises less than two hundred feet from the plain.

Coolgardie of that day resembled a mining camp on our southwestern desert—the same huddled architecture of unpainted boards, tents, corrugated iron, and burlap, the same troubles with the Demon Rum, the same atmosphere of excited hope. However, there were certain important differences. The Government had permitted unhampered sale of beer and strong liquors, but an efficient rural police clapped stern repressive measures on guns and gambling. Of the native Australian and imported Cornish miners, Hoover remarked once: "They had one great virtue in their joys; when they did get solace from the desert in drink, they never seemed to think of shooting up the town; and anyway, they had nothing to shoot with. They ran to sentiment. They'd put their arms round each other's shoulders and sing of Mother."

In place of our tough western broncos and our undiscourageable burros, the western Australian world used the camel. An encampment of Pathans, imported to drive and tend these stolid but temperamental beasts, fringed every town. Exploration and development were pushing steadily outward into the desert. Hoover made on camel-back all his first inspection trips to his company's distant properties and prospects. By night the caravan would camp in the bush, taking their water from canvas bags. "The sight of a camel," he said afterward, "makes me a little seasick to this day. What those beasts need is a gyroscope." On camel-back one simply wound in and out of the bush, guiding himself, in default of landmarks, by compass. Soon, however, the Government got round to constructing roads. This was a simple process. Surveyors ran from one camp to the next a line as straight as a Roman military highway, and workmen, following along, cut down and grubbed up the bush for a width of thirty or forty feet. In that space the wagons made their own track. Travel down those roads was almost an insanity of monotony—hour after hour with the same gray barriers of ragged bush to right and left, the same undeviating ribbon of road before. For animal life there were only lizards or occasional dwarf kangaroos; for human natives, a few Bushmen—the lowest variety of our species, and at that degenerated by first contact with civilization. In the settlements they made some trouble by trifling pickings and stealings, and helped out a little by looting the garbage cans. And yet life in West Australia had both the masculine charm that belongs to all pioneer lands and the spiritual lift that God has given to deserts. . . .

In order to keep travelers and their horses alive it was necessary to establish "water stations" along the road. In all interior western Australia no river reaches the sea. After the so-called "rainy season," the watercourses sink underground. There they stagnate as salt water; and this can easily be recovered by shallow wells. It has to be distilled before man or beast can drink it. And distillation, in a country of scant fuel, costs money; so that drinkable water sold at from three to ten cents a gallon.

When once in a blue moon it rained, every whistle in camp blew, every one in town knocked off work, and the inhabitants poured out of doors to array pots and kettles, to stretch blankets and mackintoshes—any device for catching the precious fluid of life. Then the more refined reveled in a bath—under a trickle from a five-gallon oil-can.

Hoover found himself charged with determining metallurgical methods, designing equipment, and planning means of development for ten large mines in a group of mixed ownership. The proprietors had asked for Californian methods, and Californian methods they should have. Hoover went at the job of putting them under the American plan. As he organized his working staff he sent to the United States for mine superintendents and engineers. By preference he picked Stanford men, a custom which he maintained throughout his mining days. George Wilson, Deane Mitchell, and Charles Diggles of his class answered the call, and traveled three quarters of the way round the world to join him. As fast as he could work out methods of extracting ore he had plant and equipment designed under his direction, and placed his orders with American manufacturers.

Then came a change which amounted to a minor turn

in Hoover's life. On an inspection trip from Kalgoorlie, very newest of the mining camps, he camped at that toy eminence Mount Leonora. He found a group of Welsh miners developing a prospect. He accepted their invitation to visit and inspect their workings. What he saw convinced him that they had a real mine. Isolated from the main mineral districts, it was probably limited; but also it was probably rich. He reported this to headquarters; went back for another inspection. On his recommendation the firm purchased this mine—later named the "Sons of Gwalia," from the Welsh proprietors. More than justifying his opinion, it proved one of the best properties in the West Australian field; it paid dividends for twenty years. With increased salary, Hoover was appointed to the management of the new mine, given carte blanche to develop and equip it.

During the period when he managed the "Gwalia," his firm was always calling him into consultation on the engineering direction of the group and eventually on its administrative direction. This was another turn of his life; the young engineer passed from technical work to large administration. He must solve labor problems involving thousands of men, create transportation by rail and road, find water supply. Further, he must negotiate constantly with the Government—an augury this for dealings with many Governments in many lands.

So 1898 wore away—the only year of his professional life, except 1907, that Hoover spent wholly outside of the United States. Seven years since Professor Swain, returning to Stanford from his recruiting trip in Oregon, reported to Dr. Jordan as unfinished but promising university material "a young Quaker employed as a clerk in some store in a back room of which he slept and studied up for college . . . none too well prepared but showing remarkable keenness."

That was also the year when Lou Henry took her degree at Stanford and returned to the antique adobes, the wind-tortured cypresses and the rolling blue seascapes of that old mission town Monterey. The last of the self-imposed barriers against their marriage had fallen. She had finished her education; he could support a wife. Yet this rough desert land was no place for a bride. Hoover, when he found time to be lonely, considered closing up in western Australia and looking for a job in a more habitable land.

The wheel of fate took another turn, and again the outer circumstances of his life changed suddenly, completely. The giant China was stirring, as though to wake at last. Under tutelage of European advisers and of the inspired and inspiring Sun Yat-sen, that absolute young monarch Kwang-su prepared to build a modern industrial state. Among the new government bureaus which the reformers created was a department of mines and railways under Chinese direction. They wanted a young, progressive, and able engineer, both scientifically educated and practically experienced, for expert and chief duty. None would do except an American—first, because they admired our methods and machinery, and second, because no European could fit into the political pattern. For over the face of all China sprawled diplomatic "spheres of influence."

Ringed like coyotes about a wounded buffalo, the powers were waiting for the old China to die in order that they might feast on the carcass. To select a European, even for this subordinate job, would be merely to favor one wolf over another. The Chinese consulted an eminent man, a chance visitor to China. He recommended this youthful Yankee who had risen so brilliantly in western Australia.

Hoover took little time in making up his mind. He had planned and ordered the equipment of the Gwalia; the mine stood ready to feed the mills as soon as they were finished; there was no obligation to stay. The salary of $15,000 a year and expenses had its own attractions; but even that was not the main practical point. China, it seemed, stood on the threshold of wide railway, mining, and metallurgical development. Under modern methods it might advance to a great industrial state—and he would be one of the pioneers. It seemed like the opportunity of ten lifetimes. . . . No European knew as yet that the empress dowager had already struck; that the emperor, under polite appearance of royal forms, sat an enthroned prisoner in his own palace; that the ancient bureaucracy and the fanatics of the populace were biding their time to light a hectic fire of violent reaction.

Mrs. Hoover says that on the very night when he grasped this opportunity he sent a long cablegram to Monterey, California. The answer came back at a speed which broke all records for communication with our west coast. It was in the affirmative.

CHAPTER IX

HOOVER returned from Australia early in 1899. The Chinese Department of Mines was not quite ready to begin operations; meanwhile he agreed to do a brief engineering job in California. But he had come home primarily to marry Lou Henry. When he left the university, they had an "understanding." Even before he sent his telegram from Australia, time and constancy had brought that to a tacit engagement. Indeed, when he got his first permanent job in California, they considered getting married. But Lou Henry was only half-way through her university course; and she disliked to abandon anything she set out to do. She made her own mark at the university both as a scholar and a leader. "One of the ablest women we ever had at Stanford," says President Jordan.

All their friends approved the match. They seemed "made for each other." She shared Hoover's tastes for the out-of-doors, his interest in science, his intellectual enthusiasms.

Yet, on the verge of marriage, life seemed to have raised a new barrier. Rumors of unsettled politics had reached Hoover. He felt uncertain about taking a bride to China. He knew not as yet what hardships or rough adventure his job might involve. Perhaps it was better first to look over the ground and, if he found life possible for her there, to return and get married at his first opportunity for a vacation. These scruples went the way of all lovers' doubts. Less than two days before the inevitable sailing date they determined to get married at once and go together.

Monterey had its beginning in San Carlos Borromeo Mission. As yet Spanish-Americans prevailed in the population. All the Henrys including Lou were, like their forebears, ardent Episcopalians—although after her marriage Mrs. Hoover adopted the Quaker faith of her husband. However, Monterey had no established Protestant churches, and no Protestant clergyman was available on short notice. Similar conditions had prevailed in the Spanish mission towns since the first invasion of the Anglo-Saxon. And the church had established the local custom of granting dispensations to priests for the marriage of non-Catholics. Father Ramon Mestres of the Mission was a pleasant acquaintance. He had known Lou Henry as a little girl who rode the hills on a half-wild bronco, with her pigtails streaming out behind. Called in, he took advantage of the dispensation. In his legal capacity of civil magistrate, and with a civil ceremony, he married them at the Henry house. They took a train to San Francisco and that very day sailed for China.

Hoover reported at Peking; buckled down with enthusiasm to his important and interesting new job. The progressive Chinese who governed the Department of Mines knew what they wanted. First they must develop coal and iron. With these raw materials they planned to construct their own railways, ships, and armament, and to do it independently of foreign control. Further, rumors, old records, and the scanty development of small primitive local workings seemed to prove that they had considerable deposits of copper and lead. Hoover must go exploring—look into the prospects of iron, copper, and lead, examine the coal for its metallurgical quality and its proximity to cheap transportation.

From his base at Peking he traveled far—into Manchuria and Mongolia, into Chihli, Shantung, and Shansi provinces. Sometimes he crawled by canal boat. Sometimes he ambled on horseback, with the paraphernalia of life following in carts or on packmules. Mrs. Hoover went on many of these expeditions. Her letters home sparkled with quaint details. First, as their shaggy Manchurian ponies plodded along the impossible roads, went the guard against bandits; then the Boss and his lady; then servants with household equipment, complete even to mosquito-netting. Often they camped; more often they lodged at native inns. Externally, these somewhat resembled the tourists' "pay camps" of our latter-day West. Bare, one-story rooms surrounded a courtyard; the guest must bring his own accommodations. Arrived, the servants spread bedding and lit a charcoal blaze in a tiny fireplace to heat those brick beds which are standard in Chinese homes. Then from the loads of their packmules, or from supplies bought in town, they got dinner.

The cooks had learned their technique from rich and formal Europeans about the legations; and a meal had become to them a performance as unvaried as a Taoist ritual. First must come soup; then an entrée; then a roast, and then a "sweet." Sometimes, on a hot evening, Mrs. Hoover would say to the cook, "I think we'll just have an omelet for dinner." The cook would reply, meekly, "You catch 'em;" but four or five courses would appear just the same. When supplies in the packs ran low and he had to forage, often the "Number One boy" could find only chickens and eggs. So the cooks made the chicken into soup for the first course, into variations of eggs and chicken for subsequent courses and into a sweet omelet for dessert. Then to bed on plaited mattresses laid over the brick kang; and at cockcrow the stirring of a Chinese village woke them. The children, eager to see a white woman, were already milling and whooping about the inn. To saddle; and to another day of prying into the secrets of the earth. Mrs. Hoover, who loves both adventure and science, remembers these days of her strange bridal tour as among her happiest.

Hoover's explorations proved that the world's greatest coal deposits underlay northeastern China—proximate both to the capital and to tide-water. The other minerals turned out a disappointment. He discovered no lead, iron, or copper of quantity and quality which would warrant large-scale exploitation. Nor have such been found to this day. When winter locked the roads, the Hoovers moved to a rented house in Tientsin. There Hoover, with Mrs. Hoover playing first assistant, wrote his report on the summer work.

All this time his eager, curious mind took notes not only on the mineral wealth of China but on its human life—the play of social and economic forces, the system of government, the rich history. During the long journeys by boat he filled his nights with reading; of evenings in the village inns, he talked politics, business, immemorial tradition with the mandarins. He began a unique collection of books in many languages on China and the Chinese. This, by his gift, became afterward the valued nucleus for the Chinese Library at Stanford.

That winter they dined back and forth with the European residents of Tientsin or ran up to Peking to visit with the "diplomatic set"; and Hoover began his education in the seamy side of international intrigue. Also, he became aware that the foundations of his job were crumbling away. All knew by now the situation at the palace—the emperor a gaudy prisoner, the set, powerful empress dowager in the saddle, progress already stifled. However, no one—except here and there a prophet who passed for a croaker—foresaw the hideous violence of the next summer or dreamed that the hatreds of reactionary China would make foreigners their target.

But the salary was still coming in; and future or no future, this was a most interesting job of scientific pioneering. Hoover had by now five assistant engineers. With the first breath of spring he laid out the season's work—more exploration. They plunged into the back areas, far from the European settlements on the coast. Already the fires of massacre were smoldering under all the placid surface of northern China. Then, early in the summer, Hoover was summoned back to Peking. Mrs. Hoover had come down with Chinese influenza. European residents believe that this is the same plague which killed its millions in Europe and America during the last days of the World War; and they take it almost as seriously as smallpox. There being no scientific medical attendance at the time in Peking, Hoover bundled her up and took her to Tientsin where lived a reliable European doctor. Very probably this illness of Mrs. Hoover saved Hoover's life. The fires had broken through the surface; all over the interior had begun the massacre of foreigners.

Hoover himself caught a light attack of influenza. He was just out of bed when—all China blew up. "Call it in the main one of those unaccountable emotional upheavals that sweep the Orient from time to time," he said afterward. The Boxers, with "death to foreigners" on their banners, had within the next few days assassinated the German minister at Peking, driven the foreigners into the legation compounds, ringed them with steady fire. But Tientsin felt secure; for the Imperial Government had sent to guard them thirty thousand troops equipped with European arms and under instruction by foreign officers. These forces encamped between the foreign settlement and the accumulating hordes of Boxers, thirsty for European blood. So the six hundred whites at the Tientsin for-

A REMINISCENT BIOGRAPHY 89

eign settlement, while anxious for the fate of friends and relatives in Peking, took their own situation lightly and humorously; especially after about fifteen hundred European troops—mostly Russian but including a contingent of American bluejackets—arrived as nucleus for a force to relieve Peking.

The foreign settlement of Tientsin consisted of two or three parallel streets extending for a distance of eight or ten blocks. On one side lay the river and on the other an open field. A densely populated Chinese suburb connected it with the picturesque filth of the native city, around which lay encamped the imperial army. The Russians threw up barricades across that end of the town. Civilian Tientsin regarded this as unnecessary even when missionaries, escaped by the skin of their teeth, began coming to ask refuge, and Norman Magee, whom Hoover had known at Stanford, showed up with the entire staff of a foreign college. Hoover had called in his assistants, including George Wilson, his old associate of Stanford and Australia. Coming through many an escape and adventure, they arrived unharmed.

One afternoon Mr. and Mrs. Hoover sat recuperating in their garden. For days they had heard firing to the north—the imperial troops squabbling with the Boxer mob. Now came two explosions near at hand. As they sat up and listened, the fire-bell began a rapid, excited tocsin. The whole foreign colony were running to the Town Hall, dragging their children. And rifle bullets began splashing the brick compound-walls surrounding the houses. More shells burst. Hoping for the best, they decided that this was merely the fire of the Boxers, looping over the imperial army. The authorities were considering ways and means to abate the nuisance, when a dozen panting exhausted white men in diverse uniforms appeared at the head of the street—the foreign officers, mostly Scandinavians, in charge of training the imperial troops. They broke appalling news. The Chinese army had suddenly gone Boxer. Friendly native officers had warned them just in time.

Thirty thousand troops equipped with modern arms, well furnished with artillery; behind them thirty thousand civilian Boxers, ill armed but in a state of blazing fanaticism—and to withstand them, only fifteen hundred European soldiers! These had a wealth of ammunition, happily, and a few machine guns; but only one cannon. The civilians, with accessions of missionaries, traders, and teachers who had fled to Tientsin ahead of the massacre, numbered three hundred able-bodied men. The foreign settlement boasted a home guard—which existed mainly to give an annual ball. However, Tientsin was a sporting city; search of houses and the hardware store provided a sporting rifle and a revolver for every man and for most of the women. Ammunition was scarce for these arms, and of course not uniform. A hurried council of war determined that the civilians should do sentry, police, ambulance and engineering duty, and save their ammunition against the last desperate struggle—yes, and for the women.

Hoover and his staff were the only engineers in

town; and to him and his assistants fell the immediate and pressing task of throwing up barricades, transforming the village into a fortress. Already the machine guns were milling along the Russian trench parapets; the Chinese had begun a series of tentative charges. At any moment the main force might pour from the shallow fords of the river or the alleys of the native city upon their unprotected flanks. Under the general direction of the military officers, and with the home guard and Chinese Christians who had taken refuge in the city as working forces, Hoover plugged the ends of the side streets. Needing material, he broke into the warehouses. There he found a treasure of sugar and rice in sacks, and of these substances he built his barricades.

A day or two more, and the Chinese charges grew more vigorous. Between attacks they kept up a constant harassing fire, aimless but profuse. But still they ignored the weak point which any child should have perceived—those unprotected flanks. Why, only the gods of the Chinese pantheon know. Doubtless the general was incompetent, doubtless the departure of European officers left the imperial army alone on a sea of military bewilderment. Ignore it they did, however, except for a little fire from across the river. Through the labyrinth of houses connecting the native city and the settlement, they continued to bear down on the European force at their front. The Russians and Americans, unrelieved since the first attack, were fighting asleep on their feet.

Next, Hoover and his associates stretched on the

flanks an outer barricade which would give the defense more room; and finally, they transformed the buildings at the center of the town into a strong inner fortress for a last stand.

Also, he must look out for the water supply. European Tientsin maintained a small pumping plant a little away from the town; this forced the polluted river water into a filter. To work the engine by day meant only to draw fire and might put into the Chinese mind the idea of a flank attack. Hoover and his assistants would creep out by night with sentries to guard against surprise, fire the boilers, start the engine, and run the pumps for an hour. The noise always awoke firing from across the river; bullets would rattle off from the walls. The shells—aimed not at any single object but at the settlement in general—started four or five fires a day. These must be fought with an eye to economy of water. A volunteer fire department, under the command of one of Hoover's assistants, would at the first alarm rush to the incipient blaze and beat it out with wet rags. . . . So a week wore away, and another and another.

Meantime, Mrs. Hoover, when the shells began to burst in the streets and the bullets to spatter against the walls, had taken into sensible consideration the situation of their house. It rose at that end of the street nearest the Chinese armies; from their position, the most conspicuous target in town. Edward B. Drew, American commissioner of the Chinese customs, occupied a stout house, stoutly walled, and within the inner circle of defense. He offered hospitality to the

HERBERT HOOVER, PERTH, WEST AUSTRALIA, IN 1898

Hoovers and to others who lived in exposed places. The Drew house became an American dormitory; the women sleeping on the floor of one big room, the men in another. "I didn't see much of Bert in those days," said Mrs. Hoover wistfully, two decades later. Only when news came that another civilian was hit, there was a little pause in their work. . . .

Mrs. Hoover had once reported to the doctor; had learned first aid before the volunteer corps began bringing in human wreckage from the barricades. Sometimes they had as many as two hundred freshly wounded in a day. The temporary hospital was short of everything—disinfectants, cots, bedding, bandages. Mrs. Hoover raided the meagerly stocked general stores to get cotton goods for dressings; when these supplies were gone, commandeered domestic sheets.

The Hoovers traveled back and forth from their jobs on bicycles. All the houses stood behind stout brick walls. So long as you hugged that wall nearest the firing you were safe. A cross street meant an instant of danger; you pedaled fast. In time, the vicious little "ping" of richocheting bullets became a phenomenon as unconsidered as the buzzing of the flies. In the early morning the besiegers knocked off for breakfast; and the servants at the Drew house used to go and sweep up like fallen leaves the bullets of the night. So passed a long three weeks of fighting anxiety.

The relief of Tientsin did not come dramatically like that of Lucknow—with distant pipes and a parade of troops and a hysteria of thanksgiving; although for a moment it seemed that it would. The Powers were hurrying troops to relieve the besieged at Tientsin and Peking—Japanese, Americans from the Philippines, British from Shanghai, French from Indo-China. These forces found that the Chinese imperial armies held the Taku forts at the mouth of the Pei-ho and intended to dispute the landing. There was a delay while they took the forts. But the foreign settlement at Tientsin could hear the guns at nightfall and knew they had only to hold on. Then a mixed advance force of perhaps two thousand men started up the bank, to arrive at the end of the third week. It found the settlement tired and crammed with wounded, but still fighting. In the van—balm for sore Yankee eyes—marched the olive-brown of United States marines.

And now the foreign settlement could take stock. They found they had lost more lives than all the defenders of Ladysmith, Mafeking, and Kimberley put together—a natural comparison in those days of the better-advertised South African War. Yet the hardest fighting had only begun. As more and more troops came in, the imperial army seemed to bring more and more of their forces into action.

Valiantly with the van of the first relief contingent rode four American war correspondents—Oscar King Davis of "The New York Sun," "Bobbie" Collins of the Associated Press, Frederick Palmer of "Collier's," Joaquin Miller of the Hearst newspapers. They needed quarters. Now eight shells altogether had hit the Drew house; and Mrs. Hoover, browsing round town, noticed that their own residence, conspicuous though it seemed, had gone unscathed. There was neither rhyme nor reason to the Chinese fire. So the Hoovers moved back, taking along the correspondents as guests. In another week enough relief troops had arrived to make the rear roads secure; and they evacuated the women and children to Shanghai. Also, the male civilians were free to go.

But the Hoovers felt that they were still needed. Hoover, because he knew the terrain, was attached as engineer to the colonel in charge of the American troops. Professional surgeons, arriving with the armies, took over the hospital; but Mrs. Hoover had the run of it and they asked her to stay. However, she had now a little leisure to look after her houseful of Americans.

One afternoon the correspondents were working at despatches in their rooms and Mrs. Hoover was playing solitaire in the parlor. There came from above a crash of breaking glass, a swish; then an explosion outside of the house. Mrs. Hoover, Davis, and Palmer ran up-stairs. A shell had gone through Collins's room and exploded a few feet from the gate. Bearers were carrying away the dead body of a Japanese sentry. "A close call," they said; and returned to their rooms. Not ten minutes later there came a terrific explosion. A shell had passed through the Venetian blind of a back window up-stairs, leaving a hole as round as though made by a jig-saw, had detonated its contact-fuse against the newel-post of the stairway. Fortunately, Mrs. Hoover and Palmer, in the rooms on opposite sides of the hall, sat behind shelter of their doors, and Davis up-stairs was just out of the line of fire. The correspondents still tell how they rushed through the fog of lime and smoke to find Mrs. Hoover—and there she sat, turning the cards as before. After that, not another shell struck the Hoover house!

Fear of treachery had led to a special military order; a Chinese on the streets, unescorted by a European, might be shot. One day after the relief, and in spite of this danger, Mrs. Hoover's Chinese servant came sputtering and puffing to her at the hospital with alarming news. The Cossacks, just then for the first time resting from trench duty, were looting the house. They had broken down the gate of the compound next door, and when the Chinese servant stopped them crying "English house!" they had spitted him on a bayonet.

Mrs. Hoover jumped on her bicycle and, with the servant running at the handle-bar, hurried home. The Cossacks, loaded with loot, were just emerging from her house. By the simple might of an infuriated housewife, Mrs. Hoover made them drop what they had in their hands; but she failed to notice the bulging of their boots and their breeches. The house was a chaos. They had stolen first every knife; then all feminine and dainty objects like an opera-bag, lace fichus, ribbons, embroideries. Also, they had eaten everything eatable, drunk everything potable. Her closet held a store of strawberry jam. That, it appeared, they had eaten with their fingers. Sticky finger-marks polluted all the clothes and bedding; even the walls. Her typewriter had puzzled them. Unable to account for it as a musical instrument, they had poured into its machinery a jar of strawberry jam.

At this stage of the siege the defenders fell into that state of mind which all know who know war—suspicion, hectically distorted judgment, credulity for every sinister report concerning the enemy. In a compound opposite his house Hoover had quartered a thousand Chinese officials, some of them from the Department of Mines. Rated by their countrymen as friends of the Europeans, they had fled to the Tientsin settlement; for outside of this beleaguered city the very rumor that a Chinese even knew a Foreign Devil might mean death by hideous torture. Here Hoover got his first experience in food relief. Together with Dr. C. D. Tenny, a professor in the university, he kept them alive with rice, sugar, and whatever odds and ends they could get, until the siege was over. One day a few scattering shots dropped from that direction. Hoover, who always keeps his balance, believed then and believes now that this was long-distance fire from snipers beyond the town. But war-distracted Tientsin civilians swallowed the rumor that the ostensibly friendly Chinese were shooting at them from within. Small though this colony was, it had its riffraff. That night a mob bent on lynching rushed into the compound of the friendly Chinese. Happily, George Wilson and a few other Americans got wind of this; by force of arms and justice they drove the mob away.

Then came into police power a hard-fisted provost whom the rumors had infected with war-rage. One night a messenger brought Hoover news that Chinese friends were in danger at the compound. He sped at once to the scene of trouble. He found that the provost, after some kind of rough court martial, had condemned several Chinese to be shot. In the shaken and bewildered line stood one of the officials, a Yale graduate; also Lon Etong, an inoffensive interpreter whom he knew well and favorably. By argument, by waving the American flag, by his personal pledge to see that they behaved, Hoover stopped the executions. Lon Etong has prospered; and every year since, wherever in the world they might be, he has sent Mr. and Mrs. Hoover a Christmas present.

Now still more perturbing news. Chang Yen Mao, Hoover's chief in the Bureau of Mines, with Tong Shao Ye, another friendly mandarin, had taken refuge in the foreign settlement. And this mad provost had arrested them, begun drumhead proceedings against them as snipers and spies. This time pledges and threats did not move him. Now it happened that a Colonel Wozack, who had been Russian military attaché in Peking, commanded a Russian detachment at the barricades. He knew these Chinese officials. Hoover rushed out and found him. As a soldier talking to another soldier, and as a diplomat, Wozack backed the provost down, secured release for both Chang and Tong.

Detachment after detachment, the relieving European troops poured in. At last twenty thousand of them lay encamped and intrenched about the foreign quarter of Tientsin. On July 14 the advance to Peking began with a hot and gory battle through the streets of the native city. The imperial armies fell back; the siege of Tientsin was lifted.

The Boxer war and foreign occupation in northeastern China killed of course the imperial Department of Mines. The empress and her government fled to the interior; and salaries went with them. The big job on which Hoover had built so many hopes had exploded. He was packing to return to California, when one Detring, the German financial agent for a large coal-mining company, approached him. Chinese operated this enterprise, but with a technical staff of foreigners. It was now in ridiculously bad shape. The Boxers had at the height of the disturbance seized the plant and done it much damage. The bonds—held in England, Belgium, and Germany—were in default. If the bondholders understood the situation, they might send into China representatives who would get the company refinanced and secure it protection from the grasping powers. Hoover, with Mrs. Hoover, went to Europe. He made a quick tour of the capitals, explained the situation, bent the bondholders to Detring's ideas, then passed on to California. There he prepared to start life anew.

But his destiny was always whimsical. Now it sent him back over the old track. In December, 1900, the reorganized Chinese company cabled to offer him a job at an attractive salary as chief engineer. The Hoovers sailed eastward again; settled down at Tong Shan, one hundred and ten miles southeast of Tientsin, where lay the company's works. Hoover swung into another big job of engineering and administrative reorganization. This was more than a coal mine. It made cement and operated canals, ocean shipping, even part of a railway. It employed 25,000 workers. The enterprise had never returned continuous profits; and it had of late run behind both technically and financially. The program which Hoover executed included a new harbor—Chang Wan Tow—new shafts, improved technical methods. He drew on the United States for American engineers, specialists in coal, harbors, railroads; coördinated the plan, started the work going. The property began to show profits.

All this in the midst of disturbed days. In the towers before the coal mines stood sentries looking out for bandits. As these gentry approached, the workmen withdrew behind the walls. However, they were never raided. The armies of occupation took turn about in various districts; Tong Shan saw every European uniform. In this clash between races, intentions, and ideas there arose incidents and adventures. John Newberry, one of Hoover's American assistants, tells these stories:

They had made on business a winter journey to Shanghai. They returned on an antiquated caricature of a steamer. . . . Hoover has said, "The last stage of moral degradation for a ship is the China coast. Only once did I ever know of any ship falling lower. That was in the Russo-Japanese War, when the Japanese bought from our firm some of our worn-out coal steamers and sank them in the entrance of Port Arthur harbor!" . . .

This creaking old vessel ran for days in a storm with the passengers working the pumps. Finally the skipper, in despair, ran it into Chang Wan Tow harbor, where they could not make shore for the ice. But Hoover and Newberry jumped from ice-cake to ice-cake like *Eliza* crossing the Ohio, wallowed through sleety shore waves, made land. They dried out their clothes and forfended pneumonia at a charcoal fire in a native hut. Northward from this town ran a railroad to Tong Shan, some 150 miles distant. Disorganized, like everything in China at the moment, it was used only for the occasional transportation of troops. A British military train was getting up steam for a start. Hoover, explaining who they were and how they happened to be there, applied to the India-service colonel in charge for a passage in his car. The colonel, looking over Hoover and Newberry, observing their wrinkled clothing and four-day beards, seemed to classify them as liars and tramps. "You may ride with the troops," he said—with an air of one who stands virtuously by his race, even though the specimen in question be a low and suspected person.

They tucked themselves in among the shivering Hindu soldiers. The train started, crawled, stopped. Hoover and Newberry dropped to earth and strolled forward. The engine, unrepaired since the Boxer uprising began, had broken down beyond repair—at least the Hindu engineer thought so; he was resting. Hoover diagnosed the trouble, took a mechanic's hammer, and started Yankee-fashion to fix things. The colonel, finding him at this menial occupation, felt his worst suspicions confirmed. He began ordering Hoover about. "Brother," said Hoover, "I'm the only person here present who can get you out of this fix. Any more of your lip, and I leave you where you are." The colonel sputtered; but he retired to his own private car.

Jury repairs completed, they started again. They had crawled a few miles more when they came to another halt—the engine simply could not keep up sufficient steam to pull the heavy train over the grade. The colonel, by messenger, ordered his unknown passengers to make more repairs. Thereupon Hoover and Newberry uncoupled the engine and sent word back to the colonel that they would run it down the track and look for help. They kept on running—150 miles into Tong Shan, where they notified the British authorities of this hitch in troop movements. The colonel and his regiment remained as they were for twenty-four hours. Next week, this same force marched into Tong Shan—in which Hoover was as a king—demanding billets. "Well, we'll give you a house and keep you warm," said Hoover to the colonel, "which is more than you would do for us."

In a small city some thirty miles away ruled during the British occupation an able and idealistic young officer, full of enthusiasm to improve the world. This was his opportunity. He proceeded to create in his town a régime of good government—just and unbiased courts, the first elements of sanitation, street cleaning, a police force which existed mainly to suppress banditry and graft. Hungry for change of association, he rode over to Tong Shan every Sunday and had dinner with the Americans. To them he used to confide his ambitions for reform. He seemed to be doing so well, in fact, that when in regular rotation the British troops left that region, he was warmly commended by his superiors for his distinguished service.

One Sunday night one of Hoover's Chinese servants referred to the late commander of this neighboring city: "Him velly bad man," he said. Hoover, laughing, asked for particulars. "All time squeeze, squeeze," said the Chinese; and went on to specify—this officer was head of such an organization for graft as China never saw before. His native police force had descended upon a peaceful, inoffensive, and honest suburb and arrested the head men, charging them with banditry. Then the chief of police accepted all the ready cash in town as a fine or ransom—and released them.

Hoover did not believe this, but he felt that the young apostle of reform should know what the Chinese were saying. The British officer, sent for and enlightened, nearly burst with indignation. But the next Sunday he rode into Tong Shan in a state of humiliation and almost broken-hearted depression. He had investigated. It was all true, and more. Under his very nose, the native official class had transformed his good government movement into a smooth and perfect machine for squeeze and graft!

So they lived in this masculine atmosphere, this mêlée of conflicting national interests; there were times when Mrs. Hoover was the only white woman at Tong Shan. But the job was nearing its term. The business had succeeded, was pointed to larger success. The Belgians, large holders of its securities, perceived this. Quietly, they bought out various shareholders; secured control over the British, Chinese, and German groups.

One day a representative of the Belgians appeared and took charge. There followed a bitter quarrel between the different national interests. Hoover resigned in disgust. . . . Fourteen years later these very same Belgians were pleading with our ambassador to have Hoover take charge of Belgian relief. They wanted Hoover, only Hoover!

Again he sailed back to California. Twenty-seven years old now. Well, he had advanced his education another stage. Also, he had seen China—as few foreigners have ever seen it. And life still lay before him.

CHAPTER X

DURING the five or six years after Hoover left college I saw him intermittently in California. Before he left for Australia he dropped into Stanford between flights to Colorado or Arizona. The university had as yet no hotel accommodations; so Ray Wilbur or Ralph Arnold or Theodore Hoover used to take him into the dormitory and bed him down on a sofa or a spare iron cot. By a stern edict of the founder, the electric lights went out at half-past ten. But we all kept candles hidden in our trunks; and many a night we sat until the small hours of the morning exchanging our tremendously important gossip of the campus for his lore of mines and mountains and deserts. Again, during the pauses between his journeys to Australia and China, I met him in San Francisco; listened fascinated to his account of the mining boom at Coolgardie and the siege of Tientsin. From this eye-witness I got my first horrified impression of that diplomatic mess which was festering into a world war. Probably, indeed, I carried away a picture rather too lurid; China has always shown the seamiest side of international diplomacy. If those five or six active, successful years had changed him at all from the student who led us all at Stanford, the difference expressed itself in a deepening of his powers; even his sense of humor. Looking back, however, I see that he had one added quality. Under his modesty and shyness lay an air of authority—expressed not in speech but somehow in unconsidered mental attitudes. During those exciting years of China, it seems to me, his entity came finally and perfectly into him. From that time forth he was the Hoover whom all the world knows.

His reputation had spread through the clannish mining business; and he had plenty of attractive offers. But it was time to orient his life, fix his goal. His experiences on the other border of the Pacific had given him sight of an opening as wide as a door. Our engineering practice, our machinery, our methods of organization were the best in the world. We did not know it as yet; neither the Government nor private interests were encouraging the flow of American enterprise abroad. But the outlands were beginning to know. They had seen low-grade mineral deposits, unprofitable under their own obsolete methods, yield returns at the touch of American leadership. They were demanding American engineers. That hurry call to Janin from Australia in 1897—"a young man who can install Californian methods"—it was almost a text. International engineering practice, based on the United States, drawing its intellectual strength from our soil—there lay his special opportunity.

I must hurry over the next twelve years. . . . After all, the interesting questions about a life like his are how he came to be and what finally he did; not the jog-trot between. His journeys covered the world from the equator to the arctic; but always the home port was San Francisco. His way of life in this period has given rise to the persistent reports that he was out of the country for twenty years. Even were that true, his career should be a matter of national pride. Wherever he worked he planted a nucleus of American methods, created a demand for American goods. But as a matter of cold fact and record, he spent only one of these years—1907—wholly out of the United States. The Hoovers had by now two sons; and Herbert the elder had reached school age. They must be educated at home, the Hoovers decided. By 1909, they were spending more and more time at their base in California. And by 1912 they were living in Palo Alto, San Francisco, or New York the better part of each year.

The head office of the business in San Francisco presently stretched like an expanding ripple. There was a main branch in the Empire Building, New York; and finally lesser branches ringed the world. Hoover grew with the business—or the business with Hoover. At first he figured in the mining world as a shrewd and expert technician. Then as the years went on he found, and his associates found, the true bent of his higher powers. He became distinctly a coördinator, an executive, an administrator of industrial enterprises, an eliminator of waste and folly. Says one of his oldest and closest associates: "He was toward the end a great doctor of sick companies. When a concern which ought to produce and pay did not produce or pay, after every one else gave it up they called in Hoover. He diagnosed the trouble and cured it." Quietly he rose to the top rank of his profession. Engineers do not honor their own save for eminence and service in the calling itself. That the American Society of Mining and Metallurgical Engineers has conferred on him its gold medal, the American Institute of Engineers its presidency—these are symbols of his standing.

He became, indeed, pivot-man and leader to a group of American engineers who worked internationally. A great organizer, he proves that best by knowing when to take organization and when to leave it alone. It suited the purposes of this business not to form these men into a company; to leave them mere associates, working together in loose liaison. Then, twenty years ago, we thought little about foreign trade. Such pioneers of our products and our methods would attract more attention to-day. But the only visible advertisement of their existence, during the years between 1908 and 1914, was the name "Herbert C. Hoover" on the doors of modest office suites in San Francisco, New York, London, Melbourne, Shanghai—and for long periods even in St. Petersburg and Mandalay.

CHAPTER XI

IN that period of far-flung activities between 1901 and 1914 Hoover boarded an ocean liner as casually as you or I take a trolley-car to our daily jobs. For all his voyaging, he has never become a perfect sailor; though he escapes actual nausea in rough weather, it puts him into a state where a man feels more comfortable on the flat of his back. Land travel, on the other hand, he likes. How many times he has made, between western Europe and Australia or the Far East, that voyage by P. & O. liner—twenty, thirty, or forty—he could not himself compute. At first he spent his time aboard ship in reading and study. His secretary used to stock his cabin with a miniature library—first technical works, then perhaps general literature of affairs like history and economics; and as dessert those detective stories for which he has an incurable addiction. But as time went on he found means to utilize this spare time in his business. His cabin became a floating office. There he prepared his own reports or digested those of his associates, went over accumulated correspondence, wrote on his books, thought out his problems. At Suez—first stop—a sheaf of cables awaited him. While the steamer coaled, he prepared his answers, shoveled them on the wire. He repeated the proceeding at Singapore and again at Colombo, cross-roads of the Indian Ocean.

Mrs. Hoover, who likes travel of all kinds, followed or accompanied him in so far as her boys and their education permitted. When—as in Ceylon, the Malay Peninsula, or Siberia—the actual work was too remote and rough, she established herself in the nearest center of civilization and waited. So, although Hoover did only one job in Japan, she lived for months at a time in and about Tokio.

By preference, and through necessity of entertaining, the Hoovers lived always in houses rather than in hotels; the mother-home at Stanford, like the mother-office in San Francisco, seemed to stretch a brood round the world. There were, for example, bungalows taken on brief lease in Mandalay or Broken Hill or Tokio. Two of their foreign residences the Hoovers held on long tenure, subletting them furnished most of the time, reclaiming them when the circumstances of the job required occupancy of two or three months. One was a somber little house in what is now Leningrad and was then St. Petersburg, capital of the Russian Empire; the other Red House, Hornton Street, in the Kensington district of London. This was built in the early eighteenth century as a country residence; an article in the lease still guaranteed the owner against claims for damages by the lessee's cows! But now modern London stretched about it for many a mile. Its only external manifestation was a high wall with a red gate—hence the name. Behind that, a complete surprise, lay the rusty-red old house and a garden brooded over by a great oak tree, still older.

There Hoover's friends used sometimes to see him when they went abroad. Because of this, and because he occupied it as the most convenient headquarters during the two exceptional war-years when he was relieving Belgium, many have given it in their memories a disproportionate importance. As a matter of fact, the Hoovers spent far less time in Red House than in their base at Stanford University.

But when they were there, it gathered unto itself interesting pioneers and advance agents of business from all quarters of the world. Unlike many important Americans with foreign interests and connections, the Hoovers never succumbed to social ambition. If occasionally one met "great" people at this table, they sat there not for their rank but for their wit and worth. American engineers back from building bridges for the Sultan of Afghanistan or looking into a far prospect of interior Borneo; old mushers from Nome or the Klondike with the scent of the tundra still on them; university scholars or professors—mainly Stanford men, of course—traveling to or from some abstruse search in the libraries of the Continent; Chinese business men or mandarins; skippers and ship's doctors, shipping men and war correspondents—these were staples of the companies which foregathered in this secret nook, holding serious or laughing discussion of affairs which ran as wide as the world. . . . What have we not heard at Red House!

I can mention only a few of the notable enterprises

on which he stamped his character. At Broken Hill, in Australia, men had been mining lead and silver for thirty years; the refuse from the extraction of these metals lay in dumps like mountains about the mines. These leavings contained a wealth of zinc which the methods then in use could not recover. Also great bodies of very low-grade ore still underlay the district, the lead and silver in them unprofitable unless the zinc also could be turned to account. Hoover and his associates conceived the idea that methods at command of modern chemistry could make both dumps and deposits pay. With his brother Theodore he attacked the problem. After a year or two of bafflement, of abstruse chemical and mechanical experiment, they found a successful process. Under their direction, Broken Hill erected great zinc mills. New life came into the old district, and every year since, dividends have poured out of those dumps and mines.

Kyshtim lies on the western slope of those Ural Mountains which separate Russia from Siberia. About it stretches a great wooded principality held time out of mind by a branch of the Romanoff family. There, Russians boast, they practised the art of reforesting a hundred years before western Europe ever heard of it. In the midst of this domain lay good iron and copper deposits. A company staffed and financed from western Europe, but mostly of Russian ownership, started to extract these metals. But the ores were low grade; and archaic methods failed to make them pay. The owners called in Hoover and his associates. The reorganization took account not only of mines but of every economic resource in the principality. There arrived presently an equipment of American smelters and mills. Hoover has always an eye on the by-product; and these new works dealt not with iron and copper alone. One plant recovered sulphuric acid; another distilled turpentine and recovered acetone from the woods of the great forest. This business grew to the most important metallurgical center in Russia. More than 60,000 people lived on the estate. Before, they merely existed from one famine to another. Now every breadwinner could have a steady, paying job.

And this Kyshtim enterprise illustrates one virtue which marked all Hoover organizations. He never forgot the human factor. In entering a foreign country he always considered and humored its institutions, its customs, and its mental attitudes. He made the natives forget that he was a foreigner; infused them with his own enthusiasm for the job. In Kyshtim, for example, he encouraged the population, from the exalted lord to the humblest muzhik, to look on this as their town-enterprise. About the works, Russian hovels magicked themselves into substantial houses. There followed, actually, schools. The priests insisted that the new works must be blessed—they were going to mean so much to the community! There followed a colorful religious ceremony and afterward a fête. Finally, the company, at Hoover's suggestion, sent its more expert young workmen to technical schools, in order that they might qualify for executive jobs. And notice this: when the abler of these young men branched out into their own enterprises, American methods and machines were the only kind they knew. So, as an old-fashioned German would say, "he spread our culture."

Rich, undeveloped Russia caught his professional interest. Presently he is breaking ground in another remote corner of the country—as far from his Russian headquarters in St. Petersburg as is Kansas City from New York. The wild Altai region on the border of Turkestan holds treasure in base metals, especially zinc. Here again pioneer work—roads to run, railways to construct, smelters to build, machinery to assemble, finances to regulate.

From a temperature of twenty degrees below zero in Russia, Hoover would shift to the Turkish-bath atmosphere of the Malay Peninsula. Thirty miles above Mandalay lies in Burma a most interesting deposit of metals; base and precious almost inextricably fused—lead, silver, zinc, copper, and even antimony. The region is up-ended, difficult. It was a puzzle in both chemistry and engineering which, in the course of some perplexed years, Hoover solved. Where had been jungle grew up a comfortable community of 25,000 people.

And at home—dredging at Oroville and Folsom, California, reclaiming tule lands on the Sacramento, extending gold mines at Ouray, Colorado, developing potash deposits in Death Valley, running pipe lines for oil from Midway to Los Angeles, opening copper mines at Roseland—in all these Hoover had a technical or administrative hand.

Finally, during those far-flung productive years Hoover's job impinged always on statesmanship. He must deal in Russia with the heart-breaking czarist system, in China with "spheres of influence," in Africa and the islands of the Indian Sea with imperial ambitions, in Central America with revolutionary parties. He had retained that interest in affairs stirred up by the "great frat-barb war" of his Stanford days. Though as yet in no wise a participant, he kept close and interested touch with our domestic politics; Washington was one of his ports of call. And this gave the finish to his unconscious apprenticeship for a larger career. When suddenly life thrust on him a world-wide responsibility, he was no stranger to chancelleries and embassies, premiers and foreign ministers. Still better, he understood the economic resources, the industrial methods, the business and financial organization of the twenty nations or dependencies in which he had operated. Among our formally appointed diplomatic representatives some naturally knew one or two foreign countries better than he. But none had such intimate acquaintance with so many countries. He saw them all the more profitably because he remained Yankee of the Yankees—as American as baseball or apple-pie—regarding them from the detached view of the outsider who nevertheless sits in on the game.

The true engineer thinks of adventures as a nuisance. He even dreads them, as a mariner dreads shipwreck. You're out to do a job. Generally it takes you to a far unsettled country, where there are disturbances, annoying irregularities. If nothing special happens, so much the better for the job. Hoover runs true to type. Still, there were at least—episodes. In Burma he caught a hard case of tropical malaria, came back to Mandalay, and lay long in delirium. He was tortured, tormented by a constant striving to compose poetry, in spite of the fact that the normal Hoover has never matched rhyme to rhyme. This was the only serious illness of his maturity; and his strict temperance of life, together with his native constitution, in time worked the germs out of his system. . . . Shooting across Siberia in 1905, he found that Tomsk had defied the czar, declared itself an independent republic. The populace was meeting on the public square to confirm and consolidate their revolution. They fell at once into three groups —constitutional monarchists, republicans, socialists. These argued back and forth until a sleet-storm broke. The meeting scurried to cover. Then the police emerged from hiding, took possession of the square; and the revolution was over. . . . In Chita, near Tomsk, a barber and a telegraph operator started a republic of their own. The barber had lived in the United States; so he appointed himself president. The telegraph operator had imbibed his ideas of freedom from England; he announced himself premier. This unique dual government lasted only until the Cossacks arrived. . . . A romantic interlude in the Alps. Italy has no native iron. But an archæologist, meditating on that short-sword with which Rome conquered the world, wondered where they got material for their steel? He put this question to the Italian Government. Interested, they searched records, established that the mines lay in the Alps. They found the ancient workings —and sent for Hoover. He and the family had a pleasant summer motor-tour of the mountains while he bored and assayed. It was a technical disappointment, however. The ancients had rifled the deposits.

So much for business. But before the wheel turns again and Hoover finds himself projected into a world war, let us go a little deeper into the man himself.

CHAPTER XII

LOOKING back over Hoover's development, one has the sense of a mental energy growing and rising so steadily as to overflow every boundary. More and more, his mind seemed to take possession of his being. In the Chinese period of his twenties, he was working hard enough, heaven knows. Yet the job did not absorb all his intellectual powers and curiosities. On his working staff at Tong Shan served a clerk highly educated in the native fashion. From him Hoover caught an interest in the higher Chinese modes of calculation. He found that they had carried the art as far as secondary equations, but that they approached all problems by characteristically indirect routes. And he began, thereupon, a treatise on Chinese mathematics. Before he could complete his researches he left China; but the notes for this work lie somewhere among his papers.

In 1909 appeared his "Principles of Mining," a treatise still standard in technical schools. He had written it "on the fly"; mostly during his long sea-voyages. Then a paper read at a scientific congress attracted his attention to the mystery of George Baer, or Georgius Agricola.

Agricola, a German contemporary of Martin Luther, completed in 1550 his "De Re Metallica," an exhaustive treatise on mining and smelting. It was the first written word on this subject since the Roman period, and the text-book of his profession for two centuries. American engineers interested in the history of their profession turned it over to Latin scholars for translation; but the text defied them. The technology of the Middle Ages is lost; and the terms which Agricola used had no real meaning when applied to modern process. Here was a challenge. Mr. and Mrs. Hoover, as a contribution and a diversion, set themselves to translate "De Re Metallica." Mrs. Hoover is well grounded in Latin; she brushed up. Hoover's researches in that tongue ended with his academy days at Newberg. So, with occasional assistance from such scholars as Dr. Fairclough of Stanford, Mrs. Hoover made the skeleton of a translation, while Hoover set up a small chemical laboratory in each of his various houses and began scientific detective work.

In the odd times and vacations of five years the Hoovers puzzled out Agricola's metallurgical and chemical processes, his engineering constructions, until the text, except for two or three specially involved passages, came out of the fog. And in 1912 they published their translation for private circulation among scholarly friends. It is in form and appearance—even to the humorously crude woodcuts—a replica of Agricola's ponderous vellum-bound original. And already it has acquired a collector value. Somewhere between them the Hoovers have given the feeling of mediæval Latin. Hoover's introduction shows a deep acquaintance with the culture of the Middle Ages and the Renaissance; his extensive footnotes prove his own acquaintance with the lore of mining as well as its technique; and he writes in vigorous English prose.

The bent for scholarship is one simple in his passion for Stanford University. As I have said, during all his wanderings this was the pole to his compass. He had there an impermanent home as early as 1908. In 1910 he made it permanent; established his family on the campus, entered his boys in the public schools. Herbert, Jr., was graduated from Stanford in 1924; Alan is now a student there. In 1910 he led the campaign for the Stanford Union—a club, a social center, embracing the whole university. In 1912 he became a trustee. And he has given that board active and original service. The School of Business Administration and the Food Institute are of his creation. Finally, he collected for this beloved alma mater the war library which his fellow-trustees have insisted on naming after him. This unique collection of original historical material may, as the ages go on, prove his greatest service to Stanford.

When as a boy of twenty-three he first got a salary above the bare necessities of existence, he made Lester Hinsdale a kind of distributing agent; sent him monthly from Australia a generous remittance. Most of this sum went, under Hoover's direction, to one or two relatives in process of education; and the rest to working students at Stanford who found the going hard. . . . I have this from Hinsdale, not from Hoover. . . . He maintained the habit, but he concealed it like a shame. For twenty years I have in California or New

York observed men or women of our common acquaintance sliding smoothly through a crisis like a long illness or unemployment. Then, years later perhaps, I will learn by some impulsive confession or through the process of dovetailing two remote facts, that the solvent was—Hoover.

One of his old associates in the engineering days tells of him a story which expresses much in little. On the occasion of their first meeting they left Hoover's office together. A beggar approached them, soliciting alms. Hoover refused him money, but asked for his name and address. These he jotted down on the back of an envelope—for all his efficiency he seems never to have a note-book about him.

"Why do you do that?" asked the other man. Hoover evaded the question. But the new acquaintance persisted; and drew out at last this hesitating, shame-faced reply:

"I don't like to see any one go hungry while I have enough to eat. On the other hand, I know that some of these street beggars are just professionals. So I've left a little fund with a man in the Salvation Army. When a beggar strikes me for a dime I take his address. Then the Salvation Army man runs him down. He finds lots of malingerers, of course. But there are others who really need help—and he helps 'em."

He kept his old friends; the affectionate ties of student days at Stanford remain unbroken after thirty years. And he made new friends of all the associates who remained with him long enough to reach the worth and warmth and humor under his superficial shyness.

"Attachment to Hoover," says one of his lieutenants on the Belgian job, "tends in the end toward fanaticism."

The pay-roll of those industrial enterprises which he managed or helped to manage would be a roster of the races—stalwart Americans in the mills and mines of our Far West, brawny Cornishmen in the drifts or levels of Australia, booted Russians in the forests, cement works, and furnaces of the Ural, fuzzy Tartars in the stopes of the Altai, little yellow Burmese, wearing simply a breech-clout and a hat, in the tunnels of Mandalay. All these he managed in that same spirit of understanding which gave motive-power to his later undertakings in pure kindness. He never overlooked the needs in the soul of man. He did not drive; he led.

"Every year," says one of his old associates, "he employed and directed thousands of men—yes, tens of thousands. In America, Australia, and Russia they were organized under unions. But he never had a strike."

As he drew toward the end of his vital, fighting thirties, mind and spirit were rising again to overlap their barriers. In 1912 I was returning from the Olympic games at Stockholm; and I crossed lines with Hoover, jumping from the Urals home to Stanford. During a three-day wait for a steamer we revived old memories, picked up threads of old intimacy. And on the last night we talked about his future. I cannot of course remember our exact words; but I can reconstruct their purport.

"I'm getting to the point," he said, "where I'll soon have an independent income—big enough."

"What's enough?" I asked.

"Not a great deal, as money goes nowadays," he said; "enough to live on comfortably and to be certain that the family is secure, and a margin to make sure. . . ."

"And then what?"

"I don't know exactly. But I'm already dissolving all this foreign work; the boys are taking it over. I am interested in some job of public service—at home, of course."

When I pressed him for particulars he answered at first by interesting generalities. So many problems in this world would yield to common sense, honest intention, and coöperation—the method that a good engineer uses on any big job. We were leaving to sentiment so many things that didn't belong legitimately to sentiment. We could save so much waste and effort by coördinating our activities. In such work, somehow, somewhere, a man of his experience might find place and usefulness. And one who has before the age of forty earned enough to insure him a comfortable living, should after then do something for his generation.

"It sounds to me a little like politics or government work," I commented.

"Well, I've always been interested in government and all that sort of thing," he said; "you remember Stanford. I don't know yet what it will be—but something." He was vague, for Hoover.

And as we talked that night, with Europe going on its accustomed tasks and amusements about us, the Belgian Senate was meeting in secret session to consider measures for immediate defense. We were sitting on a powder magazine and the fuse was alight. That time Europe trampled it out. Two summers later a shot from a crazy boy lit it again, this time beyond possibility of extinction. And then Fate resolved that vague "something"; again Fate decided for Herbert Hoover the decisive.

SONS OF GWALIA MINE AT MOUNT LEONORA, WEST AUSTRALIA

This shows the plant installed by Hoover in 1898

CHAPTER XIII

HOOVER had spent the winter of 1913-14 at engineering work in the United States. He intended to take a run to Russia in the spring, to consult on the way back with his engineering associates in Europe, and to return before midsummer to California. However, San Francisco was preparing for the Panama-Pacific Exposition of 1915; and the directors appointed this adopted Native Son their commissioner to arrange for the participation of European Governments. He sailed in March; traveled on this mission from capital to capital. His sons were in school at Palo Alto. When school closed in June, Mrs. Hoover packed up baggage and family and followed him. All went smoothly and pleasantly until the fatal twenty-eighth of June, when Serbian fanatics shot the Austrian Archduke and Archduchess. Europe knew what this might mean; so did Hoover. Ever since his Chinese days he had watched armaments, intrigues, and hates accumulating, had foreseen the horrible possibility of a general war. European boards of trade and foreign ministers had no time to think of an exposition six thousand miles away. He withdrew to London, wirehead for the cables of the world, and waited. A month later the worst happened; the armies moved and the blow fell.

Of course it played ducks and drakes with all international business. What Hoover thought of his own affairs stands recorded in a letter which one of his American friends, then resident in London, received from him on a day or so after Great Britain declared war: "Dear ———," it began, "I suppose we're all broke. But perhaps I may be able to scrape together a little ready money. And if there is anything I can do to help you out—" Hoover intended at the moment to remain in Europe until September, winding up his exposition business and doing what he could to save his own European enterprises.

Then by a side door he entered public life.

The war caught in its meshes 200,000 American tourists. At the first movement of the armies most of the powers closed their borders. Every Government in the world declared a moratorium on finance; no one could secure a dime from the banks. When the frontiers opened again, the Americans piled by thousands a day into England, that rim of the war zone nearest home. Most of the ships on the transatlantic run had been withdrawn; there followed a period of confused struggle for transportation. Other Americans, inexperienced in the ways of Europe and bewildered by the catastrophe, were stuck in knots all over the Continent; for they could not get enough cash even for the fare to London.

Some one must straighten out this tangle. The refugees in London met to consider ways and means. It began with a touch of comedy. An unidentified man of impressive voice and manner rose and said, "Mr. Chairman, I move we petition our Government to ask the European powers for a two weeks' suspension of hostilities, so that we may move out the American tourist decently and in order. . . ." The meeting dissolved into a roar of laughter. When it could get down to business again it appointed two eminent Americans to organize and accelerate the movement of American tourists. However, these leaders could not stay long abroad; pressing business called them home. Hoover, meantime, was doing his bit by finding for American friends and acquaintances a supply of gold, that being the only money which at the moment tradesmen and steamship agencies recognized as valid. Walter Page, our ambassador to Great Britain, knew of this; and he had heard from Hoover's own profession concerning this young man's abilities and experience. On Page's urgent request, Hoover took over the job.

This was the first time that those friends who were not also his business associates saw Hoover at work. Compared to his big engineering enterprises, I know now, it was almost child's play. We marveled nevertheless at the smooth run of his improvised engine. He concealed that machinery as he always does; gave human individuality all possible leeway; instead of commanding, led.

The Savoy Hotel had granted him the use of its grand ballroom and the whole surrounding floor; this presently bubbled like the lobby of a national convention with every variation on our American accent. Not only were the tourists coming out, but old American residents of the Continent, finding their means of livelihood gone, began scurrying for home. Most of the refugees could obtain no ready money, no matter how impressive their letters of credit. For days a British pound, worth ordinarily $4.86, cost $8.00 to $10.00 in American currency. Hoover, with ten other Americans, guaranteed an American bank in London against loss, and announced that they would cash any sort of American paper, even personal checks, at par of exchange. He raised a charity fund for those who had nothing, not even a blank check.

Thousands of young American girls were in continental boarding-schools. Their parents were ordering them home by cable; their teachers feared to let them pass through that chaos. To France, Germany, and Switzerland Hoover sent older women, who gathered up the girls in caravans, brought them across the Channel. The more adventurous among the tourists wanted to stay and see the show. They had no real business in Europe; and any mere onlooker might in the end embarrass our Government. Hoover must cajole this element into leaving. Some of the refugees were panic-stricken. Hoover must reassure them. One old lady for whom he had arranged passage told him flatly that she would not embark unless he gave her his personal guarantee in writing that she would not be torpedoed on the Atlantic. After a moment's thought, Hoover complied. "I knew," he chuckled afterward, "that there wasn't one chance in ten thousand that her ship would be harmed. If she came through all right she'd say I kept my word. If she was sunk, she'd never have time to blame me!"

He, like all imaginative and sympathetic men who

lived through the early stages of the war, found his pillow tortured by visions of the slaughter and misery that were coming. And he, like the rest of us, relieved the emotional strain by the hair-trigger laughter of war. There were little comedies at the Savoy; one in especial Hoover, with his lively and indulgent feeling for the humors in boys, has been telling ever since.

Through the crowd came marching a dozen American Indians in full regalia of feathers, beads, and buckskins, surrounding a bedraggled but very proud American boy of thirteen or fourteen. His parents, it appeared, were Poles. In August his father sent him to Poland for a visit with his grandparents. The vessel landed in Hamburg on the very day when the war broke. The tourist agency which had him in charge informed him that the border was locked; he could not reach Poland. He was too inexperienced to know about consuls and their uses; and for several days he roamed about the docks, getting lonelier and lonelier, more and more perplexed.

Meantime, a small Wild West show had been playing in Austria. When the war broke, its circus-Indians found themselves trapped and strapped. The Government commandeered most of the horses. They had to kill the others to feed their two lions. After the border opened, the authorities let them travel to Hamburg, the port at which they had arrived from America. By pooling their funds, they raised the railroad fare. But they could carry no baggage. As their Indian ring-regalia was valuable, they dressed in that, and left their American clothes behind.

So it happened that one morning the boy, now on the verge of despair, looked up to behold war-bonnets, buckskins, beads! He ran to them, addressed them in American. The leader—his Indian name is remembered as Black Feather—came straight to the point.

"Kid," he said, "got any money?" The boy had; eagerly, he put it at their disposal. Squatted on the dock, they counted it. There was just enough, with the scrapings of their own pockets, to carry them all to London via Holland.

This spectacular group lined up before Hoover. He arranged to buy them steerage passage from the loan fund. But that Carlisle graduate Black Feather seemed to have something still on his mind.

"What else can I do for you?" inquired Hoover.

"Well," said Black Feather, "you see—we took the kid's money. I'd like to be dead sure he gets it back. Can't you advance it to him? I own two hundred acres of apple orchard in Montana, and I'll make good as soon as I get home."

That night Hoover told the story at dinner. In the party was a rich American woman who had engaged a suite on the Baltic. "I've a spare cabin," she said; "ask the boy to come back with me as my guest!" But when Hoover transmitted the invitation, the little refugee shook his head and answered like a true boy.

"Thank the lady," he said. "But I'd much rather go in the steerage with my friend Black Feather!"

Early in September, Congress appropriated a million dollars to bring stranded Americans home. It was sent in gold by a battleship; but the business was nearly over before it arrived. Ambassador Page appointed Hoover to deal it out in loans to the needy.

By now Hoover's machine was running so smoothly that he might give it into other hands. The stream of tourists was flowing homeward in orderly fashion, every ship full to the gunwales. Five thousand Americans a day had passed through the Hoover organization. And this is worthy of note: It had accepted checks and other evidences of credit to the amount of $1,500,000. There was no time to look into the validity of this security; it had to assess and identify applicants simply by their looks. Yet it lost in all only $400!

Now Mrs. Hoover, who had been very busy with the Women's Committee, took her sons and returned them to their school in California. Hoover remained to close up the affair; himself engaged passage for the last week of September. But before he could sail, events hurried him to his supreme decision—for himself and for the world.

Germany had invaded Belgium. Her armies were using it as a base for their advance on France. By September she occupied virtually the whole country except the corner about Antwerp; and that fortress fell in October. Belgium was caught between the upper and nether millstones. All who—like me—saw the first advance of the German armies, felt that bar some miracle, Belgium must starve. It was the most thickly settled country, the most intensively industrial country, in all Europe. It imported in normal times 80 per cent. of its foodstuffs. At no time did its shops and warehouses hold more than one month's supply of food for the cities. Moreover, the armies, in their march through the main towns, had commandeered a great part of the accumulated supply. The British had from the first day of the war bottled up the German fleet in its harbors; promptly they put a strict "food blockade" on Germany and her conquered territories. The Allies would not open a hole in this blockade even for benefit of their little, imprisoned ally. They were trying to starve Germany out; and they had no guarantee that the Germans would not seize any supplies sent for Belgian relief. Nor could the Belgians expect any present help from their conquerors. The Germans knew, even then, that food might win the war. They themselves were not self-supporting in this respect. Taking stock of their supplies, they were preparing to ration bread and fats. Perhaps one could not expect them, in these circumstances, to assume the support of more than seven million Belgians and three million French enemies. Yet the western lines had locked on the Aisne, forecasting a long war; and Belgium was already scraping the corners of its flour barrels.

The actions which averted a cosmic tragedy started from two different quarters. In Brussels lived Millard Shaler, an American engineer concerned with gold and diamond deposits in the Belgian Congo. He saw what was coming; conceived the general idea that he as a neutral might help in opening a channel of relief. A smuggled British newspaper brought news of Hoover's work with the American refugees. Shaler had never met Hoover; but all the engineering world knew his ability at organization and negotiation, his reliability.

Here was the man to relieve Belgium—and on the spot! Scraping together some Belgian funds, Shaler hurried to London, called on Edgar Rickard, who was associated with Hoover in looking after stranded Americans, and in normal times managed the British edition of an American engineering journal. Rickard introduced him to Hoover. Hoover advised him how to purchase and load his supplies. Immediately Shaler ran into the blockade regulations. The authorities would not allow the ship to move. The fugitive Belgian Government tried to persuade the British to let it through, but without avail. Shaler came back to Hoover for more advice and help. Hoover took him to Ambassador Page; asked if the United States could not use its benevolent powers of intercession for the lives of ten million people.

There they met the other emissaries of salvation. Hugh Gibson, first secretary of our ministry at Brussels, had arrived—on the same desperate mission. And three eminent Belgians had persuaded the Germans to let them leave the country under pledge and bond, that they might ask help of our ambassador. The United States was the great neutral. By its prestige and moral power, it might break a hole in the blockade; might somehow see to it that supplies sent in for the Belgians were not diverted to the Germans. Now on this committee served a Belgian banker who had known Hoover in China. When Shaler mentioned that name, he said, "The very man." And Ambassador Page needed no persuasion. For now he had seen Hoover at work. Beyond any other American, this great engineer had the equipment for such an unprecedented, impossible job—skill at organization, experience with finance, understanding of diplomacy, acquaintance with Europe, unshakable integrity, common sense, the human touch. After an all-day conference they sent for Hoover and proposed that he take direction of an American commission to relieve Belgium.

For three days he sat with Mr. Page and the Belgians, threshing out details, imagining possibilities. And for three nights he walked the floor, weighing in the balance his own personal perplexities. I can certify to this. Between flights to the war zone I was lodging with him as his guest; and waking from war-tortured dreams I used to hear the steady tramp of his feet on the floor above. I thought then and I think now that never for a moment did he consider refusing this call to service. He was choosing, I believe, between comparative sacrifice and complete renunciation. His own affairs were in a ridiculous tangle. Two or three weeks before, he had said to a friend, "I think I'm broke. Of course, you understand I sha'n't be in want the rest of my life. I can always earn my living by engineering consultation fees. But as for having anything ahead, so that I may retire in comfort and do what I please —I guess that's over."

Then, as the lines locked on the Aisne and the war settled down for a stay, his associates began to perceive that Hoover, if he held on and played out his hand, stood to win a very great fortune indeed. In his work with mines he had specialized on base metals. He and his associates were in position to command a good part of the zinc and lead minerals in the world. And these, the materials of shells and guns and aëroplanes, were becoming as gold. No other American business man had such intimate commercial knowledge of so many countries. Had he cared alone for money and the power that money brings, he might have brought out of the war an enormous fortune—and without taint of profiteering. Carry that on to the period after the war when our enormous excess capital began flowing into all the far lands, and it is easy to see that he might have become one of the richest men in the world. . . . This is conjecture on my part; but if we on the outside saw it, Hoover also must have seen. And as for the bird in the hand, he was one of the leading engineers of the world; from fees alone, he commanded the ample professional income that comes only to leaders. Should he try to keep a hold on part of his business affairs, or let them all go? That, I think, was his quandary. Relieving Belgium would require not only the most delicate diplomacy but large operations in finance. He knew perfectly the suspicions of Europe. If he remained in active business, the charge that he was looking for concessions and advantages would hang round his neck like a millstone. Morever, this thing would demand every energy he had. . . .

On the fourth morning he came down to breakfast with his accustomed mien—pleasantly sober. We were alone in the dining-room. He bade me good-morning, poured and sweetened his coffee, looked up, and—

"Well, let the fortune go to hell," he said.

In that phrase was born the Commission for Relief

in Belgium. I felt then, I know now, that I had witnessed a significant moment in history.

Hoover spent that day in winding up his affairs. He renounced, as of date, all his engineering fees, resigned from all his highly paid executive jobs, surrendered the commercial good-will which he had been building up for fifteen years. To his associate engineers he said: "I give you the business"; and as time served in the hectic month which followed, he helped secure their election to his vacant place in directorates or companies. He would, he said, give advice on critical points, until they had the helm firmly in hand. But he would accept no more responsibility or remuneration. So, suddenly and unexpectedly, ended his career as an engineer.

Some of his fellow-directors of foreign nationality took this decision hard. He was an American; what business had he in the war? Hoover gave his grave chuckle; and in one of his concentrated moods buckled down to the big job.

CHAPTER XIV

THE Commission for Relief in Belgium was a threeply job. First, Hoover and the American ambassadors or ministers associated with him as vice-chairmen must persuade both the allied powers and the Germanic powers to let it exist and function. Second, it must initiate and organize in a desperate hurry an immense movement of commodities by sea and rail. I think I am within the truth when I say that it was the largest enterprise of the kind ever attempted by a private citizen or organization. Lastly, and perhaps most importantly, it must finance itself; must find somehow ways and means to meet a budget which grew to twenty-five million dollars a month.

During the period of our neutrality the commission steadily solicited funds for the indigent Belgians. Because of this, the world in general carelessly assumes that it lived purely by charity. That is a great mistake. The rich had to eat. A millionaire shipwrecked on a barren rock cannot use his wealth to appease his hunger. The affluent of Belgium were in a similar fix. Charity supported millions of the poor and destitute; but those vast funds which America and the rest of the neutrals gave to Belgium between 1914 and 1918 would scarcely have fed the 10,000,000 inhabitants of Belgium and northern France for two months. Providing sure and steady imports of food for every one, rich and poor alike—that was the gigantic task which the commission assumed from the day of its birth. It must operate as a food administration, not only giving to the poor but selling to the rich, and somehow making the receipts good in the markets of the world. Ultimately, indeed, the logic of circumstances forced it to requisition the products of Belgium's own soil, throw them with the imported food into the common supply, ration the whole population.

And Hoover must tackle these three problems all at once. For the moment the diplomatic was perhaps the most perplexing, but organization the most immediate. He threw together a working plan of which I shall treat later in more detail. In essence, it provided that every ounce of food which entered Belgium should be rationed out under supervision of its own American agents, these agents responsible to the commission for justice in distribution and for seeing that none of it fell into German hands.

The diplomatic problem was closely welded with the financial. The reader who did not witness the European war may find it hard to understand what barriers it lifted against the intercommunication of nations, and especially hostile nations. There was not only a food-blockade but a money-blockade. In the first conference the Belgians had proposed that they finance the broad problem of food imports—temporarily at least —from Belgian funds deposited in banks of the other allied countries. An appeal to American charity brought quick and generous response. But under scrutiny, these resources proved pitifully inadequate. They would do for a start, and no more.

At Hoover's suggestion, the State Department at Washington instructed James W. Gerard, our ambassador at Berlin, to sound out the German Government. It would admit the principle; the Americans might bring food across the closed Belgian border; they pledged themselves not to commandeer it. Walter Page approached the British cabinet. Those were the early, confused days of the war when England, which muddles through, was muddling for her life. The war-machine was only in process of building. Bureaus overlapped, crossed each other, issued contrary orders. Hoover, with Page's approval, slipped through the loopholes of this imperfect system and got direct action. By appealing to humanity, he won permission to send food through the blockade via Rotterdam. He even secured a government contribution of half a million dollars—enough to feed Belgium, at that early stage of the game, for a few days. As the work expanded, it would not have lasted a day. Captain Lucey raked together half a million bushels of wheat in Holland. Hoover found a supply of breadstuffs in England, chartered two ships for Rotterdam, that neutral harbor which lay nearest to Belgium. An underling refused them license to sail. Hoover saw Walter Runciman, chairman of the Board of Trade, in which province this matter lay. Runciman reversed the order. And on November 13, 1914, the first of these vessels landed its cargo at Rotterdam. Lucey's wheat had reached Brussels ten days earlier.

He was just in time. The little supply which Shaler had sent across in the early open days had melted like a snowflake on a stove. Brussels could go on for a week more. But Maubeuge down in the far corner, Charleroi near the great line, had reached the end of their resources. Smaller towns were actually starving. . . . Concerning that, the veterans of the commission tell a story illuminating some of those local peculiarities with which they had to deal. Hammé, south of Antwerp, had brushed the last speck out of its flour barrels. It received a supply from this first cargo. The town bakers hurried it to the ovens. Then Hammé sat down and tightened its belt and waited twenty-four hours for the bread to cool! Southerners will be amused to learn that the Continent of Europe does not recognize hot bread as fit food for man or beast.

Meantime, Hoover was stitching together his human organization. When first he approached the Germans, they asked, "Who are you people?" "We're a group of engineers, accustomed to dealing with large bodies of men," replied Hoover. "Oh, you're experts!" exclaimed the Germans; "then go ahead." They believed in specialists. Hoover had grouped round him as associates some of those eminent American engineers of international experience with whom he worked in his professional days. There still exists the roster of the original Commission for Relief in Belgium—Millard Hunsiker, John B. White, Clarence Graff, Edgar Rickard, Hugh Gibson, Millard Shaler, Captain J. F. Lucey, W. L. Honnold, T. O. Connett, and Herbert Hoover. All were Americans and all, except Gibson the diplomat, engineers. They had followed the example of him whom already they called "Chief"; dropped their own big affairs to work without profit or salary. Presently they gathered others of their kind: like W. B. Poland, who afterward gave them distinguished service as a business executive and diplomatic fighter, and Lindon W. Bates, who took charge of the purchasing in New York. Stanford University came into it presently—of course! Dr. Frank Angell, who ruled the Faculty Athletic Committee when Hoover was student body treasurer, worked through a sabbatical year as an agent in Belgium. In his hours of recreation he astounded the Belgian flappers by his agility at tennis. Vernon Kellogg had served in Hoover's student days as a professor of biology, so young that strangers often took him for a freshman. Risen now to distinction, both as scientific investigator and author, he joined Hoover and won new honors as an irregular diplomat. Caspar Whitney, author, big-game hunter, explorer, felt the thrill of the benevolent adventure, hurried to Europe . . . but I must not make this a catalogue.

The Belgians are expert social workers. Before the first food arrived they, as a result of conferences with Hoover, had founded the Comité Nationale de Secours et d'Alimentation. (Roughly translated, "the National Committee for Relief and Provisioning.") Hoover, following the old policy of his engineering days, decentralized everything he could; left execution of details to local autonomy. Committees of Belgians and Americans were created for each province; these were again dissolved into committees for each commune (county). Hoover placed American representatives in every large town, and, in coöperation with the Central Belgian Committee, laid out the detailed plans. These local subcommittees—which included the flower of Belgium—took charge of the foodstuffs as soon as they reached a distributing point, got the grain to the mills, the flour to the ovens, issued the bread-and-meat cards, saw in general to all the details of rationing. To the Commission for Relief in Belgium remained the larger administrative job. It must first—supreme task—cajole or threaten inimical elements of the powers into letting it exist; then raise stupendous funds, purchase supplies in America, find shipping, transfer the cargoes at Rotterdam, transport them to their destination in each commune.

Finally, its agents must check up receipts against consumption; be ready to prove that no American food was passing into German hands; see in general that justice was done to all.

This required more personnel. Late in November Hoover issued a call to young Americans willing to work for a bare living and for the satisfaction of saving life. Students finishing their education abroad were first to respond. Then adventurous youth began streaming in from the United States, until there were more volunteers than openings. A glorious young company, most of them served with much distinction in some phase or other of our own war. But later adventures have not blotted from their memories the Commission for Relief in Belgium; even now it is to them a unique piece of life, a solemn and great fraternity. They bore the brunt of detail; usually humdrum, sometimes for a moment picturesque. They had powers which the conquered Belgians did not possess. They alone, when some officious or ill-instructed minor official stopped and hampered the work, could exert pressure on the conquerors; they alone could settle local disputes among the people, keep the stream of provisions moving; finally and supremely, they alone could certify to the allied governments that the Germans were not dipping into the supplies.

But before the first of these assistants established himself in the sodden bleakness of conquered Belgium, Hoover was running toward a major crisis. Funds, funds, always funds! America was giving food and money as she never gave before. But it was not nearly enough. It could never be made enough. He had used up the British contribution. The few millions of Belgian money held in banks abroad—that helped but only helped. In anything like normal times the problem would have been simple of solution. But Belgium had no ready money. The seizure of the country had ruined the currency. Temporary notes, issued by chambers of commerce and banks, served the purposes of internal business; but they were valueless beyond the Belgian border. Sending even paper money in or out of Belgium constituted in the view of one belligerent or the other "trading with the enemy." Hoover conceived the idea of an exchange system to penetrate this blockade. Stripped of complexities, taken out of banking jargon, it went as follows: Permit any one, outside of Belgium, who wanted to remit to any one inside, to deposit the money with the Relief Commission. The commission, in turn, would buy food, send it into Belgium, sell it for paper currency to those who could pay, hand over that currency to the person designated to receive it. Carrying the plan farther, induce every Belgian bank or industry which had resources abroad to liquidate them and remit them into Belgium in this fashion. Or as alternative, let the larger allied powers make relief loans to the Belgian Government. But the way bristled with obstacles, chief of them an attitude of the Germans. Under ruling of the Second Hague Convention, they said, an occupied country must feed and otherwise support the occupying army. Belgium, naturally, could give no food to its conquerors. But it could give money. They had forced Belgian banks to issue paper currency and pay it to them, for this purpose, at the rate of $8,000,000 a month. With these funds they bought materials and paid labor in Belgium. To which proceeding the enemies of Germany took violent exception.

The Allies, who had entered the war upon the occasion of the Belgian invasion, and who held the money-bags, were the first and greatest hope. In October the British had set a precedent by a government contribution. But Hoover, trying this quarter, found a changed atmosphere. The blockade was growing more and more important; the military party sat in the saddle. Balked, he rushed across the mine-strewn North Sea, hurried to Berlin. Here began that series of intense arguments with ministries and chancelleries which took so much of his energy in the next two years. He bared the only weapon he had: the public opinion of the United States. "You complain that Americans are pro-ally," he said in effect; "probably they are. And why? Mainly because of their sympathy with Belgium. If you help out, by just so much do you lessen the antagonism of our country." Moved by these arguments —and by humanity—the Imperial Treasury and the Imperial Foreign Office listened, yielded, proposed a plan. As this was complicated, and as it never came into operation, I shall omit details. Briefly, the commission might draw on the internal Belgian banks, and the Reichsbank would discount these drafts for six months. However, the process was such that the funds would pinch out after a few months; and the war, Hoover saw, had settled itself down for a stay. But it would do as a start and perhaps as a lever with the Allies. Belgium's enemies had offered help. Could Belgium's allies seem less generous?

Yet, when he reached England, he found that the situation had grown worse. . . . The Germans were about to declare a submarine blockade of England; the war was rising toward another crisis of hate and desperation. Not only did a grant of funds seem less likely, but the whole undertaking stood in peril. Kitchener, then war lord of England, was an old-fashioned soldier. He saw this struggle only in military terms, not at all in social terms. Winston Churchill ruled the king's navy; and to his circle the validity and integrity of the blockade had become a religion. Both opposed the commission's very existence. The Germans, they said, ought to feed the Belgians; in the end, the opinion of the neutral world would force it. When this happened, so much less food for the Germans; therefore a quicker end. If the Belgians had to go down to the pallid gates of starvation—well, war is war. They must do their part.

Sir Edward Grey, still foreign minister, favored the commission and its work; had favored it from the first. Herbert Asquith was then premier. No one knows to this day exactly where he stood. From a friend who accompanied him, I have heard that Hoover's first interview with the premier strongly resembled a quarrel. Asquith burst out, "Young man, you're impertinent!" . . . This may not have meant anything. Trying to goad an adversary into anger in order to uncover what he really thought and felt was one of Asquith's little tricks.

At the moment, Lloyd George governed the British Treasury as chancellor of the exchequer. Hoover threw his main attack against this able, temperamental Celt. On January 21, the eve of an important cabinet meeting—the eve, too, of despair for Belgium—Hoover called on Lloyd George and made a final plea. It must have been an extraordinary battle of wits and souls—the most plausibly eloquent statesman in Europe against this grave, low-spoken Yankee who as he argues his case seems always to be dragging forward reluctant words. Even the business-like memorandum of this conversation and the confirmatory memorandum which Lloyd George requested—both now in the commission's archives—convey a sense of drama. From these documents, and the story as told by one of the officials present, it is easy to reconstruct the occasion. With his own packed terseness, Hoover told what he wanted—permission to carry out his plan for exchange, and direct help in money from the allies. Lloyd George replied with the British military view. The commission was assisting the enemy—unintentionally but none the less vitally. It was giving the Belgians food to stand more requisitions; resources to stand more monetary levies. Moreover, Mr. Hoover's work relieved the Germans from the duty of feeding the Belgians. So it was prolonging the war; for economic pressure, not guns, would win in the end. The more food the Germans gave the Belgians, the sooner they themselves would collapse. "He was wholly opposed to our operations, benevolent and humane as they were," says the commission's memorandum.

Hoover showed that the Germans had promised him to stop requisitioning food after the first of January, now past; he argued that the financial arrangement would add no resources which Germany could commandeer. He expressed his own serious opinion that Germany would not assume the burden of provisioning Belgian civilians. He quoted the views of the German military class—that they would feed the Belgians only when the allies opened the port of Antwerp; that with their own people to provision, they could not and would not take on 10,000,000 more in Belgium and northern France. And Belgium would starve. In the valley of the Meuse, Frenchmen whom the commission could not reach were already starving.

"A monstrous attitude!" exclaimed Lloyd George.

And here Hoover drew his best weapon, as he had drawn it already on the Germans—public opinion in the neutral countries, which to the European belligerents was almost synonymous with public opinion in the United States. How, if she refused this succor to her allies, would Great Britain herself figure before the world? She had entered the war—so she said—for the purpose of protecting small nations and especially Belgium. She stood the champion of democracy against autocracy. This Belgium was one of the most democratic nations in the world. It would be an ironic victory if the Belgians were annihilated in the process; if the British found the country, when their armies entered, an empty husk! Were not the British great enough to forfeit a doubtful and hazy military advantage and show magnanimity to these distressed people? The memory of that would outlast the bitterness of this war. . . . Months later and thousands of miles away, I played forerunner to Hoover with a body of important men to whom he had been misrepresented, foully and basely. As he entered the room, their very eyes expressed suspicion. He sat down, began in his hesitant way to tell plainly and reasonably what he was doing, and why. No rhetoric or emotion or tricks or fireworks; but when he left they were his partizans and adherents for life. . . . So must the magic of pure intention and pure logic have worked on Lloyd George. The most persuasive man in Europe was persuaded, and all at once.

"You have convinced me," he said abruptly. "You have my permission." Other officials of the British

Government sat listening to this debate. Lloyd George turned to them, asked them to arrange the details. This was somewhat premature; for the cabinet had to give its approval. It met that night. None knows exactly what happened, or will know until history can scan the archives of the great war. But next day Lloyd George came upon Hoover, waiting anxiously in his outer office. The cordial little Welshman slapped the American on the back and said:

"My boy, you've won!"

This was the first of those diplomatic victories by which, in the course of two years, Hoover backed the military parties of Europe into a corner. In retrospect it looks big. But at the moment it seemed doubtful. There were months of strenuous negotiations before he could set this arrangement firmly into his structure. The Allies must be convinced that the Germans had abandoned their levies on the Belgian banks. The British naval party, with whom faith in the blockade amounted to a superstition, kept up a dropping fire. Humanity being imperfect, it was manifestly impossible to guarantee that no ignorant Belgian committeeman or peasant, in some remote corner of the country, would not occasionally trade food with a German. Such trivial exchanges, even taken in mass, amounted to nothing. But always when the British naval party heard of them through their Intelligence Department, there followed a hitch in negotiations. Hoover wrote to Whitlock in March, 1915, "It is probably impossible for me to make clear to you . . . by what delicate balance this business continues, in view of the complete conviction of the British military authorities, that the whole of this effort is to their disadvantage and profoundly to the advantage of the Germans. . . . Our German friends do not always realize how easy it is to plunge us into difficulties with the English—and vice versa. . . ."

The work grew. The demand rose from $5,000,000 a month to $10,000,000 and soared on upward to $25,000,000—a budget greater than that of the United States Government in Cleveland's time! Belgian institutions in free territory could no longer carry the "outside" end of that exchange arrangement. It had grown too big. Hoover must negotiate, in collaboration with the Belgian diplomats, larger loans and subsidies from the powerful Allies. Each loan was a separate battle. The margin grew sometimes dangerously narrow. At times the commission had outstanding liabilities of $20,000,000 in excess of even its promised assets. Under the law the members of the commission were personally liable if they defaulted in payment for any shipment of food. But they kept their Yankee nerve, went on buying, and fought for the money. To the Belgians who had work or ready cash, the commission, through the national committee, sold foodstuffs at a "profit." This margin, returned to the general fund, served along with the generous contributions from America to carry the unemployed upon charity. The roster of the destitute rose from about 1,000,000 at the beginning to 1,500,000 in 1915, and, as industry faded away, to 4,000,000 at the end of the war—a plurality of the country.

And the financing of relief for Belgium was no sooner established than the invaded districts of northern France began calling for the bread of life. In that dreary winter of 1914-15 Ambassador Gerard visited the Western Front. He saw malnutrition, the beginnings of starvation, in the French population behind the lines. Like all our other ambassadors and ministers in the belligerent countries, he was by direction of our Government a part of the commission. To Hoover and to our Government he reported this grave emergency. Hoover knew it already; once or twice he had cut red tape, managed to slip through a consignment to a desperate community.

The Germans and French, agreeing for once, both wanted it done. But money—always money! Belgium was straining every resource. He went to Paris, interviewed the French Government, asked for funds—$5,000,000 a month and something extra for initial stocks of food. There followed a curious incident. The French would not admit the principle—they confirmed this attitude in writing. Their hearts bled, they said, at beholding Frenchmen in want. Nevertheless, the more food in occupied territory, the longer the German resistance. The northern Frenchmen, like the soldiers, must suffer for their country. . . . That is what they said. But that evening the head of an important French bank called and asked for details. "We are interested," he said. "We'll see what we can do and advise you later." Hoover passed on to London. Two days later he received a registered letter. "Kindly acknowledge receipt of the enclosed," it read; that and nothing more. The enclosed was a check from the London correspondent of that bank: "pay to the order of Herbert Hoover, twenty-five million francs"—in those days, $5,000,000. The French Government was not acknowledging the principle; but it was caring for its own! Later, it came out into the open.

This episode gives occasion to remark on the bookkeeping of the commission. Hoover's foresight told him from the first that he must encounter suspicions and enmities. Given the slightest opportunity, its critics would accuse the commission of peculation and graft. Therefore, it must not keep its own books. He delegated that function to the firm of international auditors which, he felt, had the highest standing for efficiency and integrity. He went farther. To an early meeting of the commission—and later to me—he said:

"Some swine, when this thing is over, is probably going to accuse us of graft. I want to be ready for him. So I'm going to pay all my own expenses out of my own pocket." He did that to the end. When, after the war, the auditors closed up a sales-and-purchase account of $928,000,000, they added a voluntary statement that Hoover had never himself drawn a cent from these funds—for traveling expenses or for any other purpose whatsoever.

Much of the money came in the same form as that check. Elements in Europe which would trust neither government nor official nor commission, trusted Herbert Hoover. Doubtless the European powers had spies on him; had combed his present and past and found them irreproachable. Also, they had met him face to face, seen him work. To doubt him was after that like doubting truth itself. No one knows how many millions came thus, addressed directly to Hoover. He never saw the money. Indorsed for him, the checks or drafts were by the accountants acknowledged, entered, thrown into the general fund; and never a cent was drawn out except upon their signature.

In 1919 the French expressed by one of their gallant gestures their opinion of the man. To the Government at Paris the auditors submitted this enormous account for final scrutiny and approval. The French waved it aside. "We have tasks more pressing and fruitful," they said, "than questioning the integrity of Mr. Hoover!"

CHAPTER XV

No sooner was the British military party reduced to quiescence than the Commission for Relief in Belgium must turn about face and fight with the Germans a desperate battle for existence.

A trivial incident set off this explosion. "I do not presume to dictate your feelings," said Hoover to his agents in Belgium, Holland and Germany, "but one thing is necessary—neutrality of words and deeds." They must carry water on both shoulders as best they could, avoiding unnecessary contacts with either the inhabitants or the Germans. From the first, he worried for fear some slip of expression, some outburst of anger, even some act of mistaken kindness, would engender a diplomatic incident. In this case the expected happened.

Rotterdam, in neutral Holland, was the cross-roads for food shipments. There the ships docked and transferred their cargoes to freight-trains and canal-boats; from there hundreds of cars and boats started for destinations in Belgium and northern France. In the Rotterdam office served a young man, lately arrived from the United States, who sympathized with the Germans. One day in 1915 three or four of the American agents in Belgium passed through the

Rotterdam office. During that early period there was much trouble and friction with minor officials and underlings. Also, very likely these young men sympathized with the Allies. Safe, as they thought, in that little patch of America, they expressed their feelings with vigorous native adjectives. War makes n... dmen of us all. That night the young man with German sympathies wrote down this conversation. He added trimmings, doubtless; and he involved many other agents of the commission in a visionary "plot." All this he transmitted to the German Intelligence Department.

Now as regards their attitude toward the commission, the German authorities fell into three distinct classes. Except for moments when an extreme military party held the reins, the central Government at Berlin favored the work. So, generally speaking, did the higher officers of the fighting zone. They understood the danger of a starving, disease-ridden, rioting population at their rear; they had that tolerance of the enemy which usually distinguishes men of the front line. In the military zone of the rear—which governed Belgium—there was rivalry and intrigue between bureaus. One party stood for stern repression; they wanted to force the Belgians to work for the Germans under threat of starvation. The other party believed in conciliation. The violent faction was for the moment in power. They had always suspected this body of foreigners, free to travel at any time into enemy lands. "Spies and secret agents!" they said. By government routine, this report came into their hands for action. Immediately they issued an order of arrest against certain leading men of the commission who were then in Belgium.

Hugh Gibson, in the absence of Minister Whitlock our chargé d'affaires at Brussels, telegraphed the ghastly news to Hoover. Meantime he argued the question, played for time. Crossing the North Sea, Hoover plunged again into negotiations. For a time he followed a blind trail; he did not know as yet the basis for the absurd charge that his men were a company of allied spies.

Relief and support came from the line itself. The quartermaster-general of the old German army had almost supreme powers. General Zöllner held that post at the time; his representative, in dealing with the commission, was Major von Kessler. These two, when they could be reached, showed justice and humanity in their dealings with the commission. Vernon Kellogg and Caspar Whitney were representatives of the commission at German Great Headquarters—"our ambassadors" the central offices called them in jest. Late in November they, Hoover, and W. B. Poland conferred with von Kessler and two of his aides. The session turned into a frank show-down. The tale of that conversation in Rotterdam had grown with the telling; the German Intelligence Department believed that our men had "tipped off" to the allies the plans for the September offensive. Hoover managed to disabuse their minds of this inference, strip the charges to a basis of fact. Major von Kessler perfectly understood the exaggerations. And he wanted the commission to

©*Harris & Ewing, Washington, from Wide World Photo*

MRS. HERBERT HOOVER

stay. A promise to keep out of Belgium all men accused of unneutral speech, a tightening of the machinery here and there, and that crisis was past. "Next!" said Poland.

In the meantime, a multitude of minor diplomatic troubles, any of which by careless handling might have become major. Belgium was sowing and reaping her crop of 1915. That, the Allies ruled, the commission must requisition and ration. And it must go to the Belgians alone—every grain and spear. Hoover and his lieutenants made the Germans recognize this principle, established machinery to satisfy the Allies. Germany was buying live stock from the peasants. That, of course, helped keep the German army in fresh meat. The British roared their disapproval. More quarrelsome negotiations before the cattle and slaughterhouses were put in control of the commission.

Now came the need of clothing. The commission sent a hurry-call over the United States. Second-hand garments, odd bolts of new materials, came back in shiploads. These the Belgian committee cleansed, renovated, made up, distributed. But the German army was running short of wool for uniforms. Second-hand woolen goods could be ground into shoddy, rewoven as uniform cloth. A complaint from the vigilant British, and a new function for the commission. It must supervise all manufacture and sale of cloth and clothing in Belgium.

The Allies were watching like hawks the quantity of foodstuffs entering Rotterdam. Not too much! Just enough to keep the populace alive. What was enough?

On that they differed with Hoover, often widely. Coached and instructed by expert dieticians, he himself became an authority on the subject. Scientifically he estimated the need; so many calories a day for a man working at hard labor, so many for a child; such-and-such proportion of proteids, carbohydrates, vitamins, and fat. Also, he watched the vital statistics. During the first year they flashed a warning signal. Tuberculosis among the children was on the rise. A growing boy or girl needs much and special nourishment. The cattle were greatly depleted; there was not enough milk. He established a special medical commission to investigate; then pried out of the Allies another increase in the allowance, established a balanced midday luncheon for babies and for boys and girls of the ravenous age. This looks simple on paper; but it was no easy job to transform all the school-houses and public buildings into restaurants! Every noontime for four years the commission fed 2,300,000 children. . . . Carrying this matter to its end, the tuberculosis rate began falling below normal. When the war closed and the whole situation could be surveyed, the Belgian authorities reported that the health of Belgian children was never in history so good as on the day of the armistice.

Northern France, lying in the zone of military action, presented a special problem. For example, the commission had to guarantee the Allies that no Frenchman who assisted the Germans in military work should receive American food. One day an irresponsible sub-officer seized at Roubaix a number of idle workmen and set them to filling sandbags for intrenchments. Crosby, in charge of this area, promptly cut off the food-supply until he could get the matter to Great Headquarters—which at once reversed the order. Each of our agents in this region must eat, lodge, travel, and work in company and collaboration with a German reserve officer. These the boys called "our nurses." Naturally such forced intimacy irritated both parties. However, when the irritation had passed, the Americans realized that these Germans had themselves become zealous partizans of the commission and its work.

In northern France the question of the native harvest was more complicated than in Belgium. Here all the able-bodied peasants had joined the colors before the invaders came. The Germans, supplementing the scant native labor, put reserve troops to work in the field and claimed part of the crop. In 1915 Hoover and his lieutenants made an adjustment which the allies approved. This was difficult—but after all, no more difficult than most of the negotiations which so complicated their job. It involved only the trifling value of $50,000,000! But the harvest of 1916 was a different story. The British saw by now that their blockade was bringing results; the Germans envisaged for the first time the possibility of starvation. Both looked over the estimates of this harvest in the fertile plains of invaded northern France. The Germans reported back to Hoover just what proportion they intended to commandeer for themselves, and just how much they would allow the commission. The Allies, likewise, notified him how much they would expect the French inhabitants to receive. The figures stood at ridiculous variance.

Hoover was used by now to that sort of thing. The belligerents always started off in a truculent mood; ground the commission and its charges for a time between the upper and the nether millstone. In weariness of spirit Hoover would edge them to grudging compromise. But now he found both parties stiff-necked, immovable. The Allies proposed to cut down the food-import into northern France to a dangerous point. Added to the amount which they demanded from the harvest, the sum total would just feed the inhabitants. Yielding 1 per cent. to the German demand meant malnutrition; yielding all, starvation.

The Germans, on their part, would not budge an inch. Suddenly, headquarters at Charleville referred Hoover to Berlin. He and Vernon Kellogg traveled up to the German capital. In his book "Fighting Starvation in Belgium," Kellogg gives a moving account of the storm which they rode out next day. The Germans, they found, were holding a conference of their lords of empire. The extreme jingo party, headed by von Reventlow, had come into power. This was the first sign of that new policy which, six months later, brought on an unlimited submarine campaign, declaration of war by the United States, the downfall. . . .

Major von Kessler, still friendly to their benevolent enterprise, broke appalling news. That morning the Berlin newspapers had published a story loaded with dynamite. Great Britain, it said inaccurately, was insisting that the whole crop of Belgium, Serbia, Poland,

and northern France should go to the inhabitants of those countries—not a grain to the German army which had helped to cultivate it. This happened at the very moment when the conference was taking up that matter of the northern French crop. It started a stampede. With two or three exceptions, soldiers and civilians alike demanded not only that the Government stand firm in its attitude on the French crop, but that if the Allies did not yield, the commission must get out of Belgium, lock, stock, and barrel. That night the conference would confirm its decision and adjourn. Only a few hours to save ten million people in Belgium and northern France; only these two Americans to do it! They could not themselves address the conference; but they could at least lobby. Man after man they plucked off in the corridors; gave him a volley of Yankee conversation. They protested that it was unfair and unworthy of reasonable statesmen to condemn this enterprise because of a temporary irritation against the enemy. They appealed to the sense of justice and humanity. And again they drew their sharpest weapon —public opinion in the United States. Did the Germans realize how our countrymen felt about Belgium? Nothing would serve better to drive the United States into the arms of the Allies than the starvation of millions of children. The rabid members of the conference took second thought, cooled down. The officials of larger vision came again into the ascendancy. Not only did they let the commission remain, but they softened the German attitude toward the disposal of the crop in northern France; accepted Hoover's own estimate of a just division. Through more irritating negotiations, Hoover managed to effect another compromise—to see that none of his charges wanted for the bread of life.

Before I finish with the high spots of Hoover's diplomatic negotiations, let me record one more incident —not for its importance but for its picturesqueness. In the summer of 1916 the French newspapers burst out with a sensational story about the enemy doings at Lille. The Germans, it said, had rounded up all the young women, carried them away for most immoral purposes. Day after day the Parisian press rang all the changes on this theme. Then one morning I opened my newspapers to find that the furor had died suddenly and completely. Not another line about Lille or its women. . . . When I revisited the commission offices in London I learned what had happened.

The famous "industrial triangle" of Lille-Turcoing-Roubaix was crammed with workmen out of jobs. They had grown restless. The Germans, fearing riot and disturbance, decided to thin out the district, to put part of the people at agricultural labor. There was some sense in this; northern France had more land than workers on the land, and part of the crop would feed the civilians. Great Headquarters sent out a call for volunteers. None responded. Thereupon it ordered that twenty thousand persons capable of agricultural work should be transported on to the land. As often happens in armies, this order came for execution to an officer who misinterpreted its spirit. He surrounded a district of the triangle with troops; on half an hour's notice, and without much regard for natural qualifications, he gathered up twenty thousand inhabitants and arranged them in caravans or loaded them into box cars. He isolated the sexes. Husbands and wives were torn apart. Women who had never handled any implement heavier than a needle went forth to hard labor with a hoe or a pitchfork. Respectable wives and maidens found themselves packed among the feminine scourings of the slums.

Two of our young Americans, Wellington and Richardson, witnessed this episode. So did three of the German officer "nurses." The Americans telegraphed a description to W. B. Poland, then in general charge of the district. He made violent complaint to Great Headquarters. Came a prompt investigation. Wellington and Richardson told their story. Two of the "nurses," tongue-tied by awe of the great general staff, hesitated, stammered, compromised. Over-Lieutenant Fritz Neuerbourg, however, had more man in him. He declared boldly that he had witnessed the deportations. The Americans spoke the exact truth. He did not criticize the order, he said; but the manner of its execution was a disgrace to German arms. Headquarters acted promptly. It permitted the deportees of the triangle to return home. Some of them, now settled on the land, preferred to remain. But five thousand women went back at once. Then Great Headquarters presented not exactly a condition of settlement but at least an earnest request and recommendation. They had read the allied newspapers; the charge that they were deporting women from Lille for immoral purposes had "got under their skins." Would not the

Americans make the allied press shut its mouth? Here was a sore point. At any time it might engender irritations perilous to the relief work in northern France. Hoover saw the allied governments. They listened to him and exercised their war-time censorship. Hence that sudden silence about the women of Lille!

Then there was the problem of shipping. Next to the diplomacies which secured its mere existence and the colossal problem of finance, this caused the commission more trouble than any other department of its work.

As the war and the submarine campaign went on, ships came into unprecedented demand. Crazy vessels resurrected from the boneyard made fortunes for their owners. The demand rose until it was no longer a matter of money but of pull and diplomatic influence. And by now the commission needed a fleet of eighty average-sized ocean freighters. The British militarist faction, especially strong in the navy, hampered Hoover's men all they could. Even when the Government in general was friendly, minor officials would throw monkey-wrenches into the machinery. After the first cargoes departed for Belgium, some underling sent a circular to the war trade clubs, calling attention to the "dangerous accumulation" of foodstuffs in Holland, warning shippers to avoid that kind of business. Hoover must get from Walter Runciman, chairman of the Board of Trade, a renunciation of such tactics, a counter-order. Skippers and owners would not sail up the dangerous Channel without insurance. That was almost impossible to obtain from private companies.

Hoover set out to bring ships chartered by the commission under the general scheme of war risk insurance. He accomplished this; but it took long trying negotiation and debate.

Also, he must secure for his fleet immunity from submarine attack. The Germans accepted this principle and dictated a plan of flags and markings. A U-boat commander could now recognize a Belgian relief ship as soon as he trained his periscope on it. Then in February, 1915, Germany declared its submarine blockade of France and the British isles. The Imperial Government laid down new regulations. It would give immunity to no ship which touched at the British isles. The Commission for Relief in Belgium must send its cargoes round the North of Scotland. The British, on their part, declared that no vessel which had not touched at England for search might pass through their own blockade. . . . There you were again—Belgium between the jaws of the nutcracker. . . . Now it was the Germans who yielded. This danger was no sooner averted than the freighter *Harpalyce*, bearing all the commission's markings, was torpedoed by daylight in the English Channel. Pressure on Hoover to make this a diplomatic crisis, a step toward dragging the United States into the war. But he always keeps his balance. He believed that the German Government, when it promised not to torpedo Belgian relief ships, meant what it said; that the submarine commander was ill-instructed, ruthless, or ignorant. Fortunately, the episode cost no lives; and he did not intend to let personal irritation imperil his needy ten million. He must minimize the incident, smooth down official backs.

As the war rose toward its climax, as the German submarines piled up their devastation, the difficulty of getting tonnage increased. The commission took steps to find a fleet of its own. In American harbors lay interned scores of available German ships. Hoover conceived the idea of using them for his purely humanitarian enterprise; and he opened negotiations looking toward this end. The Germans at first made violent objection; every one of their own ships in service of the commission, they said, released just so much British or French or neutral tonnage for war-work. But the fine-visioned Herr Ballin of the Hamburg-American Line intervened. When Hoover got both the Germans and the British to sign an agreement releasing these ships to the commission, the thing seemed accomplished. But unexpectedly the French refused to sign; and other Allies raised legalistic objections. Hoover was still hammering away at these dissenters when the German declaration of unlimited submarine warfare changed every aspect of the situation. But somehow this group of super-efficient American engineers always found tonnage, and at prices rather below the current commercial rate. Not until the maritime confusion which followed February 1, 1917, was the flow of provisions into Belgium ever halted; and then but temporarily.

This is only a sketch; it omits a thousand petty, irritating, perplexing details. . . . One morning after the war my family caught me laughing immoderately over a newspaper editorial. It said of Hoover: "His great accomplishment was the Commission for Relief in Belgium. But there, he had behind him the good-will of all the world." . . . Laughter was the only appropriate reaction.

But let me take the commission as a whole, in mass. For four years it fed ten million people; brought them through without starvation or malnutrition. It maintained a stream of 350,000,000 pounds of foodstuffs a month. It gave its charges the cheapest food in Europe. It furnished them good bread, not husks or scrapings. Germany, and later France, lived toward the end on a mélange of miscellaneous cereals, husks, and potato flour. It supplied the children milk, fats, the special foods necessary to maintain their health and encourage their growth. It carried the destitute—eventually about 55 per cent. of the Belgians and northern French—largely on profits from the affluent.

At the request of the restored Belgian Government, the commission continued its work for six months after the armistice. During this period the price of all foodstuffs was so much lower in Belgium than in other allied countries that the authorities feared international jealousy. They asked Hoover, therefore, to raise his prices! Also, with resumption of industry the destitute found work; every one could go on the "pay basis." Profits mounted to the embarrassing figure of more than $30,000,000; and Hoover, at the moment engaged in feeding half of Europe, must try to unscramble these eggs. The Belgian Government, approached, suggested magnanimously and magnificently that he use the money to establish a memorial of the relief organization. So came into being the "C. R. B. Foundation" which has created the new University of Brussels, endowed institutes of scientific research, financed the exchange of professors and students between Belgium and America. Hoover still directs the foundation. In itself this would be accomplishment enough for one man. It measures the range of his accomplishment that I must dismiss it here in two or three brief sentences!

Up to that time, the world had never seen so great an operation in public relief. When they grew larger, Hoover led them. It was the first of those food administrations which, before the somewhat hazy sun of peace rose, enveloped civilization. And the Commission for Relief in Belgium wrought a revolution in the administration of public benevolence. Hitherto, such operations had been hurried, confused, wasteful —conceived and administered in the spirit of emergency charity. This, from its first day, was managed with the shrewdness, economy, foresight, and judgment which a well-organized corporation expects of its executives. One line in the final report of its auditors tells the story. Its "overhead" during four years was only three eighths of 1 per cent. of its total expenditures. Many a charity organization in our great cities pats itself on the back when it holds down its overhead to 20 per cent.!

Finally, it occupied a high and unique position in the diplomatic scheme of the war. At the London office they used to call it in joke "the new power in Europe."

However, I prefer myself to think of it as a kind of self-governing American colony. It issued its own passports, flew on its vessels its own flag, enjoyed its own diplomatic immunities. Joking again, the office termed the representatives at German headquarters "Our Ambassadors." . . . But there was truth in this also. . . . At the direction of our Government, which took the responsibility of the guarantees, our real ambassadors and ministers, sat as honorary vice-presidents on the board. They all, especially Page, Whitlock, Gerard and van Dyke, gave valuable service in negotiating with the Governments to which they were accredited. But as time went on, the commission—and with their approval—established more and more its own contacts with chancelleries, headquarters, and foreign ministers. When in August, 1916, Hoover and Kellogg fought at Berlin that vital battle for the life of the commission, Ambassador Gerard advised them to go it alone. He felt that the commission, with the moral power behind it, would fight better on its own feet than on his back. And Kellogg has recorded how into his own perplexity and apprehension came a dart of pride!

An accomplishment without stain, this enterprise in practical idealism; the bright motive in the first two gloomy acts of cosmic tragedy; the benevolent but practical American spirit at its highest manifestation.

CHAPTER XVI

WHAT of Hoover himself in these two incredible years?

Again, as during his roving thirties, he lived on the run; used train compartments and ships' cabins as his offices; at each stop gathered up a sheaf of despatches, dumped his answers on the wire. Home harbors figured in his itinerary; he must keep watch on the important purchasing and shipping business of the New York office, must oversee and stimulate the campaign for charity funds, must report to the Government at Washington. In 1915 he found that some one, inspired by jealousy or perverted by misunderstanding, had slandered the commission to the State Department. Franklin K. Lane, he of the great heart, got him a hearing at the White House. This was his first meeting with Woodrow Wilson. Hoover cleared away the garbage and left with a warm, unqualified statement, signed by the President himself, approving the commission, emphasizing the integral part of the American Government in its work.

In Europe he made his grand tour on an average of once every five weeks. The head overseas office was necessarily in London, the shipping and financial center of the allied powers. From London he would cross the Channel to Havre, where sat the refugee Belgian Government. Some of the more important officials, however, stayed with the king at La Panne, the headquarters town. Often Hoover must hurry up to that water-soaked, shell-dotted sliver of Belgium where the army was hanging on by its toe-nails. He first met King Albert in a house that was gradually crumbling under shell-fire; that night, visited the front trenches. Thence he passed to Paris, where he conferred with the minister of the invaded regions, with the Treasury, or with Louis Chevrillon, old associate of his engineering days and now his liaison with the French Government. Across the border into Switzerland; possibly a conference at Berne; an express train at Berlin. After that, usually, German headquarters at Charleville. . . . During one of his early visits, so they told me at the commission offices, the Germans in~ited him to make a tour of the front. He had been warning his young agents to keep away from the trenches. The less they knew, the less they could be accused of telling. But the invitation was so phrased that it seemed a challenge to his courage. He must not lose face with these soldiers. He accepted, and took in the German trenches another baptism of fire.

Next, Brussels; there, between his own organization, the national committee, and the German governor-general, he must linger. On to Rotterdam, and to the passage down the North Sea. This uncomfortable and ticklish crossing he made more than forty times during the war. Across the course lay mine-fields, set down by all the belligerent nations. Even when the planters of death declared them, they were dangerous enough; but each side accused the other of strewing loose, submerged mines. The passenger boats filled their holds with empty barrels in order to keep floating in case they touched off one of these giant explosives. They crept, feeling their way; the trip took forty-eight hours. Eventually, six vessels out of seven on this run either went down or were towed disabled into harbor. . . . Acquainted with the crews, Hoover used to sign checks for his meals and settle up when he reached port. However, on one of his last crossings the steward said, "Beg pardon, sir, but I must ask you to pay cash."

"Why?" inquired Hoover. "You've always trusted me before." "Yes, sir," replied the steward; "but you see, sir, when the *Queen Wilhelmina* went down last week, several gentlemen who hadn't paid me were drowned, and I feel I can take no more such risks." . . . Once, as they were passing Zeebrugge, on the Belgian coast, a squadron of German destroyers emerged, arrested the passenger boat, took it into the harbor for search and examination. This happened periodically; no harm done except an annoying delay. But just then an allied bombing-plane soared over Zeebrugge. That knot of German warcraft made a beautiful target. It turned, circled, opened an attack. Hoover was watching the show at the rail, when a bomb, exploding off-board, splintered the deck-house behind him and severely injured a Dutch passenger. Himself unharmed, Hoover picked up the wounded man and carried him to the bed of the ship's cabin. The aëroplane, having dropped its ten bombs within a few hundred yards of the Dutch boat, soared away trailed by shell-bursts. "I too was among the casualties," laughed Hoover as he told the story next day in the London office. "I have an abominably stiff neck caused by looking upward so long and so intently!"

In an unusually severe air raid over Boulogne a large bomb exploded just outside Hoover's hotel window. Hoover, bleeding from broken glass, picked himself up and remarked: "It's a pity I haven't a uniform—I might be entitled to a wound stripe!"

Nothing in his demeanor during these strange years became him like his silence. There he was, ricocheting from German front to Allied front, from German headquarters to Allied headquarters—the only man in the world so privileged. He was even immune from that personal search so rigorously imposed on travelers in general. He has eyes in his head, an engineer's trained perception for terrain and military works, a personality which draws confidence like a magnet. The things he could have spilled! An attaché of the British Foreign Office told me after the war that whenever Hoover came in fresh from the German lines they had to bite their tongues to hold back questions. "Of course, we didn't ask them," he said; "it wouldn't have been cricket, you know." Others on both sides of the line were less honorable. But they never got out of him a fragment of a fact. Even with his associates and friends he maintained the same silence on military essentials. He would talk freely about Belgium and its unhappy situation; with humor or with vigorous western indignation he would relate his negotiations and his diplomatic troubles. But as for vital information on affairs beyond scope of his job—the same inscrutable wall which he presented to the outside world. Never once did he slip even the name of Charleville, that town where Germany kept its Great Headquarters. His silence was the price of his mobility.

The commission had at its first session elected him chairman. Neither he nor the rest, however, intended that this should be a one-man show. Indeed, it never became that. The members debated their problems in informal sessions at the London, Brussels, New York, or Rotterdam offices. But stage by stage, all these other strong, positive, and able individuals voluntarily and gladly put the larger responsibilities and decisions into his hands. They were engineers, accustomed all their working lives to handling men in regiments and brigades, to the kind of life which is a constant fight; but they recognized supreme leadership when they saw it. "At our office," said one of them, "we'd meet to consider some crisis. The rest of us would agree on a course of action. Hoover would begin thinking. You know how he does—walks up and down or looks out of the window with that knot in his forehead. Then he'd turn and announce his opinion. Often it was just the reverse of ours. We'd debate it. He'd pull fact after fact, argument after argument, out of the pigeonholes in his head, until we hadn't a leg to stand on. Even then, as we left the office, we'd say to each other, 'I think the Chief's making a mistake.' Perhaps three months later, when the affair was finished, we'd realize that he was absolutely right. He'd thought one stage farther than the rest of us.

"After he began backing the statesmen of Europe into a corner, we heard a lot of talk about Hoover diplomacy. Shall I tell you a secret? He just used open-and-aboveboard American methods—as one does when he's trying to negotiate a contract by which both sides will profit. He'd say, 'What we propose is this; here's what will happen; this is how it will affect you and us.' Now those European diplomats weren't accustomed to such direct approach. They'd dealt all their lives with the oblique method. Instinctively, they thought that in opening a negotiation a man always asked for anything but what he wanted. And while they studied and puzzled to find what he was really after—he'd put his proposition over!"

None of the staff was jealous of him; rather, they all gloried in the triumphs of "the Chief"; granted him their affectionate admiration; took personal pride in his growing reputation. That last is in itself a singular story. He had tossed aside his business and business opportunities to relieve Belgium; he was serving without salary and paying his own traveling expenses; and he seemed bent on fighting even fame. At his request, the first appeal to American people for provisions and funds went out over the name of Millard Shaler. During the crisis with the British Government in January, 1915, he did issue a strong appeal to the American people. That was a club to swing in his negotiations; necessarily it must bear the signature of the responsible head. However, he signed it reluctantly, as all his office can testify. That winter I ran back to New York in order to help stimulate American giving. Of course, we were getting all the publicity we could. Newspapers and magazines, scenting a story, began appealing for "personality stuff" on Hoover. He would stand for nothing of the sort. "Play up the need in Belgium; keep me out of it," he cabled. But those roving American correspondents who during those blind early days braved military arrest in order to report the war, saw the importance of the job and the man. They could not be restrained. Hoover, we felt, took these first mentions as a kind of affront to his personal honor. It looked—so he appeared to feel—as though he were using the misery of ten millions to exploit himself.

Yet in spite of himself his fame grew. Our diplomats abroad wrote rhapsodies on him to the State Department. European Governments awoke to his quality. They tried to load him with decorations; these, in his firm, offhand manner, he waved aside. They tried to secure his extraordinary abilities for their war-work; offered him jobs which meant money, glory, honorary titles. These too he declined on the spot; and to his private friends expressed irritation. What did they take him for? He was an American; this wasn't our war! Besides, he didn't propose to abandon Belgium. However, his abrupt refusals of honors and advantages served only to increase the esteem of the Europeans. When during the winter of 1914-15 I asked some prominent American citizen to help out a Belgian relief committee, he was likely to say: "Yes, it's a good piece of work and I'm for it; but who the hell is Hoover?" Two winters later, Hoover stood to the world the embodiment of American ideals; so far, by many a foot the most eminent American who laid his hand to the great war. In 1915 I entered the office of the commission in London to find one of the directors laughing over a despatch. "Here you are!" he exclaimed. "A little town in the Meuse district has named its main street after the Chief. He can't beat it!"

He was working in bursts of breakneck speed—diplomatic, maritime, and financial crises, of which I have tried to write so systematically, came in bunches. Sometimes on the same day shipping tied itself into a knot, governments threatened to withdraw sanctions, funds ran short. His associates worried for fear he would break down. He showed, it is true, no signs of flagging energies; but it seemed impossible that any man could carry so much without a collapse. However, he used his own common sense; rested and diverted himself during the lulls.

In this matter, as in everything else, he is individual. After he dropped baseball at the age of eighteen, playing games never interested him very much; though as a spectator he is still devoted to baseball or football. He never took up golf. In normal periods, indeed, his recreations are mostly intellectual. But he likes to build things, to work with his hands. Once, during a war-time stay in London, I found him and Edgar Rickard amusing themselves in his garden by engineering back into place a great branch broken by a storm from an old oak tree. Three years later, calling with a party at his country bungalow near Washington, I was hailed from the tree-tops. It was Hoover; he and his two boys were building a tree-house. We all took off our coats, rolled up our sleeves, climbed the ladders, and put in a merry afternoon helping—or hindering.

However, his main strength is in the touch of the earth. Often during this period he would steal a day, put into his car skeleton cooking equipment, gather up his family and one or two old, restful friends, motor into the English or French country-side. Finding a spot which gave an imitation at least of rustic seclusion, he would unship the hampers, build one of his Indian fires, cook bacon and eggs for the whole party. The hampers repacked, he would settle his back against a tree, light his pipe, and fall into a pleasantly reminiscent mood. Conspiring with him, all the rest kept conversation away from the subject of Belgian relief. He talked of old college days, of adventures in China, of his engineering jobs; or swept the party into discussion of abstract politics and pure science. As for the war, we touched only on its humors. Then home through the long northern twilight; and again he must plunge into his welter of perplexities. On one of these excursions I noticed for the first time a fleck of white at his temples. Hitherto he had looked absurdly young, even for his years.

He is never too busy to think of Stanford University. When the first agents of the commission went into Belgium he asked them as a personal favor to collect any war documents that came their way—like proclamations, pamphlets, government orders, books, and periodicals. These he stored in Belgium and shipped to Stanford after the war. As time went on and his influence grew, friends of all nations added their mites. Most of the separate items were almost worthless at the moment; but time and aggregation have made them supremely valuable. Out of this grew the Hoover War Library, unique in the world—hundreds of thousands of original, irreplaceable documents. Even to-day students from a score of countries come to study there in California the history of their own countries; and whoever, fifty years from now, writes a complete and authentic history bearing on the crisis between 1914 and 1918 must journey to those red-and-buff arches at the western edge of our white man's civilization.

Toward the end of 1916, Hoover and his forces ran into a period of calm—almost of peace. The Commission for Relief in Belgium stood established in the war-habits of Europe. Hoover even talked of resigning. "It's going along all right at last," he said. "And I've been in so many rows that maybe I've worn out my welcome. Some new man without a background in this work might carry on better." At any rate, he could come home; make America, not Europe, his base of operations. In the last fortnight of 1916 he sailed again for New York—the second trip to the United States since the war began.

CHAPTER XVII

DURING January and February, 1917, Hoover directed Belgian relief from the New York office. For more than two years he had lived like a fireman. At any moment an alarm from Paris, Berlin, Brussels, or Charleville might send him traveling again. In the solacing home atmosphere he got a comparative rest. America was curious to see and eager to honor this citizen who stood symbol for the heart of the world. In the interest of Belgian relief he made a public appearance now and then. Otherwise, he refused to be lionized.

Meantime, a strong, hidden current was running. We were no longer drifting toward the vortex of Armageddon; we were being swept. President Wilson's offer of mediation—a last desperate attempt to keep us out of war—had failed. Our diplomats knew as an open secret that Germany was building greater submarines for commission in the spring. This forecast an intensive campaign against shipping, a tighter blockade. Doubtless the German Government would impose regulations on neutral shipping which we could not accept and keep our national self-respect. The blow fell on the first of February. Germany issued her long-expected declaration. Only one American ship each week would be "allowed" to sail for England. That must travel a fantastic zigzag course and wear the caparison of a circus clown. President Wilson handed the German Ambassador his passports.

This action knocked from under the Commission for Relief in Belgium its diplomatic base. To provide for such a contingency, Hoover had already arranged that other neutrals, notably Holland and Spain, should associate themselves with the work. Their ambassadors or ministers to the belligerents sat on the board of vice-presidents. Some of these men, notably the Marquis de Villalobar, Spanish minister at Brussels, had given the commission fine and able service. We had no longer any diplomatic standing with Germany. Unless the break in relations was but a temporary estrangement, Hoover must hand over the administration of the commission, at least inside of enemy lines, to the Spanish and Dutch. Through improvised channels he communicated with Belgium, learned that the Germans would for the present permit our men to remain and work. However, more and more as the anxious month of February dragged on he saw that this was not a flurry but the first gust of a great storm. He must hurry back to Europe and arrange the continuance of feeding for these 10,000,000 people.

All passenger ships had withdrawn from the Atlantic, waiting to see which way the cat was going to jump. Hoover chafed at his inability to get a sailing—when we learned of a Spanish ship going to Cadiz. Possibly, Spain also lay within the new submarine blockade; but at least the owners thought the danger so remote that they could afford to take a chance. I too was returning to the war zone. When the American commissioner suggested that I go with him instead of waiting for a liner to Liverpool or Bordeaux, I needed no persuasion—especially since I was taking with me a newly wed wife.

So early in March we packed ourselves aboard a crazy little Clyde-built liner, resurrected for war service from some far run, and sailed to Cadiz. On this voyage Hoover varied his custom of making his ship's cabin an office. As he said, it was positively no use to work; things were so absurdly uncertain that anything you did to-day might prove waste effort to-morrow. And for the first time in more than two years, he took a real rest. Edgar Rickard, suspicious of Spanish cooking, had put into his cabin an alcohol stove, a small cooking kit, American coffee, and fresh eggs. So we prepared our own breakfasts—or rather Hoover did. When there is cooking going on, he cannot keep out of it.

After we ran into the calmer southern seas he would loaf on the boat-deck all the afternoon, swapping yarns, gossip, humorous comment with the Americans of our cosmopolitan company. Of evenings he would take a hand at bridge in the cabin.

He even managed to put the war out of his mind—the rest of us conspired in this. Fortunately for his peace of mind, the ship carried but a feeble wireless equipment. We had at first virtually no news. But a week or ten days out we must have passed close to a "talking" liner. For in atrocious French there appeared two fragmentary bulletins, beginning and ending in the middle of sentences. One announced that French cavalry had pursued the Germans, now in full retreat, through Noyon; the other that revolutionary troops were in full possession of the palace at Petrograd, that the czar was a prisoner, that Grand Duke Nicholas would probably serve as provisional head of the new Government. The allied element among our passengers went wild. In the first despatch they read a great victory on the western front—perhaps the final, overwhelming victory. The second they interpreted as delivery from the German influence which had paralyzed the czar's armies. The Russian steam-roller would roll at last!

And here Hoover showed a flash of his mental realism, his power of analysis, his foresight. The episode in France? Probably a strategic retreat. The western line of the Germans bulged unnecessarily in the region of Noyon. By shortening it they would save men. Now in the early spring, when softer roads would hinder pursuit, was the time for such a maneuver.

"Have you a map of France?" he asked. I found one in my Baedeker. He studied it, drew a line through the northern French towns. "That's their second line of defense," he said. "Probably, there's where they'll be to-night." When a week later we got our first definite news, I found that it was a deliberate strategic retreat, just as he said; and the new line did not anywhere vary by five miles from the one he had drawn on my map. This acquaintance with the German secondary defense was one of the important secrets which, during these two years of silence, he had carried deep in his mind.

The fragmentary report from Russia interested him more profoundly. All that afternoon he walked the deck with one or another of us Americans, taking little quick steps as he does when agitated; breaking out into brief bursts of speech, diving back into his reservoirs of thought. He had worked as an engineer in Siberia, the Ural, the Altai; had bucked the czarist Government in Petrograd; knew the strengths and weaknesses of this baby giant. The revolution had come at last; that was apparent. If, as the report hinted, Grand Duke Nicholas was taking the throne, well and good. Nicholas held liberal opinions; he would make it a constitutional monarchy. The Russian people, basically able but illiterate and accustomed to the symbol of a monarch, could for the present go with safety no farther than that. The republic would come in another upheaval, after a generation of popular education and experience with parliamentary forms. "But revolutions so seldom stop with their objective!" he said. And this revolution had in its ranks an element of impractical theorists embittered to the point of fanaticism by exile and persecution. They might carry events on into chaos. "Perhaps," he ventured—hesitantly, as though himself dreading to face the truth—"Russia may drop out of the war. And if we enter—you can see what a job we have before us." At the time, I put this down to a characteristic habit of mind. As I have said before, in face of a difficulty he acts like an optimist while seeming to think like a pessimist. Fearing the deceptions of hope, he looks on the dark side first. So he keeps his sense of reality and has plans ready to meet the worst. In other words, he has supreme mental courage. Therefore I took this judgment lightly. Of course, I know now that he had welded into prophecy his keen practical observation, his detached judgment, and his instinct for human nature.

An official welcome at Cadiz; the freedom of the port; news that the king wanted to see him at Madrid. Somehow, Hoover dodged that invitation. As between the Spanish and the Dutch he must maintain an attitude of strict impartiality. At the embassy he found a bale of telegrams. They carried confidential information on the attitude of our Government. It was not yet absolutely certain that we were going to declare war. But, at least, we would not resume relations with Germany. He must close up all official American supervision over this work, get his Americans out of Belgium.

Deep within him, I think, he may have cherished a faint hope of holding them on. I was staying on in Madrid to finish a piece of journalistic business; he must hurry to Paris. And that night I realized what my imagination should have told me long before—how much the Commission for Relief in Belgium had meant to the heart of him. History had written *"finis"* to that chapter; he could no longer deal directly with the German Government. Not only was he experiencing the sorrow of doing anything for the last time, but he was giving into other hands the intimate care of ten million wards for whose sake he had fought ten million devils. ... Few, I think, have ever seen him in such a mood of black depression.

When we made our declaration of war he had already joined Chevrillon in the Paris office; had plunged into a whirl of work. At all costs the commission must go on! He sounded out both sides; established the principle that it might send a food-supply up to the doors of Belgium and there turn it over to the Spanish and Dutch, who would stand responsible for its distribution. If these newcomers gave efficient service, the feeding of Belgium would go on without a hitch. Now he must get his American agents safely out of Belgium. However, the job had grown so large and complex that the Dutch and Spanish could not in a day install an expert staff. The Germans, showing a reasonable attitude, let some of the Americans stay until the transfer of the business within Belgium was accomplished. Prentiss Gray, manager at Brussels, did not come out until June.

Also, in April and May, 1917, the submarine campaign arose to its flood-height. The Germans refused immunity to such commission ships as had touched at British ports. Now Hoover could not meet them and back them down as he had so often done before. Five vessels carrying the commission's flags and markings were torpedoed in the Channel. Thirteen more, lying in British ports, refused to take the risk and sold their perishable cargo. Hoover must find replacement of ships and food. He accomplished this; nevertheless, during a month of that summer the Belgians and northern French, for the first and only time in four and a half years, went on short rations.

Meantime, the focus of Hoover's destiny had shifted to Washington. That part of the story begins a few months back. Walter Page, ambassador to Great Britain, had in his attitude toward Hoover the pride of discovery. He had watched from an intimate viewpoint the miracle of the Commission for Relief in Belgium. He had seen Hoover establish relief and food administration not as charity but on an economic basis, weld imports and domestic production into an insoluble whole, control speculation, stimulate production. Every country in Europe had learned from him; was following his methods. Indeed, certain Governments among the belligerents had tried vainly to draw Hoover into the job of organizing their war-production.

When in December, 1916, Page learned of the new German submarines, he felt reasonably certain we must soon enter the war. Washington had seen Hoover only intermittently. Page feared that neither the President nor his advisers would understand what a trump card we had in this great engineer with his talent for handling men, his knack at large organization, his intimate experience with the war. "He's the one man to take hold of our munitions production in case we have to fight," said Page. But as his published letters show, Page was not at the moment on cordial terms with President Wilson. He feared that a direct recommendation from him might have a back-kick. It happened, however, that a certain American, a friend of Page and an admirer of Hoover, was at this moment sailing home. Page urged him to see Mr. Wilson, present Hoover's extraordinary qualities and qualifications for this or any other big war job.

President Wilson listened open-minded. "You need not dwell on Hoover's qualities," he said, "I have been watching him. I'm keeping him in mind in case the worst comes to the worst. However, I'm not sure that munitions is the place for him. Perhaps he could serve better in some other capacity." Whether he was thinking even then of the appropriate job of food administrator, no one alive knows. If so, the idea lay for some time fallow in his mind. Also Colonel House admired past expression Hoover's work in Belgium. When the crisis came he added his own warm recommendation.

In April, 1917, the President called together the Council of National Defense, designed to manage our extra-military war activities. Representatives of the Allies, hurriedly consulted, declared that the primary necessities were troops and food. The council cabled to Hoover, asking him to confer with the allied experts on provisionment as to wants and ways and means. And in May, 1917—again at request of the council—he sailed through the submarine zone, bound for Washington. For two and a half years the organization which he created and led had fed ten million people in Belgium and northern France. This was an enterprise for relief unprecedented in history. But within two more years "Hoover organizations," while still carrying on the Belgian work, would be feeding more than a third of the civilized world.

HERBERT HOOVER AND A GROUP OF HIS AMERICAN AND DUTCH ASSOCIATES, ROTTERDAM, 1915

CHAPTER XVIII

WASHINGTON, during the spring of 1917, lived in a state of orderly confusion. The news from Europe during the two years of our neutrality had taught us one useful lesson: that modern war is not all a matter of armies and navies, that it imposes great sacrifices and responsibilities upon the middle-aged stay-at-homes. Much of the brains and leadership of the country poured into the capital, eager to volunteer its services. Among these eminent individuals was Ray Lyman Wilbur, a chum of Hoover's at the university and now president of Stanford. He had followed with close interest the Belgian job. Working in food conservation, and with this old friend, appealed to him. He met Hoover at the boat, accompanied him to Washington; acted for a time as his volunteer secretary.

Hoover reported to the War Council the pressing shortage of food in the allied countries, outlined the fundamental measures necessary for securing a supply. The council, nevertheless, was not yet ready to create a separate department to handle this special emergency. Secretary of Agriculture Houston had, however, done some intelligent work in preparing the farmers for "food mobilization." In the meantime, others like Wilbur were streaming into Washington to offer service under this supreme authority on provisioning and relief. Ex-members of the Commission for Relief in Belgium, unfitted by age or other circumstance for the army, put themselves again under direction of "the Chief." They were at the moment the only American experts in a brand-new field of human endeavor. He found plow-work for them to do while he waited. Able women who had helped raise funds, food, and clothing for the Belgians drifted to him by instinct. Most important, eminent men whose business had to do with provisions and provisionment came and begged to help. Hoover began to devise with them ways and means of conserving supplies, stimulating production; even to build the skeleton of an organization. At first he and Wilbur worked in a hotel suite. Then their fellow-Californian Franklin W. Lane scratched out for them a few rooms in a corner of the Interior Department.

This unofficial effort under the Council of National Defense could not last. The President saw that food was becoming most important. He conceived the idea of a separate war-department to handle the whole problem. Of course he had Hoover in mind for this job; any other choice, in the circumstances, would have been absurd. Still, he had to foil some feeble political attempts on behalf of other men.

By July a Food Administration Bill, drawn after consultation with leaders in all branches of the business involved and with Hoover himself, passed the House without much discussion or amendment. It stuck in the Senate, however, through five weeks of furious debate, often on matters extraneous to the main purpose. . . . Here for the first time appeared the outlandish accusation that Hoover, because his business in spreading American methods had taken him so much abroad, wasn't a genuine American. . . . However, in August the bill came through to the President's signature; somewhat mutilated, but still workable. The department was to be supported by an appropriation of $150,000,000. At once, $50,000,000 of this sum went to finance its first and greatest subsidiary, the Grain Corporation.

The United States Food Administration was an enterprise so large that long volumes have been written on mere single aspects. I must confine myself to its aims, its final accomplishments, and those features which best illuminate the methods and character of its leader.

When he first realized the possibility that he might be called upon to mobilize and distribute our food resources, Hoover set his thinking machine to work. He had witnessed the troubles of the Europeans. They had established hard-and-fast systems. The "dictator" took charge of the crop, rationed the people, made prices by law. There were severe legal penalties for disobedience. Nevertheless, a good part of the population evaded the rules. The business of commandeering crops, distributing bread and meat cards, policing the consumers, fixing prices by law to prevent profiteering —all required a cumbersome, inflexible, and expensive machine. The food dictator was the yellow dog of European Governments; all his fellow-citizens took a kick at him. Men accepted the job in the spirit of one who makes to his country a supreme sacrifice of prestige and career. At that, they lasted on an average about six months. During the early stages of our war, Hoover must have felt at times that he himself was making the same sacrifice.

He believed that there was a better way—at least for Americans. With our national idealism and enthusiasm we could be depended upon to fight this phase of the war not as unwilling conscripts but as volunteers. At the very first, Hoover revealed his purpose by the stand he took on a name for the office and the department. The newspapers had been carrying stories about the European food "dictators." Carelessly, those who discussed the matter with him adopted that term— even, I have heard, the President. Hoover always corrected them. That misrepresenting word wouldn't do. It was his idea, he said, that the man or committee in charge of this department shouldn't dictate to any one. For the same reason he rejected the milder terms "controller" and "director." Before the bill was drawn he settled on "administrator" as the title which most accurately expressed his conception of the job. A little, unconsidered clause, introduced at his instance, expresses the same spirit. Men who volunteered in other of the government war-departments had to take a salary, however microscopically nominal it might be, in order to comply with the law. Hence the "dollar-a-year-man." But it was specially provided in the Food Administration Bill that the employees might work for nothing whatever. . . . At the head of the affair, as things worked out, sat a kind of cabinet which the office called in jest "our fifty-thousand-dollar-a-year men." Each of its members, in order to work without salary for the Food Administration, was giving up an income at least as great as that! Following the example set by Hoover, they were even paying their own traveling and incidental expenses.

So much for the spirit of the thing; now for its machinery. Hoover said to the Senate committee which considered the bill: "My idea is that we must centralize ideas but decentralize execution." That might stand as a motto for the Food Administration—indeed, for all Hoover organizations, whether in business, relief, or government. He did not send agents of the Washington office into the States, except by way of holding conference or giving advice. Each of our national units had its State Food Controller who held leadership in his own community, knew its resources and its local peculiarities. And when, in the administrative offices, Hoover "centralized ideas," he did not shut his subexecutives into compartments. . . . He believes that most able men are all-around men; given a chance, they will generate suggestions beyond the borders of their nominal jobs. Also, he knows how to delegate authority. On appointing a subordinate, Hoover gives him the general idea, makes him responsible for results, and, so far as possible, lets him alone. Otherwise, he could never have accomplished those superhuman tasks of creation and management which marked his career between 1914 and 1920. Falling in with this method, the "fifty-thousand-dollar-a-year men" about him threshed out policies and plans among themselves before presenting them in succinct form to their chief for approval—troubled him as little as they could with detail.

Finally, Hoover believes that government, even in the emergency of a war, should not tinker with the delicate, complicated machinery of private business. It should advise, adjust, harmonize; but only in the last emergency interfere. One shudders to contemplate what harm overofficiousness or a mania for power might have wrought with a machine so powerful and complex as the United States Food Administration. The Grain Corporation expressed this idea. We must furnish food of all kinds to the Allies; but most importantly the staff of life. Also, we must protect the American farmer by preventing foreign Governments, even if they were allies, from fixing the prices against him. To perform this function the Food Administration Bill set up a kind of public company on the pattern of a private corporation. It was authorized to buy our grain crops; to borrow money; to sell its purchases. If it made profits, they went back of course to the Government. The Food Administration, the President, and Congress merely supervised its actions in a general way. It started with $50,000,000 capital. That provided entirely inadequate finances; whereupon, like a private firm in similar quandary, it went to the banks, borrowed against its warehouse receipts. At one time in 1918 it owed in this manner more than $350,000,000! Sales and purchases mounted, before its dissolution, to nine billion dollars. When finally its affairs were rounded up, it returned to the Government all the capital advanced to it and a reasonable interest thereon. This might be compared with the Railroad Administration and the Shipping Board, which cost the Government literally millions in losses! Later came the Sugar Equalization Board, sprung from the necessity of stimulating beet-sugar production in the United States and of protecting our growers. Operating on the same plan as the Grain Corporation, it bought the Cuban crop at a reasonable profit to the island planters; sold at a profit, returned the balance to our Treasury. . . . I feel almost ridiculous when I dismiss these great operations in two or three paragraphs! Already their history and economics have stood as subject for a shelf of books.

However, mention of the Grain Corporation gives occasion to mention that neither Hoover nor the Food Administration had anything to do with fixing the price of wheat in the war. True, some one had to do something! In the spring of 1917 the allied Governments, bidding against each other for the last of the 1916 crop, had forced the price up to $3.25 a bushel. The farmers got none of these swollen profits; long ago they had sold their product at the farm on a normal scale. The Allies, to prevent recurrence of this situation, combined their purchasing agencies into one organization. Henceforth, they would not bid against each other.

In Europe the grain-buyers of the powers were paying their farmers $1.50 on the farm. In Australia and the Argentine they could buy even more cheaply. However, shipping to carry American troops and munitions was a vital, primary necessity. And a freighter could transport three cargoes of grain from our ports to Europe in the time it took to carry one cargo from Australia and the Argentine. In a letter to the President, Hoover reviewed this situation, stated his opinion that the prices which the allied buyers offered were unjust to the American producer, recommended appointment of a commission, with farmers in the majority, to determine a fair price.

Therefore, in August, the month when the Food Administration formally began its work, President Wilson called together eleven men eminently representing all the domestic interests affected by the price of wheat —two labor leaders, six executives of the farmers' associations, two economists, one business man. They spent a fortnight in close conference and hard debate, and settled on $2.20 a bushel for the basic grade. The labor leaders had stood out for a price far lower than that; the final compromise figure was a little higher than the estimate of the economists and not much below the average demand of the farmers' representatives. In order not to give speculators an opening, this commission held its sessions in deep secrecy. Dr. Harry A. Garfield, its chairman; Mr. Tabor, head of the National Grange; Mr. Barrett, head of the Farmers' Union; Mr. Shorthill, Secretary of the Farmers' Coöperative Elevators' Association, and Mr. Funk, President of the Corn Growers' Association, have recently made a public protest against the campaign lie that Hoover had anything to do with this decision.

President Wilson, announcing the price to the country, as by a stroke of prescience put into his statement this line: "Mr. Hoover, at his express wish, has taken no part in the deliberations of the committee on whose recommendation I determined the Government's fair price, nor has he in any way intimated an opinion regarding that price.". . . . But any stick will do to beat a dog, especially when he is a good dog.

Wheat, sugar, and fats were the prime necessities for maintaining the European armies and civilians. Fat plays a subtle part in the human ration. The lack of it, as much as anything else, broke Germany. An impossibly long haul made unavailable to Europe the Oriental supply of vegetable oils. The American hog must meet this situation. The demand of two unregulated war years had already reduced our stock of sows far below normal; and a combination of European government buyers had of late, while draining away fodder on one hand, greatly depressed the price of pork on the other. We must stimulate breeding. In this case the Food Administration, owing to various complex considerations, did not form a subsidiary corporation but handled matters through the good-will, patriotic feeling, and common sense of the interests involved. Hoover assembled an advisory board of farmers under ex-Governor Stuart of Virginia, with representatives from every hog and cattle State. He put the problem up to this body and followed their recommendations. By making agreements between the packers and the allied buyers, he secured the prices which the farmers' committee recommended; and he limited the profit of the packers to 9 per cent. on the capital employed. Our hog-growers never made such a profit as in this period.

Following its larger policy of leadership as opposed to coercion, of shifting the major burden from an overworked Government to volunteers, the Food Administration issued not regulations but requests and recommendations. It did not ration the people; it just asked their coöperation. Generally speaking—there were a few necessary exceptions—it did not ration even the dealers.

"Ninety-nine per cent. of American business," said Hoover afterward, in reporting to the President, "gave hearty coöperation." For the large offenders among the recreant 1 per cent. Hoover's department had a device better than criminal law. The bill provided that the Food Administration might license all dealers in provisions with a capital of more than $100,000. As a last resort, it could revoke licenses. It used this club occasionally; notably against certain manufacturers who were exceeding a fair profit, and a ring of dealers who were diluting their shipments with inferior grain. In the case of smaller offenders the distributers and consumers, now volunteered under Hoover by hundreds, performed a function which criminal law was undertaking in other lands. They disciplined their own sinners. Their standard penalty was a fine, the proceeds of which went to the Red Cross.

As though Fate had for the moment turned against our cause, the wheat crop of 1917 failed; and the following winter was the coldest in the memory of this generation. I have described the depleted condition of the pork industry. Hoover's measures to increase acreage in wheat, to stimulate profuse litters of pigs—these would not bear fruit until another harvest-time. We must for the present support our national charges—our own army in France, France itself, Great Britain, Belgium, Italy, and to a certain extent the European neutrals—on the saving of our larders.

And here Hoover appealed to the people. He opened that campaign for economy, for coördination, which most Americans who did not wear a uniform remember perhaps more vividly than anything else about the war. Through the volunteers who flocked to his standards, through mobilization of a willing press, he took the public into his confidence. He hammered into them the truth about our situation. The Allies needed wheat, that most concentrated, transportable, and universally liked of all breadstuffs. They needed fats; and to supply that, we could give them pork. The Government did not ask any one to starve himself or to stint his family. But we could eat other cereals in place of wheat, other fats in place of pork. We could eliminate much waste too; and we could deny ourselves unnecessary sugar. Here was a practical way for every one to serve his country and his cause.

He mobilized not only business but journalism; gathered into his department as volunteers eminent editors, advertising specialists, poster-artists, cartoonists. These he picked with that same instinct for capacity and devotion which he had shown in selecting his business staff. Between them, these experts on public opinion evolved that motto "Food will win the war!"

resolved seemingly insuperable difficulties with one stroke of ingenuity and insight. He was always willing to coöperate: "Here is the problem; we will solve it together," he would say. While much of Washington still felt its way, he knew exactly where he was going, had already surveyed his road. The Commission for Relief in Belgium, with its tender care of starving children, had made special appeal to the sex whose deepest instinct is for creation and preservation of life. The benevolent strength and common sense and modesty of him, now that our woman leaders saw him in the flesh, solidified this sentiment. Men and women alike returned from Washington in a state of quiet enthusiasm for their leader.

Just as when he took up the burden of Belgium, he foresaw political attack and criticism. This organization, too, must stand as far above suspicion as Cæsar's wife. He owed that not only to himself but to the other able, devoted men who had given up private business to work for the cause at nothing-a-year. . . . I mention here by way of example that Julius Barnes, when without salary he took leadership of the Grain Corporation, dissociated himself immediately from all his private interests in companies dealing with foodstuffs. . . . So, following his Belgian precedent, he put in charge of accounts a reputable firm of auditors, had them keep daily supervision of the books. When the war ended, no department of the Government had its records in such businesslike and inexpungeable shape. There was not a ten-cent loophole for criticism or suspicion; and yet the Grain Corporation alone did a busi-

ness equal in amount to half our present national debt!
Now as to results.

While the American wheat crop failed in 1917, Canada did very well. That was the one bright stroke of luck. In normal years their excess would have come across the border to replenish our deficit. As it was—roughly speaking—Hoover must keep Europe going, until early summer brought the first fruits of the earth, on our economies and replacements. Then followed that trying winter, with constant below-zero temperature and a succession of blizzards. Even under normal circumstances such weather would have played hob with our lines of commercial communication. But now we were preparing two million troops for shipment abroad, keeping two million more in training camps; railroad lines groaned with their munitions and equipment. Further, the Railroad Administration had not yet found itself; there was unnecessary confusion. In mid-winter the Food Administration must needs complain that pianos, phonographs, whisky, and beer were finding transportation, while train-loads of wheat destined for Europe stood snowed in on the sidings.

January brought the crisis; probably that month marked the lowest ebb of morale among the Allies. In November the Russian revolution had dissolved into bolshevism. No more hope from that quarter, either of military aid or of supplies! As clearly as though the Germans were publishing their general orders in the newspapers, even the blinded public saw that spring would break with a supreme make-or-break offensive on the western front. And allied Europe had fared worse than it expected in conserving and collecting foodstuffs. The submarine sinkings had helped the German cause in that. Sea-transport had so dwindled that it were madness to send ships on long Australian, Argentinian or Oriental voyages. England, which would be helpless in face of a complete blockade, tried always to keep a reserve against sudden naval disaster. Lord Rhondda, British food minister, read Hoover's confidential estimate of wheat exports from the United States and Canada and cabled his alarm: "Unless Allies can rely on North American exports considerably in excess of these figures . . . we shall be confronted with a situation of extreme gravity." Dr. Alonzo Taylor, Hoover's chief field expert, cabled: "Situation in Italy is bad . . . there are areas of food-vacuum." The allied experts united in a request—almost a demand—for 1,100,000 tons a month during January and February. Such a quantity was impossible; Hoover knew that. Doubtless also he knew by old experience the diplomatic habit of asking for more than you expect to get. They were playing for a margin of safety, a reserve against some unforeseen emergency. From the accurate scientific estimates of his own agents Hoover concluded that he could pull them through on between 700,000 and 800,000 tons a month; as for a reserve, the Food Administration was preparing to mount that up in America.

By superhuman hustling to secure continuous transportation, by inspiring our people to greater sacrifice of appetite, Hoover kept wheat and beans and bacon, rice and rye and sugar flowing into Europe at the rate of his estimate. Indeed, the Food Administration, with the people behind it, did better than it engaged to do. In January the Europeans asked for 750,000 tons of wheat during the winter months. Hoover sent them 850,000 tons. Out of that short crop—which would have afforded no surplus whatever had the United States consumed at its normal rate—Hoover shipped 150,000,000 bushels—the saving of American households. Allied Europe, civilian and military alike, never even for a day lived on short commons.

"Food will win the war!"—that is like saying, "America won the war." A main factor, indispensable to victory—put the case that way. Keeping track of allied morale was one of my own wartime jobs. And I register my opinion that the pinch and fear of hunger might have turned the delicate balance, in that critical spring of 1918, to a German triumph on the west and a lost or drawn war. Had the Food Administration fallen into hands less trained and competent, had it been boggled or muddled or delayed—then disaster, even before we drew our sword fully from its scabbard. When in May, 1917, Hoover began establishing a policy and building a machine in advance of official sanction, he was getting a start for a hard, close race with starvation and defeat.

Now the crop of 1918 and the end of hand-to-mouth methods. The measures of the Food Administration and the Department of Agriculture had increased our acreage of grain by five millions; the crop promised a fine average yield. Magnificently the American people were controlling appetite, eliminating domestic waste.

The Food Administration was inventing and enforcing larger economies. Experts on threshing, by installing improved methods, added 2 per cent. to the net crop. Experts on milling, by advice and precept, introduced their own great savings. There were other ingenious devices. Australia, as I have said, had surplus wheat; but the six weeks' voyage, in that state of nautical emergency, rendered it unavailable for Europe. The administration, however, found a number of sailing vessels useless for the dangerous Atlantic run but quite practical for the peaceful Pacific. These brought to our western ports Australian grain and released for Europe just so much of our own crop. The despised but necessary American sow gives life, on an average, to nine pigs a year. Saved from the slaughter-house, she was doing her part. By intelligent handling of the Cuban crop, the Equalization Board was getting enough sugar.

As we prepared for the harvest of 1918 the food-war seemed won; the "Hoover measures" had averted starvation. Now he could accumulate reserve in Europe against a sudden unfavorable turn of events, secure ample future supply. No letting down with this program so long as the guns roared on the western front! He must act, until the very last day, on the theory that this war was going on forever. The best military opinion held that while it was reasonable to expect victory in the summer or autumn of 1919, fighting might go on until the summer of 1920—with the fresh American army bearing most of the burden. But whenever it did end, Hoover foresaw the danger of a crisis. Measured by peace standards, we were overproducing. We would have at the armistice an enormous surplus stock of perishable goods. That might bring a great drop in prices and ruin to farmers, millers, packers, middlemen—possibly a financial collapse. On the other hand, the enemy countries and the invaded allied countries had eaten their last reserve, were living on short commons. When the war ended, they would be begging for food. Here was an outlet to save the American producer while serving humanity. But before he could accomplish this, he had strong gates to force.

Then victory dawned. When in July the Americans and French broke into the flank of a German thrust at Soissons, when in August the British made a hole at Folembray, Hoover began thinking not on present perplexities and difficulties but most anxiously on the future.

With the Food Administration, he was carrying all this time the Commission for Relief in Belgium—and other burdens besides. The Council for National Defense had practically dissolved. What we called the "War Council"—the chairmen of the new departments created to meet the national emergency—replaced it. This met regularly to discuss and coördinate measures of large importance; and of course Hoover was a member. Up to April 6, 1917, he had seen the war in all its phases—diplomatic, social, financial, even military—more intimately than any other American. He had even played a leading part in the drama. In matters outside of his official province the council needed and used his experience, his calm detached judgment. In

October arrived the famous German note proposing an armistice on the basis of Wilson's fourteen points. The President asked the council for an advisory opinion on the American terms. Hoover stood out for one vital point—a clause in the agreement committing the victors to the principle of supplying the vanquished with food. For the Orient and South America had vast supplies in storage; and unless he could establish a market in Central Europe, the price of all farm products would drop with a crash. The American farmer must not suffer by reason of his great service in the war! This clause, with full acquiescence of President Wilson, went into the final terms; and from it, during the next six months, grew much history.

When the firing ceased, Hoover was already closing up his immediate affairs, packing. A fortnight afterward he arrived in Paris, authorized by the President to deal with questions of food and provisionment arising under the armistice. Four years since, with some misgivings as to the extent and difficulty of the job, he had accepted the relief of ten million war-penned souls; fifteen months since, with misgivings even more complex, he assumed the task of finding, administering, and regulating the food-supply for more than two hundred millions. As I have said, every European who attempted to control food had sailed to shipwreck on the reefs of human selfishness. . . . I lived in Paris while M. Violette played his brief part as food dictator. How the satirists played with that easily lampoonable name! . . . But in the same measure as they failed, Hoover had succeeded. His basic sanity and soundness, his faculty for inspiring confidence, his energy, his courage in daring an appeal to the volunteer spirit—these qualities and methods had made him a towering figure of the World War.

CHAPTER XIX

IN all his active, building years, Hoover had endured the hardships incidental to engineering in savage lands. "I've eaten some of the worst meals ever cooked as well as some of the best," he said once. By way of compensation he made himself as comfortable as possible between flights. He prefers a house to a hotel. Whenever he found himself settled for two or three months —whether in Europe, Asia, or America—he leased or rented an impermanently permanent habitation. This, with the help of a few portable lares and penates, Mrs. Hoover transformed at once into a home. . . . On the wall of his Washington study hangs a painting of *Mowgli* dancing with the wolves. In my mental picture of Hoover it always colors the background. . . . However, when he jumped to Europe just before the armistice, the army rule against wives in the war zone stood still in force. Mrs. Hoover, therefore, did not accompany him but returned to California.

When Hoover saw that this European trip was going to mean a stay, he rented a frivolous white-and-gold mansion at 19 rue de Lubeck in the Trocadero district of Paris, made it a coöperative boarding-house for himself and his heads of staff. From the day he entered Belgium he had been creating a body of experts at the new, peculiar, and important trade of provisioning whole populations. When after April, 1917, his men had to leave the interior of Belgium, the older among them generally took service with the Food Administration and the younger hurried into uniform. Many, indeed, pending the arrival of our expeditionary force, enlisted with the French or the Belgians. Hoover had these soldiers detached to his working force, and borrowed from the army certain higher officers of the engineering and ordnance departments who understood provisionment and transport.

As these old comrades of a perilous and benevolent adventure came together again, the house in the rue de Lubeck took on the atmosphere of a college reunion. . . . Though merely a correspondent and with no official part in the job of feeding Europe, I boarded with them between journeys to what had been the front. . . . All young, in spirit if not in years, they lived in a state of rebound from the glooms of the war. Every day some old friend of that ground stamped in, grimy with travel, slapped down his military kit, burst into vivid Americanese concerning his adventures in reëstablishing railway movement through the Italian guard on Dalmatia, wrangling a permit out of a French official, fighting to open canals across disorganized Germany, or stringing telegraph lines through Bohemia. Our dinners were symposia on the picturesque and humorous episodes in that amazing confusion which was contemporary Europe. The "Chief" sat at the head of the table, chuckling behind his pipe; when the mood was

on him, came in with a reminiscence of his own. . . .
He has, when he cares to use it, a trick of telling a story without adornment and yet with all its picturesque and dramatic values, which reminds me of Stewart Edward White's literary method.

He needed those little moments of relaxation. I have always maintained that the Commission for Relief in Belgium was his greatest miracle of achievement. For in that he worked without prestige—an unknown American citizen pitting his naked talent against kings, principalities, and powers. But in the months following the armistice he assailed the most complex and perilous job of his career. He fought now with his back against the wall. When I recall to memory my glimpses of Hoover at work in this period, I think of him as a chess master, playing twenty games at once and most of them blindfolded.

There you were: Germany starved out and still starving; what had been Austria-Hungary generally in even worse plight; Poland and those other provinces of old Russia which Germany had overrun, worse off than the Germans themselves; all southeastern Europe hungry and disorganized. The dead of winter, too; no help from native planting until summer. Even then no great relief, for seed was lacking and transportation disorganized. Also, though Hoover had demanded the withdrawal of the blockade on the central empires, the Allies insisted that it must be maintained in order to force peace.

Yet on our side of the water was food enough to supply them all, keep them going until they restored a semblance of natural conditions. And our great surplus, prepared for continued war, must find a market or our whole agricultural industry would collapse. Only the normal channels between producer and consumer were clogged and dammed by selfish blockades, unnatural finance, all manner of international rubbage and wreckage.

First, and most obviously, most of these 200,000,000 consumers east of the old Western Front had nothing which producers and middlemen could recognize as money. Gold supplies were gone or mortgaged to the victor. Austria-Hungary, for example, was managing before the downfall with flimsy paper currency, backed only by the hopes and authority of a Government now passed into history. The Succession States stamped this paper with their own markings. Thenceforth it had some slight value within the new nation but none whatever outside. The promise-to-pay of a Government without funds—pending the peace, indeed, without any official existence—amounted to less than nothing in world markets. No way, either, of exchanging products of these countries, by some uninvented device, for food-supplies from without; for they were not producing. Then again, the armistice had unloosed hate, private and national greed, all manner of uncharitableness. The Allies, hitherto bound together so solidly and nobly—at least in appearance—by the common cause, jumped back with a bound to that old international attitude which knew no common morality. Each was beginning to scramble for itself, preparing to claw from the Peace Conference every possible advantage. And they feared to make any move that was not to their immediate and obvious interest.

On our part, Hoover had the grave responsibility of averting economic catastrophe. As a measure necessary to insure us all against losing the war, the Food Administration had increased our exportable surplus of provisions from 5,000,000 tons to 15,000,000 tons. There it was—dammed. If the current stagnated too long the bottom would drop out of prices, and the distress of the farming interests would react suddenly and fatally upon our whole economic system. Abundant food supplies were now available from the Southern Hemisphere. While battering a hole through the dam of the blockade, still kept tight about Germany, he must find temporary outlets.

With breadstuffs this was relatively easy. Wheat is not immediately perishable. The sound but flexible structure of the Grain Corporation enabled it to buy on what amounted to credit, keep wheat moving toward Europe in anticipation of a brisk demand whenever Hoover's charges found means to pay. He knew that means would be found; it was only a matter of time. Sooner or later the world must hear the cry of these hungry mouths and permit him to exchange promises or mortgages on the future for food. Meantime, he did not propose to be caught with an open door and nothing to send through it; with a permission to give relief, and the relief itself three or four thousand miles overseas. As he did in the beginning of the Belgian job, he started the food moving before he knew in more than a general way how he was going to pay for it. . . . Had he lost his nerve in these crises, thousands would have died in Belgium, but millions in post-war Europe.

Meat, however, is a perishable product. We had been specializing on pork, envelope of that fat element so necessary to life and health. While we had an enormous surplus, measured by the present need it was not enough. Germany, for example, had seen her ration of this essential drop from the necessary seventy-five grams a day to twenty grams. Given a free chance, Europe would sop up this surplus like a blotter, cry for more. But there stood the dam. . . .

Yet before the Christmas of the armistice all seemed to be going reasonably well. Until then he had been fighting mainly to make a hole in the continued war blockade round Germany, and to find for her means of paying. In the middle of December, Hoover proposed an ingenious compromise for solving this difficulty. Let the Allies relax the blockade as regarded the northern neutrals—Sweden, Denmark, Norway, and Holland. They could buy food and, their trade channels being open, exchange it for German products. This would not only feed the recent enemy but help to reëstablish her industrial life. On December 24 the allied Blockade Council handed Hoover, for a Christmas present, permission to put this plan on foot. Then those military parties which caused him so much trouble in the next three months put in their oar. On the last day of the year the council reversed itself. They would permit the neutrals to import goods only on pledge against reëxport.

The Allies followed this punch in the eye with a swing to the jaw. They had signified their intention of maintaining their purchases. This would keep up the stream of buying from the American farmer. In December they had in fact ordered tentatively 360,000,000 pounds of pork products for January delivery. But on the same December 31 they canceled the order. Probably the British were back of this, as the French were back of the refusal to open the blockade. Previously they had cut their own order from 160,000,000 pounds to 40,000,000; but Hoover never felt until the blow fell that they meant this as finality. . . . Well, the weary French, having lived through four years of invasion, were a little mad on the subject of security; and the British were fighting to start up an immense, delicate commercial machine which to many seemed broken beyond repair. Repudiation, in this case, helped British business, since it revived their commerce with the Southern Hemisphere.

Unless Hoover could manage to sell American pork up to the scale of the repudiated orders, unless beyond that he could open the German and other blockaded markets, the American packers, with their unprecedented present stocks, would be unable to buy current hogs; and the farmers would fail in droves. Ruin would go on along the line—first the farmers, then the country banks, then perhaps business in general.

That January seems in retrospect such a nightmare that I wonder how Hoover can to this day look at his breakfast-bacon without a shudder. He worked us without collapse through that month by no one dramatic action but by a series of able, shrewd maneuvers. Finding little response from the British, he saw the French and Italians; persuaded or forced them to take their expected quota of 200,000,000 pounds for January—a triumph, this, of sheer power in diplomatic argument. That left the British quota of 160,000,000 pounds on his hands. Still playing on a hope, which his reason made a certainty, that the world in general or America in particular must soon arrange some way to open the blockade and rescue the starving of Europe, he had the Grain Corporation buy 100,000,000 pounds. The Commission for Relief in Belgium took 40,000,000 more—all it could carry with justice. He had restrictions removed from the sale of pork to several neutral countries. At his request our War Trade Board abated some of its regulations, and the packers, moved by both self-interest and patriotism, installed a hurried campaign to stimulate orders in countries not covered by Hoover.

These are the measures that succeeded. Others, pressed just as hard and desperately, failed—notably an attempt to get drastic and instant action on provisionment of the liberated countries by removing the blockade on them. Toward the end of that critical January he assaulted the British frontally, horse, foot, and dragoons. He proposed that they order 200,000,000 pounds of pork products for February. It would mean a surplus, true. But before long he expected to open a way into enemy and liberated territory, where they could resell. And he promised, if they did this, to expect nothing more of them after March 1.

To back his position, he had one specially sharp complaint. The "cut" of pork demanded by the British is peculiar; it will sell readily in almost no other market. And our packers, taking in good faith the tentative orders in December, had dressed 150,000,000 pounds in such form. Reminded of this, reproached with the fact that America, at their frantic request, had piled up enough food to carry the allied cause through a long war, the British retorted with complaints of American failure to finance the purchase of other materials; and they stood as firm as the Guards at Waterloo. So Hoover had to place more pork with the Grain Corporation and the Belgian relief. He urged our army to buy pork and still more pork. Many an American doughboy guarding the Rhine or waiting for the transport complained that he was "getting a lot of hog" at mess. He did not understand that he was eating to save his family in some small town or farm in Kansas or Ohio or Iowa from the consequences of financial panic. For until after the peace, none but Hoover and his closest advisers knew the full story of this crisis.

February came to its end. The eastward flow of our surplus products had gone on almost without visible hitch. The price of pork remained stable. Then in March, and after other irritating, desperate negotiations, Hoover achieved his greatest triumph of the armistice period. He broke into Germany. This—most importantly—put an end to the starving of women and children in the German cities; but as a corollary, it gave us a full and regular outlet for our surplus.

CHAPTER XX

ALL through those trying months of January and February, Hoover had been pounding away at that main point—permission to relieve Germany. In his struggle to find immediate markets for our surplus pork Great Britain was the adversary. In this other major engagement he faced France.

The world was living in an armistice, not a state of peace. Until the Allies agreed on their own final terms, until Germany signed, the blockade must remain in force. Hoover's own particular clause in the terms to Germany read: "The Allies and the United States contemplate the provisioning of Germany during the Armistice as shall be found necessary." That looked definite enough when he left Washington. And the events of the first month were such as to promise early success. While Hoover's experts, such as Taylor and Kellogg, hurried across the gloom of Germany to survey the situation, the allied Blockade Council permitted the entry of a little food—enough to relieve the situation for a few days. The new, fumbling republican government, although fighting for its life against both reaction and bolshevism, had in it enough of the old German love for meticulous method to make its own survey. That arrived about Christmas at the house in the rue de Lubeck. The Germans had for our convenience printed it in English. Having neither Englishmen nor Americans at hand to edit it or to read proof, they produced a document whose weird improvements on our language and comic typographical errors set the assembled company, on first reading, into convulsions of laughter. On second scrutiny they whistled and sobered down.

The health statistics were appalling. Already, eight hundred people a day were dying of diseases of malnutrition. Such a phenomenon, those experts knew, foreran actual, stark starvation. For months Germany had been worrying along on the shortest of short commons —for example, one sixth the amount of fats necessary to keep a people in average health. . . . Were the Germans bluffing? "A little perhaps; but not much," said Hoover. Already a direct wire connected him with Berlin; over it his experts had made a preliminary report. Further, before he left Washington he had calculated the affair mathematically. Taylor's report, fortified by independent investigations of the British and the Swedes, came to hand. It described a rise in the death-rate like that of a major epidemic; a people pale, dull-eyed, thin, under-energized, anemic, driven by sheer desperation to the verge of bolshevism.

In 1914 Hoover had the dual problem of opening the blockade for Belgian relief and finding funds. The same problem again in 1919; but with the shoe on the other foot. And this time the barrier seemed almost insuperable. Though minor bureaucrats obstructed him here and there, the major British authorities came over without much argument to his way of thinking. However, they long supported him only mildly. But Clemenceau ruled the French as premier, and Marshal Foch, with the prestige of great military achievement behind him, led the military party. These two strong, uncompromising characters, indispensable to the victory, showed smaller wisdom in peace. Clemenceau never saw the war except as a phase of a historic struggle between France and Germany, eternal unless one side exterminated the other. The extreme military element, as represented by Foch, looked only toward security—which meant, in their language, an overwhelming advantage for the next war. Notoriously, they hoped that the "peace" would give France in fee simple the left bank of the Rhine. Stephen Pichon, at the moment minister of foreign affairs, held parallel views. Neither these men nor their followers had the first, glimmering idea of economics. They believed that somehow you could starve your cow and milk her too. And so they opposed the transfer from Germany of a single mark to pay for food. The Allies would want all German resources for reparations. The military party regarded the blockade as a means of keeping Germany meek during the period of the Peace Conference; so that no matter how harsh the terms, her starving representatives would sign on the dotted line.

For two early years of the war Hoover had kept the route to Belgium open, in face of opposition from German and British militarists, by threatening them with public opinion in the United States. That weapon was now dulled; and his French opponents knew it.

During the past two years our wrath against Germany had risen to white heat; and we were still in no gentle mood. For the moment, Hoover could not expect any strong backing from home. He had for resource only pure reason and pure humanity.

With these he hammered now this point in the iron ring, now that. Did the French, he asked, wish to accomplish their ends by starving women and children even after the armistice? Would they leave that blot, for all future eyes to see, on the pages of their history? Would they perpetuate in the structure of Europe this occasion for another war? They hoped to get from Germany reparations for the hideous devastation wrought in their own northern provinces. Well and good. But how could a people work when they did not eat? Leave the situation as it was, and Germany must go to pieces. There must follow years of expensive work at restoring the industrial structure before the Allies could count on any reparation payment. Finally, communism of the Russian type was making headway in Germany. Hunger and despair were its best allies. With Russia and Germany gone bolshevik, could the French and British resist the infection? All these arguments stood on a sound basis of sincerity; the last no less than the others. Hoover believes that hunger and industrial disorganization propagate the culture in which the germs of bolshevism grow to epidemic proportions; that if the Allies in the crucial days of the Russian revolution had kept her people fed, her industries going, her lines of transportation running, they would have saved her to liberal democracy.

He won the British to his active support and then the Italians; but not the French. And the Germans themselves were sometimes an embarrassment rather than a help. The new republic was only partially seated in control of Germany. The general staff was still engaged in demobilizing the army and in negotiating with the Allies over military questions arising from the armistice. And they arrogated to themselves the right to speak for Germany in other matters.

Presently, Hoover received notice that two officers of the general staff who had served in the administration of civilian affairs in occupied Belgium were en route to negotiate with him over questions of food-supply. Now Hoover believed that the only sound policy was to support the new republic; and that it should have the prestige of conducting such business. Further, these two representatives of the general staff were peculiarly obnoxious to him personally. They had belonged to the "party of repression"; they had caused the Commission for Relief in Belgium infinite anxiety and trouble. Like all men of energy, Hoover has a temper—which he usually keeps pent up behind a steel barrier of control. When he read those names, it exploded. "Go to the devil," he said, plainly and simply; adding that he would treat with the representatives of decent Germany, but not with such as these. Even the delegates finally chosen bungled their end of the negotiations. Constantly they represented to the Allies the danger of political collapse if Germany continued to starve. This was no bogy; but they made it seem so— gave the French ground for an accusation that they were drawing bolshevism in and out like an accordion.

Hoover, however, had mustered the major forces on his side. But now the French, out-argued and out-maneuvered, fell back on the tactics of obstruction, seeking to delay action until after the peace. When on January 17 the Allies and Americans met with the Germans at Trèves and extended the armistice for another month, he had a practical proposal of advantage to both sides. The revival of free traffic on the high seas had effected an unexpected shortage of ships. The Allies in restoring their own economic life needed more tonnage. Germany had many idle vessels, blockade-bound in her docks and in neutral harbors. Let the Germans release these to the Allies, on condition of receiving relief. He suggested as a start 200,000 tons of breadstuffs and 70,000 tons of pork. One third of the tonnage was to be used for carrying this food to Germany; the rent from the rest would help to pay for it. Also, he proposed relaxing the blockade rules against exportation of certain German products.

The French virtually accepted the principle as regarded ships. But they would allow no exports except on impossible terms; and they resisted every suggestion for "taking money out of Germany." They proposed instead "a loan by the Allied and Associated Governments." This was merely a device to block the wheels. Only the United States had money to lend. And in face of our enormous foreign commitments, Congress would not authorize another cent—the French well knew that. The American, British, and Italian economic experts at this conference added to their report a strong recommendation that the blockade, which now amounted to a disease in the economic structure, be relaxed for the neutrals and in great measure for Germany. This the French refused to sign.

Total failure so far; or at best a moral victory. And meantime, Germany was wasting away toward disintegration. Hoover continued his hammering. "Up to date not a single pound of food has been delivered to Germany," he informed the American delegation in a confidential memorandum. ". . . The uses to which the blockade on foodstuffs is being put are absolutely immoral. . . . I do not feel that we can with any sense of national honor or dignity longer continue to endure this situation. . . . I wish to solemnly warn the Conference as to impending results in the total collapse of the social system in Europe." This was on February 19, and already he had seen another conference talk itself into a vaporous nothing. That time the Germans had asked for 670,000 tons of foodstuffs to complete the harvest year. It was little enough.

The French made a counter-proposal which looked like a concession. They would permit entry of 370,000 tons to cover six months, in exchange for release of the German ships. However, they would guarantee this arrangement only for a month at a time. Hoover would have been contented with that; he believed that at each expiration he could renew the agreement and so worry on until the peace. But the German delegates balked. It appealed to them only as a trick to get their ships cheaply. And they would not have dared, after such a transaction, to face their own people. Fenced off from the world for five years, educated on propaganda, Germans did not know that Germany was now in the council of nations a mere cipher. Another adjournment; and nothing accomplished.

Now Hoover changed his tactics. The affair had been kept, probably with purpose, in subcommittees like the Blockade Committee and the Allied Food Council. All through the Peace Conference the French underlings worked under strict discipline. Whereas the American experts would dispute policies with their superiors, whereas certain British delegates rebelled at times, the French, whatever their private opinions, took program. He must join battle with his main adversaries—Foch and Clemenceau. That seems easy. As a matter of fact, the leading Europeans of the conference had intrenched themselves behind such an entanglement of red tape that he found it supremely difficult. There were more negotiations, seemingly fruitless, more strong notes and expressions on the part of Hoover, before on March 4, 1919, the Supreme Economic Council managed to pass the buck squarely to the Supreme War Council; which included not only the "Big Three" but the experts of all the delegations.

That meeting of the Supreme War Council in the Quai d'Orsay was long a diplomatic secret. Hoover had behind him a majority of the delegates. But a majority was no good; only a unanimous decision meant anything at all. And Foch, Clemenceau, and Pichon sat like rocks. In a formal report, Lord Robert Cecil virtually laid down the object of the meeting. Should the victors relax the blockade to let food into Germany?

Foch opened debate. Such a measure, he said, amounted to "disarming the allies." Hoover rose and replied with one of his reasonable, convincing utterances; plain speech, the emotion behind it only dimly perceptible. Then, as he sat down, Lloyd George swept in like a charge of cavalry against a wavering line. Four years before, as I have told already, Hoover had fought against him for existence of the Commission for Relief in Belgium. On that historic occasion Lloyd George had taken much the same attitude as Clemenceau was taking now. And Hoover had persuaded him, wrought in him a sudden conversion like that of a revival. Henceforth the Welsh preacher-statesman, to whom moral emotions make appeal, alined himself as an admirer and partizan of Hoover and his work. Now he stood beside his old adversary and burst into eloquence. Only a curt synopsis in the official record of the conference preserves it to history; but Britons who heard it call this closet-effort one of his greatest speeches. A technician of oratory even at this moment, he pinned the thing down with concrete instances—told what the British army on the Rhine was witnessing daily of starvation and distress; prophesied a mutiny of sentiment and perhaps of action if such oppression continued. Tottering army morale—that Clemenceau could understand. He, not Foch, had decision of this affair; he was supreme representative of France at the Peace Conference. For once the Tiger knew when he was beaten. He gave grudging ground.

Five days later Hoover was sitting at Brussels with the German delegates, signing an agreement to deliver food in return for the use of German ships. That open meeting had a dramatic quality—the Germans in their threadbare clothes answering with monosyllables and keeping their eyes on the table; Emil Franqui of the Belgian National Committee, who had for four years taken orders from the conqueror, sitting now a victor at Hoover's right hand. The press of the world gave it eloquent description. But the real climax of the battle to feed Germany came in the earlier meeting at the Quai d'Orsay.

The affair was not wholly settled. None had yet arranged a means of financing the operation. Finally, the Germans were permitted to pledge their gold reserve against future payment. But Hoover did not wait for that. The moment Clemenceau yielded, he was diverting food-ships from other nations to Germany, unloosing the reservoirs at Rotterdam. He accomplished delivery of hundreds of thousands of tons a month— in the first thirty days, all the huge accumulated stocks of pork products. It checked at once the rising deathrate; it began the restoration of stability. Five months more until her own inadequate harvest—had Germany gone on for this period unsuccored, men, women, and children would have died by millions not only of malnutrition but of unmitigated starvation. Before that, however—hunger, bolshevism, the dismantlement of Europe's workshop, an allied invasion of desperation, economic ruin for a whole continent, chaos! In this supreme battle, Hoover fought not only to forfend an economic crisis at home and to succor a beaten enemy but to save civilization.

In the midst of all this came criticism and recrimination from America. He must almost apologize to his own people, so ardently burned the war-hate still. In March he issued one of his most vigorous documents to explain why we were feeding Germany. "From the point of view of my western upbringing, . . ." he wrote; "because we do not kick a man in the stomach after we have licked him. From the point of view of an economist, . . . unless the German people can have food, can maintain order and stable government, there is no hope of their paying the damages they owe the world. . . . We have not been fighting women and children and we are not beginning now; . . . no matter how deeply we may feel at the present moment, our vision must stretch over the next hundred years and we must write now into history such acts as will stand creditably in the minds of our grandchildren."

Let me finish here with the German affair. When the great food crisis in Europe was passed, there remained the universal problem of the undervitalized European children who, unless we wished to see the strength of a continent sapped, must have special nourishment until happier times. America acted generally in the spirit of large charity. Congress gave to this work hundreds of millions. But as the bill passed the Senate, an amendment provided that none of these funds should go to countries which were our enemies during the war. . . . I know not what Hoover thinks of this; but myself, when I remember it, I have no heart to criticize Clemenceau. . . .

Hoover must find other means; and again he went

to the people. All through the war the American Quakers had been working in their own way to succor the unfortunate, to rebuild devastated towns and districts, to preserve normal life. They had now both experience and organization. Hoover sent for these people of his own faith, asked them to take up the task of feeding the German children. With his advice and backing, with the prestige of his name, they opened an appeal to charity in the United States. Later, he organized his own campaign to raise money for their use. Before the work ended he had poured $8,000,000 into their treasury. And until 1922, when even this emergency was over, they gave virtually all the children and nursing mothers of Germany those special foods which averted the danger of a stunted, undervitalized new generation.

CHAPTER XXI

As though in a spirit of irony the Peace Conference, even while the British were repudiating pork orders and the French blocking his efforts to succor the old enemy, had made Hoover administrator of the economic restoration of Europe. At his suggestion the conference created the Supreme Economic Council. In this body, all the powers were represented. Sitting as American member, Hoover at first took his turn as chairman, and became eventually its executive head. Even his individual job involved problems beyond that of the immediate food-supply. For example, his work in eastern and southern Europe, hereafter to be described, broadened out to include starting up trade, commerce, industry, national economic life.

John Maynard Keynes, the British dissenter of the Peace Conference, has described him as sitting "with the air of a weary Titan" as he watched short-sighted self-interest boggle the peace. Titan he is, but not usually weary; perhaps he looked so because the proceedings made him tired. As more and more the decisions of the negotiators seeped out of conference rooms, as it became apparent that this peace was to be made on political terms and without any sound regard for economics, Keynes himself resigned in protest. When the raw, unrevised terms of the proposed Versailles treaty were laid before this body, most of the experts—even those who had supported the attitude of their supreme representatives—stood appalled. It was unsound, unworkable. But Hoover believed that the Allies and Americans should sign. The social and economic structure of Europe was tottering. Another six months of discouraging delay and it might fall. The important thing was to let the people go to work. Time and future trouble would smelt the fallacies out of this document. However, on the eve of Versailles, Hoover and other American experts—notably Norman Davis—did succeed in trimming away a few of the more uneconomic terms. He supported the League of Nations—with the Senate reservations. As regards this issue, he rowed in the same boat with Republican Presidents Taft, Harding, and Coolidge, and with most of the current Republican candidates.

And all through that exacting, irritating, important half year he was keeping relief running to the eastern and southeastern fringes of Europe. The struggles to avert disaster from the American farmer and to break through the blockade into Germany furnished the heavy dramatics of his work during this period; the southern and eastern jobs, for all their tragic importance, have here and there a lighter and more amusing touch. Virtually all the Balkans needed food immediately and vitally; all the new Baltic states of Poland, Estonia, Lithuania, and Latvia; all the empire that had been Austria-Hungary. To meet this emergency he had been buying provisions through the Grain Corporation and starting them, in advance of financial arrangements, for northern and southern ports. The means to pay were found with reasonable promptness. In February, 1919, our Congress appropriated $100,000,000 for general European provisionment and opened negotiations for loans with such new nations as we could recognize diplomatically. For ten nations and nearly a hundred million people this solved the financial problem. But it did nothing for riven Austria—starving, as she does everything else, gracefully—nor for Hungary. Congress had stipulated that no part of our appropriations or loans should go to help the nations on which we had made war. Hoover's struggle to succor these remnants of an empire was only a little less trying than his battle to reach Germany. But this also he accomplished.

And, as I have said, the European Food Administration was no sooner settled down to its work than it found both powers and necessities expanding. Even to get their imported provisions through, Hoover's men must open traffic on the railroads and canals. Presently the job involved starting up production. Coal was heart of this problem; and our European Food Administration became also a fuel administration. The private hostilities of new nations clawing impotently at each other with feeble imitations of war, ran barriers across great rivers like the Danube. By arranging tentative treaties between states not on speaking terms, or by hammering at the main conference, Hoover and his subsidiary diplomats like Kellogg, Taylor, George Barr Baker, Colonel Logan, Colonel Goodyear, Colonel Grove, Colonel Haskell, and Captain Gregory, opened a way for their own goods and then for general trade. In the same way they arranged for the exchange, across closed borders, of surplus foodstuffs for coal, raw materials, even manufactured goods and railway rolling-stock. Eventually Hoover drew more than 1500 skilled American business men and engineers from the reserve element in our army. Presently, they became virtually the economic directors of Europe. . . . During the dreary, disorganized period of the armistice these were the only positive official measures toward restoring normal production and commerce.

Forth from the house in the rue de Lubeck went the messengers of practical benevolence to big jobs of hard, close, perilous work varied now by amusing adventure. First, they must open telegraphic communication between the principal European cities. In a month they had a complete system working between Helsingfors and Constantinople, with main stations at Berlin, Prague, Vienna, Warsaw, and Paris, and way stations everywhere. There followed miracles of efficiency in restoring rusted, unrepaired railroads to life and movement, and linking up traffic across borders which had been closed for four years.

In the remnants of Austria-Hungary they fought their hardest battle, achieved their greatest triumph. The old efficient imperial railway system of 12,000 miles, a unit before the war, was split among five nations. Each was scrambling for the battered, worn-out rolling-stock; each at first refused to let a train from any other Succession State pass its frontier. It amounted to paralysis. No food supplies could move; in the dead of a very cold winter, municipalities were freezing. Hoover was appointed to resolve this tangle. Colonel Causey took hold. By guaranteeing the return of all rolling-stock, and further by a combination of diplomacy, energy, and sheer Yankee bluff, he relinked the old system, restored schedules.

But without fuel, railroads cannot run nor municipalities keep warm. The main source of coal for this corner of Europe—at the moment the only source—is Silesia. Production there had virtually stopped with the armistice, and stocks were near their end. With a sigh of resignation, Hoover got himself appointed to take on this new burden. Here Colonel Goodyear, as aide in the field, executed his policies. Through difficult negotiations with four nations or embryos of nations, with owners, with trade-unions, he restored production—and in time.

Next, a medical job. Typhus, which thrives on hunger, destitution, and disorder, broke out all along the Russian frontier and spread like wildfire westward. At height of the epidemic, there were 600,000 cases. Send for Hoover again! He took the job of organizing war on the lice which carry this disease. He raided our Army Medical Corps and Red Cross for experts; he mobilized the endangered peoples themselves; he borrowed delousing equipment to the value of $10,-000,000 from all the armies—including the German. And in three months typhus was almost extinguished.

As soon as they had finished their survey of Germany, Taylor and Kellogg passed on to Warsaw, made a rapid estimate of the urgent need in Poland, Estonia, Lithuania, and Latvia. That most distressful corner of Europe deserves a separate paragraph or two. Invaded, held tight by the conqueror, it was during the war only a larger Belgium. While it produced a greater proportion of its own foodstuffs, the German armies were helping to till the fields and taking of course their part from the crop. Even before we entered the war, Hoover was struggling for a chance to relieve those captured Russian provinces. But he encountered special diplomatic and geographical difficulties. Among the nations of the world, Poland was neither fish, flesh, nor good red herring. Nominally, Russia owned it, while Germany held it in pawn. Actually, it loved the nation of which it was a geographical division as little as it did the conquerors. It had, to express its collective will, no government of its own, no diplomatic corps. Also, it stood far from the center of events. Belgium, though separated from the allies by a wall of steel, was nevertheless closely adjacent to Great Britain, France, and the seaboard. Allied spies could keep watch on food-distribution, ascertain if the Germans were dipping into it. But supplies for Poland must pass over German land or through that end of the Baltic where Germany maintained her own blockade. The Allies would not take risks with an accumulation in German territory. Hoover was still at work on this problem when our declaration of war made American relief impossible.

Meantime, Poland and the other old border provinces of Russia had lived as by scraps from the scant table of a poverty-stricken master. Temporary disorganization followed the armistice. Not only were the stable elements busy in resisting bolshevism, but a half dozen little "settling" wars had arisen. While Germany and Austria were fading away through malnutrition, that corner of Europe was starving outright. Even before he saw his way to finance the operation, Hoover jammed cargoes of wheat and pork through the Baltic. When the first of the ships unloaded, women and children scooped up dirty leavings of flour from the docks, boiled it dirt and all into porridge, ate it ravenously. To the end of the armistice period, Poland, Lithuania, Estonia, and Latvia, owing to their distance, to the little wars, to the Russian menace on their eastern border, caused the European Food Administration constant perplexity. . . . Hoover's workers and agents went forth with their passports of course, but also with a special pass which requested all and sundry to grant them movement and facilities. This, in order to impress sentries, bore a gold seal and the signature of Herbert Hoover. Often when an American presented his passport at a border or a line, the soldiery merely waved its bayonets; but when the officer in charge deciphered Hoover's signature on the special pass, he came to salute. Even in those far regions that name meant the bread of life. More than once our boys ran a supply-train through two hostile lines which lay intrenched sniping at each other!

The background of the work in the tangled Balkans was almost as tragic. Also, hazy borders, conflicting claims to territory, the birth-struggles of nations, the

"All right; you can surrender to the United States, can't you?" inquired the captain pertinently. "And if you do, I'll give you all a good paying job." After further conference, they decided that they could. The company clerk had a trick of fancy penmanship. At the captain's orders, he created from the red ink and colored wafers in his field-desk a gaudy and imposing document by which the parties of the first part gave themselves as prisoners to the party of the second part —viz.: the United States of America. But suddenly an afterthought struck the captain. This proceeding might get our Government into some unimagined diplomatic trouble.

"Strike out 'United States of America' and substitute 'United States Food Administration,'" he ordered, suddenly. "It will look all the same to them."

It did. The belligerents signed, stacked their arms. One faction commanded by the company clerk, the other by the chauffeur, they marched down to the port and went to work. But trouble broke out at once; epithets flew, hidden knives came out of inside pockets.

"They're squabbling again over the point of honor," reported the interpreter.

"All right—split 'em up," ruled the captain. "Put one faction on day shift, the other on night shift!"

Then there was the serio-comic episode of Béla Kun and the Archduke Joseph in Hungary. Austria and Czechoslovakia, when the Habsburgs fell, immediately set up republics. But Hungary, monarchist by habit and belief, sat paralyzed. For the moment she had no government whatever. Béla Kun, a communist adventurer, thereupon declared the soviet republic. Through a combination of circumstances too complex for description, the union-labor and moderate Socialist elements at first granted him lukewarm backing. In a few days they grew heartily sick of him. A mere hint of aggressive support from outside would give this element a lever to overturn him. Meantime, the impression that Hungary had gone bolshevik might in that critical period work much mischief. Hoover, after conferring with the leading spirits of the conference at Paris, wired an ultimatum to the effect that Hungary would get no food shipments so long as Béla Kun held power. This was not so drastic as it seems. The granary of the old empire, Hungary had for the moment enough provisions; the immediate difficulty was getting transportation between farms and towns. This measure sufficed; Budapest bounced Béla Kun. That left Hungary again without government. "You could have taken the throne with a pop-gun." Archduke Joseph, a minor Habsburg, did just about that. Again a dangerous situation: a Habsburg on a Balkan throne was but prelude to a new, confused, devastating war. Again Hoover saw the temporary masters of Europe; got permission to act. Then he wired to Captain Tom Gregory, Stanford '99, his agent in Hungary, another stiff ultimatum —no more food and no more railway communications until Joseph got out. He ordered Gregory to deliver this at the palace, and at once to report the answer.

Now the European Food Administration had started off with a telegraph code of its own. To this the suspicious allied powers objected. All messages, they said, must be in plain language. Hoover yielded the point. But the boys in the field beat the game by using American slang for important communications. . . . One eminent European statesman figured in their code as "Mutt." . . . So to Hoover, waiting anxiously at Paris wire-head, came this message:

Archie on the carpet three p m stop through the hoop three five
GREGORY

Now the peace; transportation and industry coming slowly back to life. But the economic organization, though on a somewhat different diplomatic basis, kept up its work until the harvest in August. From Latvia on the north to Albania on the south, from Poland on the east to Belgium on the west, it chased away the specters of starvation. "How many lives have these Hoover organizations saved since the armistice?" I asked a European who knows. "Ten million at a minimum," he replied. "But if you said twenty million, you'd probably stand within the truth."

He would have taken, had he been allowed, a responsibility still larger. Believing firmly that hunger is the growing-ground of bolshevism, he considered the case of Russia. In 1919 the national life was at lowest ebb, distress at its maximum. Not only were the innocent starving there, but it seemed possible and probable that provisionment, even yet, might restore Russia to sanity and representative democracy. That job, even in its first diplomatic approaches, required handling by the neutrals. At Hoover's suggestion, Nansen the great Norse explorer and philanthropist got sanction from the Peace Commission to make a preliminary survey of Russian conditions. Then, authorized by Hoover, Nansen sent a parallel request to Lenin, dictator of Russia. After some delay, Lenin's answer came back. It began with a diatribe against the capitalist system and capitalist governments. Of course, Lenin had to put that in to keep his face with the boys! But mixed with these fireworks were expressions which left the door open to further negotiations; a kind of half consent. However, neither Hoover nor Nansen knew this until long afterward. For the despatch had passed through the Foreign Office of a certain allied power. Just then Admiral Kolchak, leading the Russian czarist forces, took Tomsk in Siberia. That was only a temporary success; but to many it looked like the end of the soviet republic. And some one in the aforementioned Foreign Office, making his own interpretation of the situation and of Lenin's purport, gave it out as a flat, offensive, unqualified refusal. And that was that!

At last the strain relaxed. Europe was coming back toward normality. But there still remained one pathetic, grievous burden on the kindness of the world. Over most of Europe the children were in much the same condition as in Germany. Undernourished through four years of war, they got no real relief from the peace. Europe supped with poverty. Owing to the depletion of herds, special foods such as milk and fats were scarce, as was also the surplus necessary to sturdy growth. Whole nations such as Poland stood in danger of a rickety, tuberculous new generation.

Now before we finished, 15,000,000 tons of American food came across the Atlantic for the salvation and stabilizing of Europe. We had given magnificently—in charity, in government contributions, in loans. That fount was running dry. Hoover, however, had foreseen from the first this special need. And after the gifts and loans stopped, he managed to stretch the congressional appropriation to finance the relief of European children.

His experience in Belgium had taught him that work of this sort must proceed under supervision. You cannot get results by dumping the supplies into the towns and distributing it among the families. A certain proportion will administer it unscientifically. Selfish adults will eat it themselves. In Belgium he had set up the institution of a full, extra public meal for children. He spread his tables in school-houses and town halls; and the best women of the community served them. On the same plan he fed and restored eight million undernourished children in Poland, Lithuania, Latvia, Rumania, Germany, Serbia, and the knot of new nations which had been Austria-Hungary. This work went on from the winter of the armistice to that of the peace—indeed, far into the period of reviving production and commerce.

CHAPTER XXII

INTERLUDE now: by September, 1919, the work of organization was done. Though Europeans in tens of millions still lived by virtue of his work, the masterhand could give over the helm. "Hoover organizations" more resemble a living thing than a machine. He lays them on sound principles which always take into account the human factor, staffs them with able men who will work on self-initiative; the time comes when the creator can rest and let his creation simply function and grow.

To the people of Europe he had become as a superstition. In a dozen different lands, waiters and peasants and small shop-keepers, pouring out to me their heterodox opinions on their own Governments, would pause and add: "Ah, if we only had your Mr. Hoover!" And Europe, had he permitted it, would have turned his life during that summer of the peace into one long ovation. He dislikes to have any one make a fuss over him. This proceeds, as does all his shyness, from an intense inner sensitiveness. Besides, he was brutally busy. Standing on platforms, receiving plaudits and oratory, takes time.

He had declined from the first all official decorations. But appreciative Europe found other ways.

The Belgians, even while under heel of the conqueror, had fashioned in his honor a whole collection of those medals at which their artists are so adept. Other nations imitated this device of gratitude. Somewhere in the midst of his relief work the King of the Belgians invited him to headquarters—for a business conference, Hoover thought. The American found the king surrounded by his cabinet and counselors; and one rose and bestowed on him the title "Citizen and friend of Belgium." Lille and Warsaw struck municipal medals in his honor; Warsaw immortalized him in a public monument. From Estonia to Belgium, streets dropped their old names to become "Hooverstrasse," "Via Hoover" or "Rue Hoover." More appealingly still, letters of appreciation and thanks, signed by the citizenry of whole municipalities, poured into his houses and offices even for years after the peace. I have heard that the signatures on these touching documents add up to four million.

And the high as well as the lowly paid him unqualified, generous tribute. Not one figure of the conference but many called him the single statesman of the war period who came out of the struggle with untarnished credit. Some of these men had fought him blind in the interest of their own Governments or factions; but they admired nevertheless his powers and his intentions. With Latin grace, Attolico, Italian food director, symbolized and summed up their corporate opinion. As Hoover prepared to depart from Europe, Attolico sent him for a farewell present a reproduction of an old Greco-Italian coin. Around its obverse ran a wreath of ripe wheat. And with it came this message:

". . . I salute your departure with very great emotion. It is of the greatest concern to me that Europe should lose a man of such driving power as you. You are a man of *bonæ voluntatis* in the biblical sense, and nobody has more deeply than myself appreciated the fundamental honesty of intention and the love of humanity which have been the basis of your unfailable success. I regret your departure all the more because I feel that my country and myself lose a very dear friend. My only wish is that on the other side also you may find your way to devoting yourself to the reconstruction of the world. . . . I take the liberty of sending you a small memento of your work and our connection. It is of no intrinsic value. The original of the Pæstum coin of which I am sending you a reproduction is in the National Museum of Naples and recalls an era when wheat was plentiful in Italy! And it has been due to you that Italy has not lacked wheat, which is the basis of our life, during the war."

Poland, however, trapped this shy bird. Circumstances and difficulties in that far corner of his invisible, benevolent republic demanded one last visit of inspection before he sailed for home. And he found himself at Warsaw guest of honor to a touching demonstration. The Government, with poetic appropriateness, turned out not its armies but a hundred thousand children of the capital and its suburbs—they whom the "Hoover luncheons" were building back to strength and normal vitality. The poor little eyases were very ragged. But the Poles, like the Belgians, put a brave face on poverty; they had covered their patches and tatters with gay ornament of colored paper. Carrying Polish and American flags or banners inscribed in his honor, their ranks filed past for a whole afternoon. A confused wild rabbit coursed into the field. Boys will be boys; these little Poles broke ranks, ran after it, by some miracle cornered it, fell on it in a struggling scrimmage. Then, the proud captor holding his captive by the ears, they marched across the field, presented it to Hoover. . . . His heart was very full that afternoon, I suppose. And the hunting of a wild rabbit must have evoked his own childhood among the Iowa hills. His eyes filled. . . . Then suddenly he turned to the Polish dignitary at his side.

"It is only an hour until dark," he said. "From how far have these children come?"

"From as far away as twenty miles," was the answer.

Without a word, Hoover left the official party and hurried for a half mile along the line opposite to its direction, shaking hands as he went. Even the Americans in the party did not at first perceive his object. He was speeding up the ceremony—seeing, so far as he could, that none of his little charges should go home in the dark!

That was his last official act in Europe, his farewell; three days later he boarded the *Aquitania*, homeward bound. And the incident seems to me dramatically apropos. It revealed the man. Knowledge of suffering and wrong strikes at once the very tender core of his heart. Especially if the tale somewhere involves moral heroism, it brings, more often than the world knows, that initial reaction of moist eyes. But the emotion stops there; translates itself not into tears but into action. "What can I do?" he asks himself; and the mind once more takes control. Henceforth while others weep, he works!

Home now. In September, 1914, he had bought passage by steamer and rail to California. He was five years in arriving—five years as strange as any man ever lived on this planet. I have neglected in this chronicle to dwell on the brutal strain and effort of it all. Probably no other leader of the great war worked and thought so hard and so continuously. During the period of the Food Administration in Washington, sometimes he sat down to his desk by half-past seven in the morning; and often at midnight his light still burned. Assistants ten or fifteen years younger found that they could not follow his pace. "Where he gets that inner strength," they said, "the Lord knows!"

Lewis Strauss, his secretary during this period, tells about one of these long days a story which illustrates Hoover's vitality. Having begun work at half-past seven in the morning, they left the office at half-past seven in the evening. Strauss, worn out, got a quick dinner, tumbled into bed. Arriving at the office next day, he found that his desk had been unlocked and rifled of certain important and confidential papers. "Enemy spies!" he thought; and was about to telephone to the Secret Service, when Hoover entered.

"I picked the lock of your desk after dinner last night," he remarked; "needed some of those papers."

"How late did you work, Chief?"

"Oh, about one o'clock I suppose," replied Hoover casually. And fresh and bright-eyed, he plunged again into the job.

He had lived, too, under constant emotional strain. True, every one who worked long on intimate terms with the war experienced that drain on his inner forces. But the human background to Hoover's work was all so gloomy! No relief of heroics or parade or deeds which stir the blood; just visions of emaciated hands stretched out to beg the bread of life—tales of quiet misery. Now that it was all over, a cloud settled on his spirits.

However, he was back with the family again. Since the Germans crossed the Belgian border, he had seen them about as seldom as a soldier on active duty. The boys were all this time in school at Stanford; Mrs. Hoover had seen her husband only in brief visits, which for three years involved running the submarine zone. Also, they were preparing at last to settle down. Eight years before, they had approved the plans for a new house. Now, on the golden hills above the red tiles of Stanford, they fulfilled that old dream in the first of their many habitations which—because they had built it—they could call their own.

There were old friends, too; and amusing domestic episodes. For example, the Hoover boys grew interested in the lively and noisy frogs which inhabit the marshlands about Palo Alto; trapped a menagerie of them. These they installed in their "frog hollow," a kind of sunken bowl bottomed with an artificial pond of their own construction. For each inhabitant there was in the bank a separate and individual hole. At feeding-time the boys gave a peculiar whistle. The frogs came to associate this noise with dinner. Utter it, and comical heads suddenly blossomed all over the bank. Hoover himself used to show off this box of tricks to visitors. . . . There came, too, the pleasant duty of escorting the King and Queen of the Belgians, his old friends of wartime, over the Far West. The cloud lifted.

But his countrymen showed no more disposition than Europe to let him alone. Into the new home at Stanford poured enough invitations to make the next winter a continuous ovation. Finally, Hoover acknowledged and declined them all in a document whose humor proceeded from its mild burlesque of an engineering report or a college syllabus:

> I plan to adhere to the following rules for one month:
> *First*—
> (a) That I will reply to no telephone calls, and my secretary has directions to explain in the most amiable manner that I am spending a month with two vigorous small boys. . . .
> (b) That I do not myself read any communication that exceeds one page. . . . These rules are solely for my own good.
> (c) That I must decline the honor of speaking at . . . public meetings to which I have received invitations. . . . I am not a spellbinder and I am satisfied that the American people will be gratified to find a citizen who has retired from public office who wants to keep still . . . this rule is for the public good. . . . My family is building a "palace" containing seven rooms and a basement, a kitchen, and a garage, all on the university campus. The old cottage is good enough, but we all

think we can build a better house than anybody ever built before, and every American family is entitled to this experience once in a lifetime. . . .

Briefly, then, he reviews the jobs before him. First, rendition of a two-billion-dollar account for his operations in the Supreme Economic Council—"We are not afraid of this settlement; no one can collect these sums from us. If there were six fewer ciphers on these figures, I might be worried." Then a report to Congress on the exact details of expenditure of the one hundred millions appropriated for relief in Europe; and the routine of handing back eighty-five or ninety millions of this sum in obligations of foreign Governments— "I hope this will be an agreeable surprise. Most of Congress thought the money was gone forever, but voted for it anyway." Next, a report on the economic measures taken under his direction since the armistice; then arranging the endowments made possible by the surplus left from the Belgian relief work; finally, directing from this side the continuous feeding of four million children in eastern Europe. And he concludes:

Fifth—
I plan to return to California a month or two later if I can advance the above matters satisfactorily. I shall then continue to attend to my duties:
    (a)   Head of a family;
    (b)   Trustee of Stanford University;
    (c)   A member of the committee of the European Children's Fund;
    (d)   The head of the Belgian Foundation above;
    (e)   The completion of the "palace" above referred to; and

A REMINISCENT BIOGRAPHY 253

(f) To support activities under (a) and (e) from my occupation as a consulting engineer and my income from pre-war savings.

All subject to the reservation that nothing more turns up to irritate my conscience or peace of mind.

I offer this intimate disclosure of private affairs in order that no further inquiry on this subject will be needed, and so that it may be seen that I contemplate no mischief against this commonwealth. . . .

Statement *Fifth* (f) of this lightly humorous and profoundly serious document needs expanding. I have described that dramatic moment in early October, 1914, when Hoover, impelled by sense of duty to accept the job of Belgian relief, threw to the winds his prospects of a very great fortune indeed. He resigned that day as administrator of twenty or thirty industrial concerns; dissociated himself from business. However, in some of the mines for which he served as directing engineer he had invested his savings of twenty years. Under other management one or two of them did reasonably well in the war. For five years he drew no salary or fees from his public work or from any other source whatsoever. He paid his personal and traveling expenses to the last red cent; and as he rose to the rank of a world-figure these necessarily increased. He had to break into his capital. He could cast up accounts now; and he found that he had just a competence. When we talked on his future back in 1912 he set his aim, so far as money went, at enough to keep him and his family in reasonable comfort for the rest of their lives and to provide a margin "for safety." The remnant of his fortune did not meet those terms; never again was he so rich a man as on that day of renunciation in 1914. His not excessive salary as secretary of commerce has made a welcome and necessary addition to his private means.

Now, however, avenues to fortune opened in every direction. With his prestige, his world-wide fame, his reputation for getting results, the mere name at the head of a big company would have yielded him hundreds of thousands of dollars a year. Already American capital was flowing abroad; on almost any wave of that tide he could have ridden to millions. Some of the offers were almost fantastic. But until he accounted for every dollar of the public funds which he had handled, until the last European orphan departed from his communal tables, he stood as a public servant; he could not cast over this work a shadow of a suspicion that he was using his position to make money. For once he drifted along on the surface of things, resting.

But his friends did not rest. Where originated the first Hoover-for-President boom no one exactly knows. It burst spontaneously and naturally. Here he was, the one statesman of the war who had emerged with full credit; the idol of the subordinates who had fought with him for the relief of Belgium, for conservation of our food supply, for relief of a hungry two hundred million in Europe; the war-leader of our women. The Democrats, very hard up for a candidate, took the first positive action. Frank Cobb, editor-in-chief of "The New York World," fired the signal-gun; came out squarely for him as President. Now

Hoover, as all his old and intimate friends knew, was always a Republican. It was born and bred in him. West Branch, where he lived as a boy, had only one Democrat.

In our dormitory debates at Encina Hall during his student and early-graduate days he had argued furiously for the gold standard as opposed to the Democratic measure of free silver. We knew, further, that he had remained a Republican. In 1909, for example, he joined the National Republican Club; which membership implies adherence, both practical and theoretical, to the party. He found himself serving in the war under a Democratic President. Well, so did many another eminent Republican—and for that matter, millions of Republican doughboys. The Democratic party and President represented us before our associates and our enemies in Europe; the volunteer official of a country engaged in making war and peace must in honor give the commander-in-chief loyal adherence—or resign.

At the moment, Hoover was conducting a drive for the destitute children of Europe. He had no political ambitions; partizanship, with the prejudices which it engenders, might injure this vital enterprise. And, as I happen to know, he had no political ambition. His friends heard of Frank Cobb's intentions. At Hoover's direction and as a matter of fairness, they carried to Cobb the word that Hoover was a Republican, intended to remain a Republican. "Well," said Cobb, "that's a blow. But we're independent on this sheet!" And he announced at the head of his editorial page that the "World" wanted Hoover for President, be his party Democratic, Republican, or Independent.

When he could honorably resign his war job, Hoover issued a brief statement. He was a Republican; always had been. This did not stop his fanatical friends, even the Democrats among them. Hoover smiled, tried to check them, reluctantly abandoned the attempt. He never took the campaign seriously, and was much relieved when it was over; but, after all, to pour cold water on such generous enthusiasm was like exploding the baby's toy balloon! There is very little doubt that the country as a whole saw with the instinct of democracy that he was the great figure of the moment. But when Wilson lost his hold on the country and the Republicans began to scent a sure victory, others began building up formidable organizations. The little band of enthusiasts entered at last a convention where an unpacked gallery rose with such fervor to Hoover's name that Hugh Brown of Nevada (Stanford '96), who seconded him, never made his speech heard. "It was like talking against a boiler factory," said Brown. But clamor of the galleries did not affect that particular convention. Hoover's high tide was thirteen votes.

The summer brought a dying spurt of work. For example, the affairs of a nine-billion-dollar business like the Grain Corporation are not wound up with one flourish of the pen. That passed. And now at the age of forty-six Hoover must orient himself, determine what he was going to do with the rest of his life. The glittering avenues to fortune were still open. But he has never cared for money as money; and he had tasted blood. A summons from President-elect Harding solved the problem. The abortive campaign of his friends in 1920 had demonstrated Hoover's hold on the country; and his talents were manifest to all. Such a member would strengthen and popularize any administration. Harding called him to Florida, offered him a place in the cabinet. It is characteristic of Hoover that he chose the one which seemed at the moment least important of all—and therefore the one which afforded the greatest opportunity for service to these United States. On March 4, 1921, he took the oath as secretary of commerce.

CHAPTER XXIII

RECENTLY, Darling the cartoonist published a "View of Washington." In the foreground of every vista walks the same figure repeated over and over again: Hoover the leader of American domestic commerce; Hoover the agent of our export commerce; Hoover the nurse of radio and civilian aviation; Hoover the patron of waterways; Hoover the foe of unemployment; Hoover everywhere. It tells the story in one eye-flash, better than I can in one sentence, of Hoover's seven years in the Department of Commerce. These activities are all parts of a definite program for national welfare so complicated that I cannot set them forth in chronological order, nor dwell long on any one item. However, at the risk of making myself tiresome let me begin with a bald, running summary.

I have said that Hoover, on entering the cabinet, chose the least esteemed post of all—Commerce. He saw there an opportunity for real service. Intelligently managed, it could contribute more than any other department in our Government to the recovery of our economic life from the disease of war. "Commerce," as he found it, comprised the six bureaus of foreign and domestic commerce, fisheries, census, standards, Coast and Geodetic Survey, and navigation, together with the Lighthouse Service and the Steamboat Inspection Service. They were loosely knit; and their character at the moment is best expressed in the words of a Washington wit: "Lighting the lamps along the coast and putting the fishes to bed." Since then, either by transfer from other departments or by creation of Congress, Hoover has taken over the Bureau of Mines, the Bureau of Patents, the All-American High Commission and the radio division. The old, moribund bureaus he has raised as from the dead; the new he has endowed with life. And he has directed them all toward the main, invariable end of help, use, and comfort to the American people.

Also, he has served for seven years as handy man to the administration. It was Hoover whom the President, during the hard times of 1921, assigned to direct the important Unemployment Conference. It was Hoover who presided over the St. Lawrence Waterway Commission. It was Hoover who accepted the job of stimulating development of our water resources. It was Hoover who investigated our dangerous increase in traffic accidents and, by arranging coördination between the States, instituted one remedy.

He served on the Foreign Debt Commission and on the Advisory Committee of the Washington Arms Conference. He is chief administrator of the $20,000,000 national fund for research in pure science. He organized, and he still conducts, that useful and effective movement for spreading individual home-ownership known as "Better Homes in America." He acted by Presidential appointment as chairman of that

Colorado River Commission which settled an interstate quarrel of twenty years' standing and agreed on the Colorado River Compact. He presided, again by appointment, over that International Radio Conference of seventy-four nations, which settled the principles of treaties to govern this new force in civilization. He organized in 1922 and 1923 Russian famine relief, and saved perhaps 15,000,000 lives. He was appointed in 1927 to direct relief measures in the Mississippi flood, our greatest peace-time calamity.

And so on and so on. . . .

How does he do it all—one man, and a calm, unhurried citizen at that? Of course, sheer ability is essence of the answer. He has the capacity for close, consecutive, all-embracing thought. His intense mental curiosity still serves as handmaid for his high powers. For thirty years that acquisitive mind has been gathering treasure in knowledge of this country and of the world. Finally, above any other administrator alive he knows how to save waste motion by decentralizing organization. With the uncanny instinct of the practised engineer for the uses in human material, he selects good men, grants them responsibility and authority, inspires them with loyalty—and lets them alone.

Among these "outside" activities, perhaps the most important to the American people was his attack on the problem of unemployment in 1921. We all know the situation—a sudden post-war deflation, millions of idle men. Hoover—very busy at the moment with reorganization of his own department—recommended to the President an unemployment conference of eminent business men, manufacturers, labor leaders, and economists. Appointed to deal with an emergency, it proceeded under Hoover's guidance to one of the greatest coöperative efforts ever undertaken in the United States. Federal, state, and municipal governments organized to undertake and to accelerate public work. Manufacturers agreed to institute jobs of cleaning up and reconstructing their plants; and to "stagger" their employment so as to give as many people as possible some wages each week. When the people began to recover their income, they began also to buy. In three months the wheels were turning again; the backbone of hard times was broken. European Governments have struggled with this problem for years, but never in history was there such swift solution. The conference went farther: studied unemployment down to its very roots, gathered data which will serve invaluably in future crises.

As for the department itself, that least-considered stem of our Government in 1921 ranked by 1926 as one of the first two or three in usefulness and importance. Not only has Hoover developed the separate bureaus in detail, but he has coördinated many bureaus to a great general purpose—coöperation with all elements of the community to lessen fluctuations of employment and to stabilize business. And he has done this without increasing the number of government employees or piling up expenses, but by—well, how *does* Hoover do it?

Some of the subsidiary bureaus I can afford to dismiss with brief mention. Though they serve a vital purpose, they have smaller public interests than some others. There are those maritime agencies, the coast survey which provides sea-charts for our navigators; the Bureau of Navigation which lays down rules of the road, inspects our ships, sees that they carry proper life-saving appliances; and the steamboat inspection which looks after engines and boilers. Our millions of seafarers do not know what careful guardianship broods over them night and day. And in Hoover's term we had no great disaster attributable in any degree to failure on their part.

The Bureau of the Census deals, of course, with statistics. Time out of mind, it has counted noses every ten years. Always, it had its in-between period, when it functioned mildly if at all. Hoover has found uses for those slack years. He has set the bureau to revamping and compiling statistics for practical use—guidance to business men, farmers, manufacturers, and laborers. To-day it is the greatest fact-finding institution in the world.

The Bureau of Fisheries, at the inception of Hoover's term, confined itself to a purely scientific study of aquatic life. Hoover transformed it into a live, practical organization to safeguard marine fishing and promote game fishing. Warned by this bureau of the danger to our Alaskan salmon industry, he steered through Congress the legislation which prevented its destruction, put it on the road to recovery. Hoover is himself an enthusiastic angler. His wise and witty speech on this topic before the Izaak Walton League is a fisherman's classic. And under his direction this bureau, coöperating with hundreds of fishing clubs, has attacked the problem of preserving our game fish. Assisted by acts of Congress, it has put this work on a wide and systematic basis. The Alaskan job has assured us a permanent supply of salmon; the work for our amateurs will give recreation to ten million people.

The Bureau of Mines, since it came under the wing of "Commerce," has expanded in the direction of assuring safety in underground workings. Its inspection, its scientific investigation, has decreased every year the roll of mine accidents.

When Hoover took hold, the Bureau of Patents was eighteen months behind its work of passing on the applications of our inventors. In 1927 it was only six months behind; and its experts told Congress that by the end of 1928 they expected to pull even with the work. Encouraged by Hoover, the All-American High Commission, representing the Latin nations of our continent, has signed an agreement to protect our trade-marks and copyrights.

However, these are but details in the picture. It is in the Bureau of Foreign and Domestic Commerce and the Bureau of Standards that Hoover has done the original work which raised the Department of Commerce, even during the first two years of his incumbency, to major importance.

CHAPTER XXIV

WHEN Hoover took over the Department of Commerce, foreign trade was just drilling along. It was a fine thing to have—so American business seemed to feel—but it would take care of itself. The Bureau of Foreign and Domestic Commerce maintained agents abroad. They did what they could to make themselves useful and helpful. But the bureau as a whole lacked policy and definite objective. Hoover, he of the worldwide experience, conceived foreign trade in different and more positive terms. We could and we should find broader and stabler outside markets for our goods. As he saw this problem and opportunity, it linked up with his plan to stabilize and extend employment. Also, in creating more demand for labor, increased foreign trade would stimulate the home market for our agricultural products. The high purchasing power of American workmen would serve our farmers better than the low wages of foreign labor.

Looking into the matter with his customary discrimination, he established one guiding principle. In goods requiring much labor, we cannot compete with Europe. But we can compete in high-quality products manufactured by our mass-methods. This principle established, he convened two hundred leading manufacturers, held counsel with them on the strategies of foreign trade.

They agreed on one principle. While trained economists had their uses in the general scheme, selling goods and encouraging the selling of goods was a job for specialists. Hoover acted on their advice. Under the old policy, our commercial representative in Paris or Madrid or Buenos Aires had gathered information promiscuously on opportunities for American trade. This was dumped without much system into the department at Washington. To find anything of use in his specialty, the business man must needs burrow. Hoover decided to divide the work on lines not of geography but of specialties. Gradually, he set up thirty or forty "commodity divisions," dedicated to definite trades, such as steel, automobiles, foodstuffs, canned goods, and textiles.

At the inception of this work he went to the trades themselves; consulted their leading spirits and the officers of their organizations concerning needs, wants, obstacles, ways and means. When with their aid he had formed a general plan of campaign, he asked each to nominate from its own ranks a representative who combined ability, knowledge of the business, and experience in foreign salesmanship. The men so chosen he appointed directors of the commodity divisions. Virtually without exception, they made serious sacrifices to take these jobs. Most of them had been earning and could earn in the future two or three times the meager government salary. But Hoover, who has himself given so much of his energy and talent to benevolent and common causes, has the art of inspiring sacrificing in others. Few of the appointees refused the honor. With the same enthusiasm that they used to put into selling combined harvesters or structural steel or California fruit for private firms, they peeled off their coats and went furiously to work.

These commodity divisions, seated in the departmental building at Washington, are nerve-centers for the new system which Hoover created in 1921. The eyes and hands toward which the nerves reach out are our commercial attachés, trade commissioners, and special trade committees abroad. Under the new dispensation the commercial attaché has become almost as much a star reporter as a diplomat. It is his job to gather facts which have a practical use; statistics that mean something. He transmits news of general trends, yes; but beyond that a bewilderment of detail—the special tastes of Touraine and Lombardy or the Chilean coast for American prunes or shoe-blacking or plows; the standing, commercial rating, and general reliability of the firms with which the American exporter must needs deal; the temporary condition of markets; official or private obstacles which the green exporter is likely to encounter; the methods and tactics of competing firms from other nations.

Beyond that, he serves as a super-salesman for American trade in general. A Government announces a big piece of construction work. Here is an opening for American machinery; perhaps for an American contractor. A Government or a private enterprise announces a new railroad. It will need rolling stock, structural steel—commodities in which we compete with the best. The attaché gets the news, often in advance of its general publication. It goes to Washington and thence, by channels presently to be described, directly, promptly, and impartially to the trade. Beyond that, the attaché collaborates with our ambassadors and ministers in negotiations over unfair trade restrictions or phases of trade which impinge on diplomacy. Finally, he is forever adjusting tangles into which, through ill luck or ignorance, American importers have got themselves. This work ranges from pushing a million dollars' worth of goods through the customs to ascertaining the best means for collecting a bad debt.

Ahead of the attachés scout the trade commissioners, finding and feeling out new fields. They have penetrated, since Hoover began sending them forth, to districts as remote as the upper Amazon and the border of Tibet. They have met their adventures in these savage lands—all part of the day's work. And some of their reports, like one on interior China a few years ago, are economic classics. Finally, in special cases and special emergencies, commissions of experts go out to make a general reconnaissance. Notable among these is a survey of raw materials, issued at the time when the British rubber monopoly threatened our tire industry, and of incalculable permanent value to American commerce.

These facts, opinions, and observations go into the department at Washington. Thence, collated and given meaning, they issue to service of American business through the local offices of the department. Here is another Hoover improvement on the old machinery.

Before he took hold, the Bureau of Foreign and Domestic Commerce had 200,000 inquiries and applications for information a year. This piece of business was rather cumbersome. You wrote to the department. It dug through its files, and in the good time of a government bureau the answer came back by mail. That is, provided the department could answer. Such a process was all too slow for Hoover. He strung across the country from New York to San Francisco a chain of sub-offices—six in the beginning, grown since to twenty-three. The inquiring business man now writes to the nearest office, or visits it in person. The inquiries have increased from 200,000 a year to 2,400,000—multiplied themselves by 12. And that is saying nothing about the quality of the replies.

Any dispenser of information knows that certain rubber-stamp inquiries are repeated again and again. For such, the local offices have the data canned and ready. Answers to questions a little more difficult they can generally dig out for themselves. Especially knotty ones go to Washington; whence the answer comes back with a celerity unprecedented in government transactions. The questions range, of course, from the tremendously important to the trivial; from that of the manufacturer contemplating a million-dollar selling campaign in South America to that of the small specialist who wants to know if hairpins are wanted in China. But to the business man looking abroad, the department can give and does give all that he needs to know. It will tell him what competition, native or foreign, he will encounter, what wholesale and retail prices

A REMINISCENT BIOGRAPHY 269

he must meet, what formalities he must observe. It will inform him concerning local peculiarities which he must humor or against which he must be on his guard. It will give him the standing, reputation, and rating of the importers with whom he must deal. It will describe the banking system from which he must obtain credits.

Often during the early years of Hoover's administration an agent of American business, returning from a "boosting" trip abroad, dropped into the department for some omitted fact or figure. And after looking over their stock of information on his special commodity, he would remark: "Except for personal contact, my trip was wasted. I needn't have gone beyond Washington. You fellows have more than I could get in a dozen trips." Now such a man need not go even to Washington. There is in the nearest big town a sub-office of the department which can give him information just as accurate and complete. The dissemination of useful information extends farther than that. To a list of establishments which have applied for it, and whose good American intentions can be trusted, go confidential bulletins which treat with foreign crises bearing on their business, with special problems and—notably—with the operations of crooked or irresponsible foreign firms or individuals.

Above all this sits Hoover, the strategist of the campaign; he who, as an engineer in private practice, has planted American products and installed American methods in most of the countries with which his subordinates are dealing. His experience, his wide point of view, his amenability to counsel and advice, serve him in giving wise direction to this campaign for greater and more stable American commerce. Still, as in the days of the Belgian Commission when he backed the European militarists off the boards, he "sees one turn further than the other fellow." For example: Before the war most of our advisers and admonishers on foreign commerce told us that we should never get anywhere until we altered the packing of our products, and even the products themselves, to suit the individual fancies of diverse foreign peoples. It was almost an axiom. Hoover gave that proposition his cool, detached scrutiny and found it faulty. "Our strong hold in commerce and manufacturing," he said in effect, "isn't the special or individual or fancy. Other nations can beat us there. Where we lead the world is in moderate-priced goods turned out in enormous quantities by machine methods. If we keep on delivering an honest product, made American-fashion, packed —with due regard to climate—American fashion, foreigners will realize finally that our goods, in spite of their unfamiliarity, are better and cheaper." And so it has turned out. When American automobiles, manufactured by "continuous" machine process, began flowing into Europe, the natives preferred their own hand-made, especially designed product. But compared with native cars at the same price ours had so many merits and conveniences that they swept the boards. Now nearly 90 per cent. of the automobiles which come out from behind tariff walls and compete in the open international market are American made.

Before the war, Great Britain financed the world. Through circumstances not of our creation, we have succeeded to that office. Ahead of our exports has run a flood of American dollars. This creative capital, by raising the productiveness of foreign peoples, increases their purchasing power; there follow more sales for our business men, more employment for our workers. Except in a few instances where such loans were against the interest of the American people, Hoover has steadily encouraged this movement.

Much of Hoover's work with the Department of Commerce is imponderable. It reaches so far into the future, runs so deep in our economic structure, that one cannot tag it with a money-value. But this campaign for extending and solidifying our foreign trade furnishes an exception. I have asked not only experts of the department but informed outsiders how much he has added to our national export trade. It is guessing, of course, but not such wild guessing after all. And they say, generally: "Oh, about a half billion dollars a year!" Some of them call this the minimum. And these fields which he has broken to the plow may yield their richest harvests in the future.

So much for export trade. But, as Hoover himself has said, American prosperity can in many ways be measured by the volume of imports. We export agricultural products and manufactured goods; we import raw materials. If the inflow of such commodities as rubber or sisal or platinum be clogged or restricted, American industry suffers. During Hoover's term with the department it has fought and won its notable battles to protect the consumer of imports. For in half a dozen products necessary to our industry or our national life, foreign Governments or commercial combinations have tried to establish monopolies of one form or another, and to make American consumers pay the price.

Most famous and notable among these attempts was that of the British rubber monopoly—virtually a government undertaking. Owing to our great and flourishing automobile industry, we consume 70 per cent. of the world's raw rubber. And until lately we have produced, in our whole continental and colonial area, only 3 per cent. of our supply. Our rubber came largely from British possessions in the East Indies. In November, 1922, the British growers, under legislation by the Imperial Government at London—the Stevenson act—arranged to restrict the output of each plantation to 60 per cent. of its normal production in 1919. Immediately the price jumped from 36 cents a pound—which price the British had declared fair—to $1.21 a pound. It played hob with our tire industry. The British had us.

Hoover was already meditating on this subject of foreign monopolies at the sources of our imported raw materials. Now he was compelled to fight a decisive battle. He sent his experts forth on the famous world-survey of raw materials. They paid special attention to rubber. On the East Indian source of supply they gathered facts and figures both searching and accurate. Stocked with this ammunition, Hoover went up against the British Government. Negotiation, however, served not to modify their attitude but only to stir up the government-controlled faction of the London press. Hoover, who in 1919 had figured in their columns as a super-efficient archangel, became now a black devil of Yankee greed. Thereupon he turned his face homeward; instituted what amounted to a buyers' strike. From the workshops of the tire manufacturers to the garages of the ultimate consumers passed Hoover's motto: "Wear tires to destruction." Manufacturers found how they could employ second-hand rubber to a degree hitherto considered impossible. Between 1925 and 1926 the sale of tire-repair materials increased by 37 per cent. We had 2,360,000 more automobiles running in 1926 than in 1925; yet between the two years the sale of casings decreased 16.6 per cent. and of inner tubes 22.6 per cent. Theoretically, the Stevenson act enforced a price of 36 cents a pound. By the time Hoover brought this matter before Congress it stood actually at $1.10. Then, owing to these measures, the demand for foreign rubber came down like a pricked balloon.

We import about 900,000,000 pounds of rubber a year. At 32 cents a pound, our annual bill was about $300,000,000. At $1.10 a pound, it would be nearly a billion dollars a year. But under the impact of Hoover's assault the price fell to 30 cents a pound. The Stevenson act, a piece of economic folly, was defeating its own ends. It was doing nothing for British planters, and it was throwing the East Indian business bit by bit into the hands of the Dutch. And many of the British planters now agree with Hoover.

Meantime the department was taking measures to render our automobile tire industry permanently independent of foreign monopoly. Since we consume the rubber, why not grow it? The survey of raw materials considered not only the existing sources of supply but possible sources of future supply, American owned. Hoover's agents ranged the meadows of the Philippines, the uplands of the Amazon country, the jungles of East Africa. The enormous Ford plantation in Brazil stands in a district which the experts of the department explored and recommended as suitable land for rubber growth and a "white man's country." Their work has stimulated rubber-growth in the Philippines. The Bureau of Standards and other departmental agencies have looked into the possibility of growing on a commercial scale the guayule or rubber-weed in our own Southwest—and found something in the idea. It takes a baby tree about seven years to reach full bearing. By the early 1930's we shall be producing enough rubber, under American ownership, to avert control of our supply by any foreign monopoly.

This was Hoover's hardest and most successful fight to prevent foreign monopoly. But with other tactics, he has won battles in other fields. He broke the attempt of Brazil to dictate the price of coffee—the famous "valorization plan" which at one time almost inspired a buyers' strike. The Chilean nitrate monopoly bears especially hard on our farmers. By encouraging artificially produced nitrates he has rendered it comparatively ineffective. That dangerous combination is now crumbling. Also, he has shielded our farmers from raids on their pocketbooks by the Mexican sisal monopoly and the Franco-German potash monopoly. The latter, too, appears a little sickly since it went up against Hoover.

CHAPTER XXV

THAT period between the slackening of Hoover' European job in 1920 and his call to the cabinet ii 1921 was a comparative rest. But he could no mor abandon the habit of creation than an artist on vaca tion can inhibit his eye from seeing the world in com positions or plots. At some time during this interval] took a railway journey with him. The talk driftec from comment and gossip to ships, shipping, and the problems of sea-transportation. As though I had pulled a trigger, his mind began to shoot. From his twenty years of experience with ships, he sketched out an ideal ferry-like service with cargo-liner types of ships. Before the porter came for our bags he was webbing the back of a stray envelope with maps of trade-routes, figures. . . . He never carries a notebook. When he wants to preserve a useful but fleeting idea he covers the first piece of paper at hand—if there be nothing better, the margin of a newspaper— with hieroglyphic notes. In the days of the Food Administration Lewis Strauss, his secretary, used every morning to go through his chief's clothes like a pickpocket and salvage these important bits of crumpled paper.

During this period Hoover the private citizen began to develop two ideas which Hoover the government official cultivated into important functions of his department. In February, 1921, the Council of Federated Engineering Societies met in a hotel at Syracuse, New York. As their newly elected president, he read a kind of inaugural address. This meeting attracted very little attention at the time. Yet Hoover's paper had perhaps a more profound and beneficent effect upon American commerce than any piece of formal legislation enacted by Congress during our generation. It was a discussion of the waste in industry and especially of that poignant human problem, the waste through unemployment. Even before the war, when Hoover was merely an engineer in private practice, his mind had been running on that subject. I have recorded elsewhere a conversation in 1912, wherein he dwelt on the faulty coördination of our industrial system. And from that quietly inspiring paper arose two actions. First, and perhaps most important, was a study of the phenomenon of those business cycles which bring waves of unemployment, together with suggestions for their mitigation. Second was an investigation, by a commission of our more able engineers and economists, of the waste through imperfect coördination in industry. Perhaps that term "imperfect coördination," as Hoover used it, needs defining. It refers not to faults of individual industries but to leaks and flaws in the joints between—things which the industrial body has always wanted to remedy could it but find the way. It had, like most of his theories, a practical bearing on public welfare. The more you save to industry as a whole, the lower the price of goods. The lower the cost, the more people can possess them.

As a matter of fact, when he faced the engineering council he had already started action toward solution of the last-named problem. In 1920 he had secured to this end a modest endowment from private sources. Now fifty eminent engineers and economists, working without recompense, started a rapid survey of our wastes and the possibilities for remedy. They completed the job in six months, by which time Hoover sat at Washington as secretary of commerce. It showed that about 30 per cent. of our industrial motions amounted to waste motions. Without hampering legitimate competition, without interference of government, we Americans could by perfect coördination save thirty billion dollars a year—and add thirty billion dollars' worth of goods to our comforts. That sum, 50 per cent. larger than our whole national debt, seemed staggering, astronomical. And indeed the engineers who made the report put it forth as an impossible ideal, for to attain it we should need perfect human instruments. But even allowing for the human factor, they estimated that we might eventually save ten billion dollars a year—which is large enough.

Established in the cabinet, Hoover set about to make this engineer's dream come true. And a recent Department of Commerce report gives the text of the story:

> It seems worth while at all times to reiterate the fundamental purposes of this campaign. The objectives which underlie it have but one purpose; that is, to maintain American

standards of living for both workers and farmers, and to place production on a more stable footing by enlarging consumption and export markets through reduced production and distribution costs. The high standards of living enjoyed by the American people are the result of steadily mounting per capita productivity. There is only one way to further advance these standards, and that is by improved methods and processes, by the elimination of waste in materials and motion in our production and distribution system. The moral and intellectual progress of the Nation is not the offspring of poverty or low living standards. The incentives to crime decrease with increasing security; the opportunity for education and the growth of understanding are the products of economic progress—not of economic degeneration. Devotion to economic improvement whether in individual effort or in improved methods enlarges the field of leadership; it is not a stimulant of idle or luxurious living.

Just as twenty years ago we undertook nation-wide conservation of our natural resources, so we must today even more vigorously sustain this campaign of better nation-wide utilization of our industrial resources and effort. More especially is this the case in view of the many complex forces which have arisen from the war, and particularly the difficulty of maintaining our situation as against the competition of a world of lower standards overseas.

The term "elimination of waste" is subject to some objection as carrying the implication of individual or wilful waste. In the sense used in these discussions elimination of waste refers wholly to those wastes which can be eliminated solely by co-operative action in the community. It does not refer to any single producer, for in the matters here discussed he is individually helpless to effect the remedy. Nor does the elimination of such wastes imply any lessening of fair competition or any infringement of the restraint of trade laws. In fact, the most casual investigation of the work in progress will show that its accomplishment establishes more healthy competition. It protects and preserves the small units in the business world. Its results are an asset alike to worker, farmer, consumer and business man.

It may be worth while repeating the major directions for

national efforts as they were outlined by the department at the beginning of the undertaking:

1. Elimination of the waste imposed by inadequate railway transportation, by improved equipment and methods, and the establishment of better co-operation.

2. Vigorous utilization of our water resources for cheaper transportation of bulk commodities, flood control, reclamation, and power.

3. Enlarged electrification of the country for the saving of fuel and labor.

4. Reduction of the great waste of booms and slumps of the "business cycle" with their intermittent waves of unemployment and bankruptcy.

5. Reduction of waste in manufacture and distribution through the establishment of standards of quality, simplification of grades, dimensions, and performance in nonstyle articles of commerce; through the reduction of unnecessary varieties; through more uniform business documents such as specifications, bills of lading, warehouse receipts, etc.

6. Development of pure and applied scientific research as the foundation of genuine labor-saving devices, better processes, and sounder methods.

7. Development of co-operative marketing and better terminal facilities for agricultural products in order to reduce the waste in agricultural distribution.

8. Stimulation of commercial arbitration in order to eliminate the wastes of litigation.

9. Reduction of the waste arising from industrial strife between employers and employees.

One thing at a time, however. Hoover tackled first the waste in those perplexing, lawless areas lying between individual establishments in the same industry. In the Bureau of Standards, which he inherited as part of the departmental machinery, he set up the Division of Commercial Standards. It included a half dozen men assigned to work on "Simplified Practice." Nominally a small and inexpensive cog in our Federal machinery, this bureau made itself as important an instrument for national economy as any government ever knew. Hoover proceeded on that same theory of government in its relation to business which made the Food Administration such a furious success. Do not coerce; encourage. Employ as little formal legislation as possible. Work by voluntary coöperation. Regard the Government, in relation to the industrial system, as an adviser who, being also an outsider, sees the game broadly and impartially but never even advises unless it is asked. The office of Simplified Practice has said to business: "Here we are; this is our idea; now what can we do for you?"

The idea on which the office of Simplified Practice began operations was in its main lines not at all complex or esoteric. In almost every department of industry manufacturers were making too many sizes and designs of everything. Let us see, therefore, how many unnecessary sizes and designs we can eliminate! Take as an example that industry which the division was first able to tackle—paving-brick. When Hoover's men made their first survey, our manufacturers were producing sixty-six sizes. Any child can see that there was no sense in this. Diverse calibers of paving-brick did nothing to improve the beauty of our cities. In order to furnish replacements for pavements already laid in this bewildering variety, manufacturers must keep special machinery in commission, must lose time in "setting" it, must tie up capital in stock of odd and little-used sizes. The same principle applied in other terms to the middlemen. They too must keep extra and odd sizes in stock, thereby losing the annual interest on just so much capital. And as always happens, the burden was passed on to the ultimate consumer.

When the paving-brick manufacturers of the country first made application for this new service of government, Hoover went at the matter as he always does in similar cases. First, his men joined with the manufacturers' men to go out and gather the facts. Then he called together outstanding representatives of the producers, the manufacturers, and the consumers in our municipal governments. "Almost any human problem can be settled," Hoover has said, "if you can get all the interested persons together in one room and make them talk it over." By mutual agreement, the paving-brick interests reduced their number of sizes from sixty-six to eleven; then, by successive annual agreements, to seven and eventually to five. Later, the division tackled in the same manner and with the same successful results the problem of common building-brick. The manufacturers and architects and contractors reduced the sizes from forty-four to one. All this looks simple, foolishly obvious; yet at one stroke it saved millions of dollars to industry and the consumer. Great ideas are usually very simple.

The next national industry to apply for service of the division was bed manufacture. The manufacturers, distributers, and consumers of beds, springs, and mattresses reduced their sizes from seventy-four combinations of lengths and widths to four. The retailer need no longer carry bedspreads, mattresses, and springs in two dozen sizes, need no longer employ a plumber and a tailor to make them fit—all at the expense of himself and the consumer. And now for the first time this important movement toward increase of national wealth swam into the ken of the newspapers. Somehow, simplifying beds tickled the comic sense of our paragraphers and editorial writers. This served a useful purpose—it advertised the job. The business community learned that simplified practice was on the map. The rush to Washington became almost an embarrassment.

Next, the division began its longest and most important job—assisting in straightening out the lumber industry. This enterprise had an aspect more important even than elimination of waste in stock and material. No American needs to be informed on the shrinkage of our forests and the consequent danger to our watersheds. For reasons too complex for treatment in detail, our lumbermen were strewing the clearings with rotting odds and ends of wood which a saner arrangement of dimension in the finished product could save. The importance and intricacy of the interests which make, sell, and use lumber rendered this task extremely difficult. However, by 1924 the industry had eliminated dozens of unnecessary sizes. Session after session, bills to regulate lumbering and save our forests had come before Congress and with no practical effect. This agreement proved that industry can do such things voluntarily and without compulsion of law. For it worked, smoothly and magnificently. The associations which represent our lumber business estimated recently that the annual saving affected by these "Hoover measures" amounts to the staggering total of two hundred and fifty million dollars a year. And the consumer is the main beneficiary.

On the same terms and by the same methods the division had by the end of 1927 helped to straighten out the kinks in eighty-six American industries, some as familiarly known as beds, lumber, hotel chinaware, steel bars, and hospital supplies and some—like plow-bolts—important but generally unknown. . . . Who stops to realize that to-day all nuts and bolts of the same dimension will screw together? A few years ago every maker had a different thread. As a consequence, our dealers carried hundreds, thousands, and even millions of unnecessary pieces.

Never in the course of this quietly revolutionary undertaking has the Department of Commerce applied an ounce of coercion; nor has it "gone out for business." Simplified Practice has announced its own existence to the industrial world and waited for the customers to come in. How much this sensible idea inexpensively applied has saved to American industry during the past six years, no one exactly knows. However, ten of the eighty-six industries have of late estimated their annual saving through simplification. The total runs past two hundred and eighty-six million dollars—about the amount of those recurrent tax-cuts over which Congress fills so many volumes with oratory. And an economist who has been following the operation makes, as to the saving in all the eighty-six industries, a guess-estimate of six hundred million dollars a year. The work, necessarily slow, has only just begun. Says Hoover: "There is a great area still untouched in which the application of these waste-elimination measures might save not only millions but billions."

Of course it will take time. And the Department of Commerce cannot do it all alone. Already many business associations have taken the cue and are applying simplified practice on their own account. However, Hoover has woven so tightly into the fabric of American society this method and principle—government by coöperation, not by regulation—that whoever succeeds him must go on with the work or confess himself a failure.

As I write, the experts of the division are looking into a score of other industries, some of them most important—like automobile tires and structural steel. It has not altered its method. First comes the invitation from the industry itself. Then follows a survey by experts from the department and the industry; then a series of conferences wherein all the interests involved thresh out their ideas; and at last, usually, a sound and final agreement. Sometimes the problem is in detail so complex as to make chess look like matching pennies. For example, when you start to simplify automobile tires you must deal not only with the tire-manufacturer but with the automobile manufacturer. Now body-designers have so calibrated their wheels as to blend into the general design of the car, and with no regard whatever to any standard of tire-sizes. Frequently the variation between two makes is not more than half an inch—a difference so small as to have no bearing on the proportionate beauty of the car. But it may cost millions of dollars a year to manufacturer, middlemen, and consumer of tires. So, beginning with the tire-makers, Hoover's simplification experts must go on to deal with the whole automobile industry.

Economists are writing treatises on this important movement in American commerce; the annual report of an important New York bank refers to it as "a new and constructive economic force"; yet in the biography of the man who originated it all I have room only for these few paragraphs—so full has been that life! But before I dismiss this subject, I might dismiss also the idea that "simplification," as fostered and practised by Hoover's Department of Commerce, means standardization—blue-printing American life. In this work Hoover has drawn most carefully the line between the essential and the non-essential. Here are two automobiles, their bodies the best expression which the American craftsman can accomplish of beauty in manufactured commodities. With their designs, simplification does not meddle. But their body-bolts have two different "pitches" of threads. No one, contemplating the automobile as a whole, sees the end of the bolts! Yet those variations of pitch make it necessary for manufacturers, garage-owners, and service stations to tie up just so much aggregate capital in stock. In the jestful matter of beds, simplification does not in the least dictate design or coloring or ornament. The maker may turn them out as plain or as fancy, as tasteless or as beautiful, as he wishes. Simplification merely dictates that the inner area, where the springs and mattress fit into the frame, shall adhere to a few standard dimensions. So, among other savings, we avoid that trouble and expense of remaking an oversize mattress to fit an undersized bed which every householder has experienced at least once in his life.

Nor does simplification presume to touch at all that special class of commodities whose main merit is art craftsmanship. In reducing the stocks of hotel china from seven hundred sizes and objects to one hundred and sixty, the division did not deal with decoration but merely with shapes and sizes; and did not presume to touch those special varieties manufactured for the luxury-hotels. Indeed, most of the commodities to which it has given its beneficent services are like nuts and bolts—invisible. The plumber who goes back from the job to his shop for a piece of material has been for forty years a standing newspaper joke. Why does he go back? Because if he carried with him enough parts to fit the variety of connections that he is likely to find in the plumbing of a single household sink, he would have to take along a ten-ton truck. There never was the slightest sense in this diversity; it was just a bad habit into which the business had fallen. And that, too, the Division of Simplified Practice is in process of straightening out. Simplification of plumbing systems will not by so much as one nail or shingle make American homes less individually beautiful; but it will make them less expensive and immeasurably more convenient.

During the first five years of Hoover's administration this work dealt primarily with production. Of course, distribution and consumption came into it incidentally; when the Division of Simplified Practice reduced the stocks of manufacturers, it rendered the same service to wholesalers and retailers. Distribution is traditional among economists as the most wasteful division of industry. In 1923 and 1924 Hoover began to get at that special problem through the Bureau of Foreign and Domestic Commerce. Choosing the wholesale grocery business as a model, it made a preliminary survey. As any one might have suspected, it found that the wastes in distribution were even greater than those in production. For example, manufacturers had long known the costs of their own operations to the last penny; wholesalers generally did not. The typical middleman was carrying "lines" which, unknown to himself, lost him money—was stretching his business to include remote customers who paid no better. The first result was an "atlas for wholesalers," by study of which progressive firms have learned where and where not to send their salesmen—so effecting great economies. Later, these experts made a study of retail trade, that branch of business notorious for bankruptcy. And "Retail Store Problems," issued subsequently by the department, is the "best-seller" among its publications.

Professedly, however, these measures only skimmed the surface. Having at last secured an appropriation for the work, Hoover's investigators began a thorough survey of our distribution system. For this purpose he has divided the country into nine economic districts. The report on the southeastern district was finished in 1927; in 1928 his men were working on the northeast and southwest. When this job is done, the department will have the facts. Then Hoover, or whoever in future carries on his policies, may bring about such adjustment-by-agreement as he has already effected in eighty-six of our manufacturing industries. This is one of those "great areas still untouched in which the application of waste-elimination measures might save not only millions but billions."

So much for the first movement which sprang from that meeting of the engineers in February, 1921. Probably the other has affected American commercial life of to-day and to-morrow just as benevolently and profoundly. On the gloomy winter day when Hoover faced the assembled engineers in a Syracuse hotel, we were sinking toward the very depth of a financial depression. In the war and the brief period of hectic, unnatural demand which followed, we had blown up American industry like a balloon. Now the balloon was pricked; and the deflation brought widespread distress. Unemployment, which grew acute in the autumn of 1920, was by the spring of 1921 rising toward its peak. Manufacturers, wholesalers, and retailers found themselves on the one hand grossly overstocked, and on the other facing a "buyers' strike." Given the inflation, this deflation was bound to come. In fact, when during the armistice period Hoover broke the European blockade and opened a door for our surplus farm products, he averted its premature arrival.

Economists have long known and studied the

phenomenon of the "business cycle." A period of prosperity, then a slump; another period of prosperity, then another slump; misery of bankruptcy and unemployment alternating with blatancy of extravagance and waste—it goes in the rhythm of an intermittent fever. No sensible farmer, manufacturer, dealer, or laboring man likes this rhythm. He prefers long stability of conditions. None was quite certain of the causes. Now, when the disease was in its acute stage, seemed the best time to study its symptoms and to search for a remedy.

In September, 1921, six months after his induction into office, the new secretary of commerce found himself in a position to act. Industrial distress had reached its absolute peak. I have said that the President, upon his recommendation, called the Unemployment Conference. Hoover served as chairman. In our past history such assemblies had usually contented themselves with a few platitudinous resolutions, a little muck-raking, or perhaps some recommendations for temporary palliatives, sound or unsound. This one took the measures for immediate relief which I have described already. Then, inspired by Hoover, it went on to get at the root of the evil. He obtained a gift of $50,000 for the necessary incidental expenses. Then he formed a committee of industrial leaders, labor leaders, and sound economists, under the chairmanship of an eminent business man. For six months these unpaid volunteers gave all their spare time to study of the problem. Their final report to Hoover was unanimous as to the main conclusions. As in 1921, so always, these distressing slumps followed a period of hectic inflation. It was best to begin remedial measures when the inflation first made itself apparent. Out of their wisdom and experience they enumerated the signs by which a coming inflation manifests itself. And the best remedy seemed to be light, more light—sound scientific collection and collation of facts, publicity of these facts in the right quarter. If the Government would in some manner keep watch for the signs, would, as the danger signals flashed, inform certain pivot-men of our industrial army—notably the credit bankers—we might nip inflation in the bud, thereby preventing the distress and disorganization of deflation.

Whereupon Hoover infused new life into the old Bureau of the Census. He instituted in it a monthly survey of current business, which went farther and deeper than any similar investigation ever undertaken by any Government. American business gave hearty coöperation; yielded up not only the basis of bare statistics, but larger and more valuable information concerning rates of production, stocks on hand or in transit, the drift of prices, the volume of sales, the trend in money rates. The first of these reports, formally sponsored by leaders in American business, was issued from the White House in 1923. And it came, probably, just in time. For according to the signs and omens discovered and described by the fifty experts, we were starting another of those inflation periods which are prelude to a flop. The pivot-men, warned, adopted such measures as reduction of credits; the

Federal Reserve banks—when rightly used a valuable safety-valve—acted after their own fashion. The incipient boom died a-borning.

Hunt, the economist, has called the original report of the committee "the most important economic investigation ever undertaken." But the work did not stop there. The committee on business cycles carried on. Supported by private funds and with coöperation of the Department of Commerce, it has undertaken an investigation whose results may prove equally important to the commonwealth and to scholarship. In 1921 the patient was ill. That was the time to study the disease and to find a remedy. Since then, the erstwhile patient has lived, moved, and had his being in a condition of riotous health. No nation ever enjoyed such abundant and stable prosperity as the United States between 1922 and 1927. The physicians of our body politic have discerned no symptoms of that inflation which precedes a flop. And economic phenomena without parallel in history have marked this period—such as a wide distribution of comforts and an advance in real wages.

Some of these phenomena have puzzled the economists. For example, ever since Smith and Mill laid down the principles of their science the law of supply and demand has stood as an axiom. When demand rose, prices rose; when supply rose, prices fell. But now—well, a recent advertisement of a very popular car tells the story. "Owing to the unprecedented demand for our four-door sedan," it reads, "we have been able to reduce the price" . . . What does it all mean—this and a dozen other contradictions of old-fashioned, accepted economic principles? More pertinently to the ends and purposes of the average citizen, how can we perpetuate such conditions? The new survey will try to answer these questions.

The investigation of 1921–22 was, as I have said before, like a diagnosis of a patient in the agonies of his disease. This resembles one of those health-insurance plans of the modern insurance companies. It goes over the patient when he is in health; finds, so to speak, what makes him well. Further, it explores his system for the tendencies which may lead to disease. While it has its great scholarly importance, the new survey aims primarily at a practical object. Once the principles are known, the Department of Commerce may proceed in its own way to apply them for the increase and continuance of national prosperity; as it did after the important report of 1922.

When Hoover stepped into the Department of Commerce, he had just built the house at Palo Alto. Fresh from that experience with plumbers and carpenters and building codes, he added a small Housing Division to the machinery of his department. He had seized the appropriate moment, as he usually does. Suspension of new construction and of repairs during the war-years had caused a shortage of housing; yet paradoxically millions of idle men were walking the streets. That could not last; and as business revived, we should probably witness unparalleled building activity. Now, at the start, was the time to encourage saner, better-coördinated, more economical building. On this subject Hoover has his own sound theories. He believes that every family should at least attempt to own its own home. This makes for immediate happiness, for stability, for the more general distribution of wealth. A few measures designed to bridge that gap between the housing-shortage and the unemployed millions—and Hoover was off again, this time with the Better Homes movement, whose beneficent influence has touched nearly every community in America. "To relieve the shortage of houses inherited from the World War, to decrease construction units and costs, to stabilize business through expanded home construction, to improve the character of homes and promote home ownership"—that was its professed object.

So far as large economies are concerned, this job has interplayed with the work of simplified practice in the Bureau of Standards. The lumber business, where simplification has wrought its greatest saving, has of course a direct connection with any building problem. So has plumbing and steam-fitting, with which the experts of the department began wrestling in 1927. Along the way they have introduced the characteristic Hoover economies into manufacture and distribution of a dozen commodities used in building —such as steel lath, window glass, window sashes and frames.

However, the department has worked more widely than that. For the first time, perhaps, the ancient and honorable trade of building begins to see itself as a whole. As Dr. Gries of the department says: "The giant is awakened. He knows that his arms and his legs are a part of him. He knows that no matter which member is injured, he suffers." Nowhere has Hoover inspired wider or more hearty coöperation than in this movement to lessen the wastes of construction and to secure for the future a better-built America. The architects have as a class responded with special enthusiasm. Even before Hoover took up this work a national organization among them had set itself to drawing plans for sounder, cheaper, and more beautiful American homes. They aimed not only at reducing costs and increasing convenience, but primarily perhaps at eliminating the expensive and hideous "ornamentation" which disfigured so much American architecture of the past generation. Hoover has incorporated this endeavor into the basic structure of his scheme for better homes. And his own experts, collaborating as always with the most intelligent and able outsiders, have done wonders in devising or approving methods of new construction which combine safety and beauty with economy.

With both employers and labor of the building interests, Hoover took up at the very first that problem, old as the trade, of seasonal employment. As a result and always by mutual agreement, the building interests arranged to save as much of the repair work as possible for the ordinarily slack winter season; thereby giving steadier employment to skilled and unskilled workmen by hundreds of thousands. Moreover, they have studied together the question of winter work;

established that more construction than to any one previously had seemed possible can go on during the cold season—and applied this knowledge in practice. During the winter of 1923-24, for example, there was one third more new construction than in corresponding months of the previous year. Not only did this increase income but—because the railroads and factories found continuous employment for their plants—it lessened costs. For a century governments and boards in all lands had wrestled with that problem. But it was too big and complex for any one group to handle alone. Hoover, by combining the efforts of every affected element, has come nearest of all men to finding a solution.

When the building and housing department began its survey, it discovered a woeful and wasteful diversity in building codes of our municipalities. Sometimes their specifications were lax to the point of danger. More often, perhaps, they overemphasized the factor of safety, so rendering construction unnecessarily expensive. Transmuting research into practical results, the department, after many scientific tests, after much conference with experts, drew up a series of ideal building codes for various types of construction and especially for individual homes. In some items, as for example certain kinds of walls, this new code while insuring safety permitted a saving to the builder of from 10 to 20 per cent. More than one hundred cities of the United States have embodied these principles into their municipal laws.

Nor has the department forgotten the ultimate consumer—the man of small means who plans to build his own home. By the "Better Homes in America" movement, organized in 1922 with Hoover as president, it has carried the movement to the people. This unofficial society operates through local bodies, locally financed, to encourage home ownership, sound methods of building and beauty, economy, convenience of design. It uses generally the familiar, effective American method of "drives" and ballyhoo. Beginning in 1922 with fewer than 300 local chapters, by 1927 it had grown to 3600 chapters. Annually, in hundreds of cities it conducts a "week" with exhibits of model small houses and lectures by experts. Through it the department has circulated to the number of 325,000 its all-embracing pamphlet "How to Own Your Own Home."

Of late, this movement has passed rapidly into the rural communities. All over the country housing experts are touring the farming districts, giving instruction in principles of economical, sound, and yet beautiful construction. Scarcely a county in the United States but has profited either in physical appearance or in pocket by this single enterprise of our secretary of commerce. And as for its main object—own your own home—the result stands forth in the recent statistics of building. In 1920, 27.8 per cent. of our total construction consisted of individual residences; but by 1926 the proportion had grown to 48.7 per cent.

Pleasant, uncrowded, and secure surroundings are as important to the owner of the new home as his design. Until the last decade or so, American cities grew up haphazard. The fine residence district of today was often the factory district of to-morrow—a process involving disturbance and immeasurable loss. Now and again, after some sweeping disaster like the Baltimore and San Francisco fires, our larger communities considered putting themselves back on the map after some permanent plan—but almost always the impulse went no farther than planning. Haste and expediency rather than foresight governed the rebuilding.

In 1916, however, New York city took positive action by adopting a zoning law. Boiled down to its essentials, this set aside certain parts of the city for certain definite uses. Notably, great areas were designated as residence districts. In these no one, without unanimous consent of the property-owners in a given block, might install any new factory or business establishment. Further, this act so regulated the height, shape, and construction of building as to serve the health of the community and give light to the streets. Immediately after that the war imposed a moratorium on all such plans for municipal improvements. Hoover, assuming office just at the dawn of a new building era, foresaw universal danger to residential neighborhoods. Unsupported, the home-maker would be the sport of the land speculator. He formed at once the Commission on Zoning. Following that method which is almost universal in his public enterprise, he had experts survey the situation, make a critical examination of the proposed remedies, and issue a general report. That was the basis of a "zoning primer" which told all that any city official or public-spirited citizen needed to know about this problem, and which the National Association of Real Estate Boards circulated wholesale. Further, the department drafted a standard zoning act for use before state legislatures. In five years twenty-eight States had made this the basis of new laws. And now 580 cities, towns, and villages of the United States—half of our urban area—have adopted zoning plans based on the facts and recommendations gathered and issued by the Department of Commerce. Along with its other benefits, this movement has eliminated a great waste of money and effort.

But zoning is only one feature in intelligent arrangement of a modern community. Enthusiastic subordinates in the department wanted to start at once toward the larger objective of city planning. "One thing at a time," replied Hoover, and held them back. Then, after the lesser work had been going on for a year or two, he made an address at a large real-estate convention. When he spoke on zoning and touched lightly on city planning, he felt a thrill of interest in the house. "The big fellow," said one of his veteran subordinates, "has an uncanny sense of timeliness." Evidently, he felt that the hour had struck; for on returning to Washington, he said to the housing department, "Go ahead." And the movement for sane zoning, initiated by the Department of Commerce and carried forward by thousands of business or civic organizations all over the United States, is blending into a nation-wide movement for more convenient, more economical, and more beautiful arrangement of our cities.

It is possible to estimate in cold cash the enormous benefit which such "Hoover measures" as simplified practice have conferred on our industrial commonwealth. But when it comes to this high endeavor for the comfort, permanence, and beauty of our future America, one must abandon even guessing. Though it has eliminated much waste in tearing down cities, one must measure it chiefly in spiritual terms of security and contentment and happiness. Really great peoples are always great builders. And for centuries to come, American building will bear Herbert Hoover's mark and imprint.

CHAPTER XXVI

THIS chapter must serve perforce as a catch-all. History cannot pass final judgment on Hoover's work at Washington until he and you and I are long dead. Enterprises which seem momentous in 1928 may have passed to oblivion by 2028; and acts which seem trivial now may have achieved by then an unimagined importance.

There is radio. When Hoover issued to WBZ the first broadcasting license in history, this invention seemed to the public in general just a laboratory trick, a minor tool of navigation or a child's toy. Hoover saw farther. In 1921 he called it publicly the most important new instrument for intellectual communication since Gutenberg began casting movable type. And even before the furious development of radio, he perceived a danger and a need. Wave-lengths, "the channels of the air," were limited. Government control must preserve them to the people. "This," he said, "is just as important as to keep our channels of navigation open for ships."

The only radio communication as yet recognized by law was that between vessels at sea, over which the secretary of commerce had a right of regulation. Using this authority for a start, Hoover called together representatives of all elements interested in radio broadcasting. From this grew a series of annual conferences which worked to find effective methods of traffic control, to develop this new liberal art, and to preserve public interest. As radio grew in importance and popularity, further legislation became vitally necessary.

Hoover laid this emergency before Congress and urged that now, at the very beginning, we should so draw our radio laws as to preserve public rights. He himself worked out the main principles of the legislation which Congress finally adopted; including the Radio Board. His foresight averted chaos in the air.

Then there is commercial aviation. In 1924 Hoover assembled a committee representing the infant industry, to report on the best means and methods for its development. At the time, Europe far excelled us in civilian flying. The department drew on their experience; made a thorough and accurate study, for our benefit, of the European industry. When President Coolidge appointed the Morrow board to look into military aviation, Hoover presented a program of commercial aviation as a strong and effective reinforcement to the military arm. The Government had for 150 years given service to nautical transportation; why not do the same for aërial transportation? Let us begin with the national airways—lighted routes, landing fields, charts. Let us provide airports in all the important towns. With these facilities, private enterprise would create a network of commercial lines and, as an inevitable consequence, a great manufacturing industry. This would be in itself a powerful, useful reserve; by proceeding in this manner, instead of manufacturing as a purely military measure, we would save literally hundreds of millions. Europe had generally built up its commercial aviation by government subsidy. Hoover opposed this principle. He believed that, given the fundamental services described above, Americans would develop the new industry on their own initiative.

Congress, persuaded to make the try, passed the act establishing in the Department of Commerce a Division of Aviation. It had authority to carry out this program. Commercial aviation in America passed at once from an embryo to a live organism. By June, 1928, we shall have 7500 miles of lighted and marked airways; and in daily mileage of flight by commercial aëroplanes we shall exceed all Europe. Manufacture of aëroplanes has passed from red figures to black; by the end of 1927 the industry was operating more than a hundred plants. This sensational growth has cost our Government nothing more than a modest sum for maintenance of the airways. The post-office now makes an annual profit on the mail contracts.

For thirty years the West had agitated the question of developing the mighty, perplexing Colorado River. Most Americans, probably, know by now something of that problem. Periodically, the Colorado looses a devastating flood, endangering the lives and property of 100,000 people who live along its lower courses. Impounding the river for flood-protection implies the creation of vast water-power. It should be done—to that principle all interested parties adhere. But quarrels among the seven States which border the great river had paralyzed action. They fought continuously in the courts; twice the matter reached the United States Supreme Court. Early in his term, Hoover found himself chairman of a Colorado River Commission comprising representatives of the seven divided States. This body held hearings all over the West, and ended with three weeks of pow-wow in a lonely lodge of the southwestern mountains.

By now the affair seemed a hopeless tangle. But by concession after concession, Hoover edged the belligerents into an agreement so wise and practical that no one has challenged its equity. However, when this agreement came to ratification by the seven States, some of them tried, as a consideration for signing, to force concessions on other controversial questions. Consequently, not all of them have ratified. Viewed simply on its own merits, this is a great piece of constructive statesmanship. Important enterprises like the Boulder Canyon dam await settlement of those quarrels in the Southwest.

Here, Hoover served the far-distant future. He serves even better with his work to create an extensive, coördinated system of internal waterways. At the period when he entered the cabinet, higher wages and increased cost of supplies had necessarily raised all railroad rates. These increases penalized especially the mid-western farmers. They must pay more to send their produce to market, to bring goods to their farms. Gigantic waterways, heaven-made avenues for cheap transportation, netted the Middle West. But

A REMINISCENT BIOGRAPHY 305

the units of this potential system were unconnected and unorganized. Hoover proposed that the Mississippi and its greater tributaries should be improved and joined up into a modern system of waterway transportation. This, as he saw it, would connect the Great Lakes with the Gulf, Pittsburgh with Kansas City, and—through laterals—Chicago with St. Paul. Reaching the St. Lawrence through the Great Lakes, it would finally link the Atlantic and the Gulf.

Experience and experiment on one complete stretch of the wide, coördinated system which he envisaged proved that water transportation could in great degree reduce freight-rates on farm products. And this, as he saw the problem, would not work injustice to the railroads. A quarter of a century from now, when we have added forty million souls to our population, we shall need to work our transportation resources full blast; there will be business for all. Congress has accepted and indorsed the idea; the system is under active construction. This was not Hoover's own idea, of course. For thirty years prophets false and true have preached waterways development. But Hoover gets things done. He helped the people of the Mid-West to visualize their problem; he inspired the Government to action.

And twice since he entered the cabinet, life has called him back to the old trade of relieving stricken humanity. In 1920 and 1921 a serious drought, with famine in its wake, struck Russia. Such disasters, on a lesser scale, were periodic in the old empire. But very probably disorganization put the crown on disaster;

for just then communism was at flood tide and government efficiency at its lowest ebb. In July, 1921, cosmic disaster stared Russia in the face. And at this point Maxim Gorky appeared in Riga and telegraphed a frantic appeal to Hoover as the one man who could solve the problem.

If you look over the chronology of the Department of Commerce you will find that Hoover was at the moment busy with reorganization—carrying a dozen heavy tasks. But always he can find time for another job.

With President Harding's approval, Hoover accepted the burden; started as of old to raise funds, arrange transportation, organize personnel. As usual, finance was the first and greatest job. Russian relief cost, eventually, $75,000,000; of which he strained $15,000,000 in gold out of the Soviet Government. The rest came from the United States. It was not all dead loss to our people. These vast purchases helped to lift the price of American corn out of the ditch, to relieve our farmers of the Mississippi Valley.

But at first sight it looked difficult. We were in our post-war slump. American charity, both private and official, had been strained to the breaking-point. Unemployment had risen to its maximum. Congress was in no mood to grant Europe any more funds. However, the Grain Corporation had accumulated $20,000,000 profits. Hoover asked Congress to grant this for Russian relief. There was some opposition in Congress itself, some slander from outside, before he secured the appropriation. He stimulated and assisted our philanthropic religious bodies to raise funds; scraped together the residue of funds in the old American Relief Administration and threw them into the pot.

But as usual he set the machinery in motion before he had an assured supply of fuel. Within a week after Gorky's appeal his agents had moved on Riga, Russia's peephole to the outside world. There they met representatives of the Soviet Government. Even in this grave emergency, official Russia was suspicious and hostile. But after a few days of hot debate, the Americans and Russians signed an agreement. First, the Soviet Government bound themselves to release the American prisoners whom they held in Russia. Then they granted the Americans control of our supplies and freedom of movement and assumed the cost of distribution within Russia. Five days later our workers were in Moscow, digging through filth and misery to find living and working quarters. They started at once a survey which proved that this famine was not a figment of the imagination but a real and terrible disaster; began the organization necessary to their benevolent task.

For details of the field work I must refer the reader to H. H. Fisher's book on the Russian famine. From Belgium to Armenia, from the first call out of Brussels in 1918 to the last shipment to the Levant in 1923, Hoover's men never tackled any other job so ticklish and so melodramatic. That two-fisted soldier Colonel William Haskell, who learned his trade under Hoover in Rumania and Armenia, took charge in

Moscow. The job involved not only distribution of provisions but the restoration, so far as it could be restored, of a rotting, rusting transportation system. Haskell and his men encountered all the mental obstacles which one would expect when West meets East and capitalism tries to work with communism. Owing to sheer bureaucratic incompetence or to official theorizing on a situation which required practical action, there were periods when a dozen provision trains lay stalled on a siding; when Haskell, in despair of getting relief through diplomacy, must issue the ultimatum—"start something or we get out." At times, the administration had to meet and face down orders of wholesale arrest as "counter revolutionaries" against its Russian employees. Toward the end, it must struggle to prevent the Soviet Government from exporting native food "to restore economic life" while feeding its own people on American charity.

Along with the famine came the danger—nay the actuality—of pestilence. Typhus, smallpox and such diseases are scotched snakes for us and for the western European countries; but they lurked always just below the surface of Russian life. Now they burst forth —especially typhus, that co-conspirator with famine. Another rush season for Hoover. He secured three and a half million dollars' worth of supplies from our surplus army medical stores, begged a contribution from the Laura Spelman Rockefeller Foundation, managed other funds so as to squeeze out a few million more. And the Americans took on the familiar, disagreeable job of establishing hospitals for the sick, of delousing, inoculating, and sanitizing the healthy. In six months they had pestilence under control.

Our young agents, heirs of the men who founded in Belgium this new craft, struggled through two years during which dreariness alternated with melodrama. They lived often in towns where accumulated filth lay ankle deep. They faced pestilence, of course. Several had close calls with typhus; and Harold Blandy died of it. Philip B. Shield disappeared as though the earth had swallowed him—probably murdered. They witnessed at times incredible horrors. They lived in a constant state of apprehension for the safety of their native assistants. And from the Siberian border to the Black Sea, they governed districts as large as our Northeastern States over which this strange turn of international destiny gave them virtually power of life and death.

By the summer of 1923 the disaster was over. It is hard to estimate how many lives Hoover's promptness and wise administration, plus the devotion and efficiency of his working staff, saved to their normal term. An estimate of fifteen million would perhaps be no exaggeration. As usual, he had a heart for the children; along with wheat and bacon, the relief imported condensed milk by the car-load, got it securely into the systems of the rising generation through the old familiar device of special meals. And all this time the Relief Administration supplied Russia with the seed for her scant harvest of 1922, her abundant one of 1923. When the crisis was over, the soviets gave Colonel Haskell and his aids a complimentary dinner.

And though the Third International continues to use us for the awful example, under all this bluff lies perhaps a warm memory. . . .

Four years more; and at last his own country called to Hoover the Reliever. The Mississippi flood is so recent that I need not describe it. When in April President Coolidge appointed him chairman of a committee to deal with the human factor, the first crest had reached the upper part of Mississippi. It had cost already two or three hundred lives. Refugees had fled to the hills by tens of thousands. Their more fortunate neighbors were helping them as best they could. But the work went on unsystematically. And every one knew, now, that the worst was yet to come.

Hoover touched flood-relief with his magic hand. Immediately, life-boats and crews were speeding westward from the Atlantic coast, aëroplanes winging from the army and navy fields, coast guard vessels speeding up the river-flood, carpenters in a hundred yards throwing together emergency boats, Red Cross units entraining for the Mississippi. Then, like one of those trick moving pictures, lines which signified nothing by themselves jumped together into coherent meaning. Ahead of the flood moved Hoover's forces in perfect coördination. Volunteers under the state flood directors warned the inhabitants out of dangerous areas. They did not all move, humanly. Indeed, when the crest reached the conservative Acadian districts, very few moved. But as the levees broke or the inundations advanced at their resistless pace of three miles an hour, the aëroplanes buzzed overhead, scouting for men, women, and children marooned on roofs or sections of levee, for animals getting ready to swim. Behind them came the mosquito-craft to the actual work of rescue. And on the highlands of a thousand miles broke out the Red Cross camps, under Hoover—sheltered, sanitated, supplied with everything necessary to life. In two months these forces effected or supervised the removal of 700,000 refugees. Only six lives were lost—fewer than the probable toll of automobile accidents had the roads remained open. Prompt medical work with disinfectants and the needle prevented the epidemics which usually curse such migrations. Indeed, the health of those 700,000 was better than in normal times! ... I reported this disaster. I wrote then of Hoover: "It was like seeing a master play billiards. You may not know much of the game, but you recognize supreme skill when you see it."

I, who have followed Hoover on his great European jobs, would like to leave him as I saw him one May morning of 1927—standing on the tottering Melville levee, his aëroplanes scouting overhead, his mosquito-fleet scurrying below, a group of prominent citizens about him listening to the wise, quick, terse directions which were bringing order out of chaos. It symbolizes the man, that scene—"The one tranquil among the raging floods," the transmuter of altruistic emotion into benevolent action. On that side of him his friends and intimates base their fanatical affection. It is a warm and witty and very human Hoover that they know; a creature of vibrant sympathies. In a smaller and more intimate way, this nature expresses itself by acts of personal kindness which it were not decent to catalogue here. He has given its larger aspect verbal expression in his "Children's Bill of Rights," which our Child Health Association has spread over all America. For whether it be the underfed waifs of the war or the neglected of our own country, no appeal for a child ever failed with Hoover. And while he works with machines and factories and railroad lines, these insensate things are not his America. He sees a nation of men and women and children whom government serves only as it brings them more security and comfort.

But after all, his importance to our people at this moment derives from his work as secretary of commerce. He took a dead, rudimentary department, whose importance no one else recognized, and transformed it into a major agency for increasing and stabilizing our national economic life. The eyes of our generation, I suppose, cannot yet clearly see this job in all its magnitude. When a secretary of the navy takes a run-down fleet and builds it into a power—there is something visible! We behold its new armadas in our harbor; and any child can understand its comparative figures of guns and tonnage. But such work as Hoover's lies buried deep in the economic structure, invisible to most eyes. Perhaps another generation may perceive more clearly its influence and results. There is for this feat of constructive statesmanship no exact parallel in history. And for a roughly similar example of a cabinet minister who has brought a lifeless function of government to abundant life, we must go back to our origins and study Alexander Hamilton's work with the Treasury.

Stated in other terms, he has lifted engineering to its highest level. Publicly and privately, he has often spoken on the widening importance of his profession. When as a boy he worked in the drifts of the Sierran mines, the engineer concerned himself only with minor tactics of the industrial struggle. He estimated the cost and selected the methods for sinking a shaft or digging a ditch or building a dam; then he went ahead and sank or dug or built. Gradually, engineering expanded to a higher function. It began to use callipers and calculus upon companies and industries as a whole; to discover by experiment and calculation where they were wasting effort, where missing opportunity, where blanketing efficiency with tradition. Now comes Hoover, to apply the same method to the whole industrial structure.

Perhaps one nation tried it before; perhaps pre-war Germany was aiming a little blindly at the same thing. Only she was employing law, regulation, the goose-step—the autocratic method. Here precisely comes a Hoover stroke of genius. That is no method to give permanent results with any set of civilized, modern human beings, least of all with Americans. From the dawn of his public work he has made full use of the volunteer spirit; has never commanded, but persuaded and led. He carried that method to wider use in the Food Administration, when fourteen million families, instead of obeying legal regulations, followed Hoover requests. He has brought it to full flower in the Department of Commerce. That eleven-story building in Washington, that string of offices across the United States and the world—they and what they contain are only a skeleton. It is the business community, giving hearty coöperation, which clothes it with flesh. An investigator for a foreign board of trade expressed his amazement at that collection of current facts, estimates, and statistics on which the department bases most of its work. "How do you make your business people open up their books in this manner?" he asked. "We couldn't, even if we threatened them with jail!" The variation of this method with that so commonly applied in Europe is expressed in that word "make." Hoover does not make any one do anything. He inspires volunteers—from the able men who direct and staff his departments to the farthest human outposts of our commercial structure.

He is engineering our material civilization as a whole; and that without goose-stepping the human spirit, blue-printing the human soul. Even though the work fall at times to blind and incompetent successors, it must go on; for he has shown a new way. To this larger and general purpose he has subordinated his other powers. It was at one time the fashion on Capitol Hill to remark that Hoover was no politician. But since some of our elected representatives noticed that above all other members of the cabinet he gets his appropriations through, we have heard less of that! They meant, really, that he was not primarily a politician. The true statesman is seldom that. Politics is to him not a main end but a useful tool.

These are some of the reasons why the department of his shaping has stood since 1921 unique among national boards of trade and ministries of commerce; why officials from all over the world more and more cross oceans to study it; why a British statesman burst out in a mood of frank irritation: "We have to fight not only American foreign trade but the American Department of Commerce!"

www.ingramcontent.com/pod-product-compliance
Lightning Source LLC
Chambersburg PA
CBHW032001220426
43664CB00005B/93